The Principal's BACKPACK

Tips and Tools for Managing Yourself

(So You Can Manage Everything Else)

NANCY KARLIN FLYNN

Copyright © 2024 by Solution Tree Press

Materials appearing here are copyrighted. With one exception, all rights are reserved. Readers may reproduce only those pages marked "Reproducible." Otherwise, no part of this book may be reproduced or transmitted in any form or by any means (electronic, photocopying, recording, or otherwise) without prior written permission of the publisher.

555 North Morton Street
Bloomington, IN 47404
800.733.6786 (toll free) / 812.336.7700
FAX: 812.336.7790

email: info@SolutionTree.com
SolutionTree.com

Visit **go.SolutionTree.com/leadership** to download the free reproducibles in this book.

Printed in the United States of America

Library of Congress Cataloging-in-Publication Data

Names: Flynn, Nancy Karlin, author.
Title: The principal's backpack : tips and tools for managing yourself (so
   you can manage everything else) / Nancy Karlin Flynn.
Description: Bloomington, IN : Solution Tree Press, [2023] | Includes
   bibliographical references and index.
Identifiers: LCCN 2023019938 (print) | LCCN 2023019939 (ebook) | ISBN
   9781958590058 (paperback) | ISBN 9781958590065 (ebook)
Subjects: LCSH: Educational leadership. | Principals--Social conditions. |
   Self-management (Psychology) | Time management.
Classification: LCC LB2806 .F584 2023 (print) | LCC LB2806 (ebook) | DDC
   371.2/012--dc23/eng/20230517
LC record available at https://lccn.loc.gov/2023019938
LC ebook record available at https://lccn.loc.gov/2023019939

Solution Tree
Jeffrey C. Jones, CEO
Edmund M. Ackerman, President

Solution Tree Press
President and Publisher: Douglas M. Rife
Associate Publishers: Todd Brakke and Kendra Slayton
Editorial Director: Laurel Hecker
Art Director: Rian Anderson
Copy Chief: Jessi Finn
Production Editor: Miranda Addonizio
Proofreader: Sarah Ludwig
Text and Cover Designer: Julie Csizmadia
Acquisitions Editor: Hilary Goff
Assistant Acquisitions Editor: Elijah Oates
Content Development Specialist: Amy Rubenstein
Associate Editor: Sarah Ludwig
Editorial Assistant: Anne Marie Watkins

DEDICATED TO
MY PRINCIPAL
COLLEAGUES

Acknowledgments

Jim Roussin, Leadership Catalyst Coach and Executive Director, Generative Learning: While I have written more than seventy thousand words in this book, I am truly at a loss as to how to adequately express my gratitude for all of your listening, guidance, and advice throughout my journey. You taught me what it means to deeply reflect on my practice, cognitively reframe situations, and always find solutions. And last, but not least, thank you for saying: *Somewhere in all of your journals, you have a book.*

Suzanne Kaback, Associate Professor of Education, Saint Catherine University: I am incredibly fortunate to have had such a strong school-university partnership with you for so many years. You have my sincere thanks for reading the very first draft of my book, providing such thoughtful feedback, and encouraging me to go ahead and submit it.

Becky Pedersen, Principal, Saint Paul Public Schools: You are truly the definition of a super ally! Thank you so much for always being there. *Super* understates our decades-long friendship and our commitment to unconditionally supporting each other as we navigated our careers, opportunities, and hectic lives. Our daily texts, emails, and phone calls and the amusing, crazy, inexplicable, and celebratory conversations made us laugh, cringe, and ultimately learn from each other. As we always said: *You just can't make this stuff up.*

Jackie Rogalski, backpacker extraordinaire: I am so grateful for our friendship and for having such a strong woman in my life. You've taught me everything I know about backpacking and navigating the (real) trail. Thanks for being there every step of the way.

Miranda Addonizio, Solution Tree editor: My sincere gratitude for your patience, guidance, feedback, enthusiasm, and sheer warmth throughout the entire process of completing this book.

The entire Solution Tree staff: Thank you for the opportunity to publish this book.

Solution Tree Press would like to thank the following reviewers:

Kimberly Calcasola
Assistant Principal
Granby Memorial High School
Granby, Connecticut

Abbey Campbell
Principal
Silver Creek Primary School
Sellersburg, Indiana

Jed Kees
Principal
Onalaska Middle School
Onalaska, Wisconsin

Ian Landy
Position District Principal of Technology
Institution School District 47 (Powell River)
Powell River, British Columbia, Canada

Katie Madigan
Director of Student Services
Longfellow Middle School
Fairfax County Public Schools
McLean, Virginia

Faith Short
Principal
East Pointe Elementary School
Greenwood, Arkansas

Dawn Vang
Administrative Assistant
Pembroke Elementary School
Virginia Beach, Virginia

Visit **go.SolutionTree.com/leadership** to download the free reproducibles in this book.

Table of Contents

Reproducibles are in italics.

About the Author	xi
Introduction	**1**
Prepare for the Journey	1
About This Book	2

Chapter 1: Mapping Your Route — 5

Tip 1: Get Organized — 6
- **Tool:** Priority Score Worksheet — 6
- **Tool:** Share the Load Spreadsheet — 9
- **Tool:** Thinking and Productivity Styles Reflection — 10

Tip 2: Set Goals — 13
- **Tool:** SMART Goal Template — 13
- **Tool:** The Why of My Goal Process — 15
- **Tool:** Progress Report — 16

Tip 3: Make a Decision — 17
- **Tool:** Two-Tine Litmus Test — 18
- **Tool:** Start With the Why Process — 19
- **Tool:** Concern and Influence Organizer — 19
- **Tool:** Fishbone Diagram — 21
- **Tool:** Heuristics — 22

Tip 4: Know Your Purpose — 23
- **Tool:** Your Ikigai — 23

Tool: Values Organizer	24
Tool: Four Archetypes Reflection	26
Tip 5: Psych Yourself Up	28
Tool: Personality and Temperament Self-Reflection Chart	28
Tool: The Big Picture (Staff Chart)	31
Summary and What's Next	32
SMART Goal Template	33
The Why of My Goal Process	34
Progress Report	35
Concern and Influence Organizer	36
Values Organizer	37
The Big Picture (Staff Chart)	38

Chapter 2: Packing Your Bag — 39

Tip 6: Put Safety First	40
Tool: Emergency Procedures One-Pager	40
Tool: Role-Playing Scenarios	42
Tool: U.S. Homeland Security Website	43
Tool: Psychological Safety Assessment	43
Tip 7: Know the Laws	45
Tool: Web Resources for Laws	45
Tool: Law and Policy Reference Guide	46
Tip 8: Discover Your Strengths	48
Tool: Strengths Self-Evaluation	48
Tool: Strengths Assessments Organizer	49
Tip 9: Create a Network	52
Tool: Hire a Coach	53
Tool: Find a Super Ally	55
Tool: Critical Friends Process Worksheet	55
Tool: Join a Professional Organization	57
Tip 10: Study Your Boss	58
Tool: My Boss Under a Microscope Organizer	58
Tool: Contributions Chart	60
Tool: Four Ds Process Worksheet	62

Summary and What's Next	64
Emergency Procedures One-Pager	65
Law and Policy Reference Guide	66
Strengths Self-Evaluation	69
Strengths Assessments Organizer	70
Questions to Prepare for Being Coached	71
Critical Friends Process Worksheet	72

Chapter 3: Navigating the Trail — 73

Tip 11: Stay Calm	76
Tool: Mindfulness Techniques Organizer	77
Tool: Binaural Beats	79
Tool: Office Yoga Poses	80
Tip 12: Keep Your Balance	81
Tool: The Full Plate Activity	82
Tool: Just Say No	83
Tip 13: Listen Up	83
Tool: Six Levels of Listening Survey	84
Tool: Four Purposes of Listening	86
Tool: Listening Blocks Worksheet	86
Tool: Feedback Tendency Tracker	87
Tip 14: Express Yourself	91
Tool: Approachable Voice Versus Credible Voice	91
Tool: Right Voice, Right Time Worksheet	93
Tool: Well-Dressed Hamburger	94
Tip 15: Stretch Your Limits (But Know Your Limitations)	96
Tool: KFG Bracelet	97
Tool: Stop Light Grid	98
Tool: Grit Score Reflection	100
Tool: Setting Boundaries Worksheet	101
Summary and What's Next	103
Right Voice, Right Time Worksheet	104
Stop Light Grid	105
Setting Boundaries Worksheet	106

Chapter 4: Unpacking Your Bag — 107

Tip 16: Give Yourself Some Grace — 108
- **Tool:** Self-Compassion Survey — 108
- **Tool:** Self-Compassion Exercises — 109
- **Tool:** Pathways to Enhancing Your Mindset — 110
- **Tool:** Cognitive Reframing Worksheet — 112

Tip 17: Reflect on It — 114
- **Tool:** Journal Writing — 114
- **Tool:** Ladder of Inference Process — 116
- **Tool:** Decide, Enact, Analyze, Reflect Model — 117

Tip 18: Laugh About It — 118
- **Tool:** Laughter Yoga — 119
- **Tool:** Humorous Media — 120

Tip 19: Recharge — 120
- **Tool:** Your Happy Place — 121
- **Tool:** Unplug and Disconnect Tracker — 122
- **Tool:** Nature Log — 123

Tip 20: Celebrate! — 125
- **Tool:** I Honor Cards — 126
- **Tool:** Celebrations Questionnaire — 126
- **Tool:** Accomplishments Checklist — 127

Summary and What's Next — 128
Cognitive Reframing Worksheet — 129
Ladder of Inference Process — 130
I Honor Cards — 131
Celebrations Questionnaire — 132

Conclusion — 133

References and Resources — 137

Index — 147

About the Author

 **Nancy Karlin Flynn, EdD,** has been an administrator in the Saint Paul Public Schools district for twenty-four years, serving as an elementary, junior high, and middle school principal. She is passionate about coaching, mentoring, and reflecting on leadership practice with aspiring principals as well as those with all levels of experience as a school leader.

Flynn created LeadersHike!, a professional learning workshop for school leaders based on this book, to combine her passion for coaching and her love of nature and hiking. Flynn was a contributing writer for *LeaderTalk*, an online blog through CASTLE and Education Week, and has published articles in *Learning and Leading With Technology* and other technology-related journals.

Flynn earned a bachelor's degree in business administration from the University of Connecticut, a master's degree in educational technology from the University of Nebraska, an education specialist degree in educational leadership from the University of New Mexico, and a doctorate in educational administration and policy from the University of Minnesota.

To learn more about Flynn's work, visit www.leadershike.org.

To book Nancy Flynn for professional development, contact pd@SolutionTree.com.

Introduction

I stood atop Mount Sinai as the sun peeked over the horizon. I was a college student exploring the Middle East when I happened upon the opportunity to climb this biblical landmark. I wasn't exactly prepared to climb a mountain, as I didn't have any hiking boots or hiking gear, but it was an adventure I couldn't pass up. I stayed at a monastery at the foot of Mount Sinai and rose at midnight to begin the ascent. The idea was to spend the night climbing so that we would hit the summit at sunrise. In lieu of a flashlight, I used the starlit sky to guide my steps up the mountain. When I reached the summit, just in time to watch the sun rise, I remember the exertion of the climb matching the exhilaration of standing atop a mountain. It was exhilarating on two counts: first, I had climbed a mountain; second, it was the very same mountain upon which, according to the Old Testament, Moses received the Ten Commandments.

I have been backpacking on trails and through mountain ranges all over the world since then, and each trip combines those forces of exertion and exhilaration. Even with the proper gear, climbing mountains is an uphill battle. Many people question why, when I have a challenging job as a public school principal, I seek out challenges as a way to unwind from the grind of the job. The answer: I revel in the balance of exertion and exhilaration. It's a delicate balance. If exertion outpaces exhilaration, the trip can be exhausting and unfulfilling, and even dangerous. If there's not enough exertion, the feeling of accomplishment, and thus exhilaration, is greatly diminished. It is the same with the principal's job.

I am extremely mindful of purposeful self-management. For principals, a lack of self-management can lead to exhaustion and put our health in jeopardy. On the other hand, if we don't exert enough force, we will accomplish far less than what we desire. The purpose of this book is to provide tips and tools for managing oneself in order to achieve and maintain a level of equanimity as a school principal and ultimately to be an effective school leader. These tips and tools are not just for surviving but for thriving as a school leader. When you have your self-management dialed in, you will have much more time and energy to work with and appreciate your staff's qualities. Throughout your journey as a school leader, you will work with people of different races, ethnicities, genders, sexual orientations, religions, and political views. Embracing those differences is essential to creating a welcoming, inclusive environment that functions at a high level. By embracing differences, you seek to understand and honor the perspectives of others.

Prepare for the Journey

I pack very intentionally for my mountain treks, keeping in mind that I carry everything on my back for hours, and sometimes days, at a time. I balance the essentials for survival with what I can comfortably carry. And as I pack, I keep in mind that every liter of water I carry adds a little more than two pounds; yet without water, I don't survive. When I consider what I need to survive as a principal, I think of all of the self-management tools I have picked up along my professional journey. These tools are in a figurative backpack that I carry throughout the school day as I trek through halls, classrooms, playground, gymnasium, cafeteria, and buses. Carrying these tools gives me the confidence to manage whatever the school wilderness bestows upon me at any given time. I need a clear head and all the necessary gear and tools that will help me manage myself as I navigate and contend with whatever the day brings.

Hiking and being a school leader might seem to have little in common, but both demand readiness for anything and everything. We don't know exactly what we're going to encounter, be it beautiful or beastly. When trekking through mountain passages in remote areas of the world, it's essential to be prepared for the potential of the elements. Once, in the middle of the Swiss Alps in July, my hiking group encountered a fierce snowstorm. Barely able to see, we rummaged through our packs for gloves, hats, and anything that would keep our body heat from escaping. I took out my nice, new, tight-fitting gloves (tight-fitting to allow for dexterity), but my hands were too wet and cold to even get them on. Since then, I am sure to pack gloves that are large enough to put on easily with cold, wet hands. Just as in the wilderness, panicking is not an option when the "storm" hits in the building. There will be days as a principal that, no matter what you think you are prepared for, something new will come along and hit you like a snowstorm you never saw coming. I never thought, for example, that I'd find a loaded gun in the backpack of a seven-year-old, but it happened.

To manage yourself, you must know yourself—both physically and emotionally. It means understanding how to care for your own physical and emotional health and well-being. In a survey conducted during the COVID-19 pandemic in 2021, researchers asked 631 Minnesota principals what supports they would find most helpful at that stage of the pandemic; 73 percent chose staff mental health resources as their first answer, and only 9 percent ranked mental health resources for themselves as most important (Pekel, Kemper, Parr, Evenson, & Zhao, 2022). As principals, we're typically more concerned about the welfare of others than we are for ourselves.

Though it was once less visible, we're hearing a lot more about mental health these days, as well-known people like elite athletes and celebrities come forward to share the circumstances surrounding their own mental health. Mental health is getting a lot of attention through all sorts of media outlets. As principals, we are also under enormous pressure, and while it doesn't get that kind of media attention, managing yourself under pressure is crucial in our profession. Billie Jean King (2008) once said that "Pressure is a privilege" (p. 101). She explains that with every success come certain pressures that go along with it, and the pressure that comes with that success must also be seen as a privilege. King (2008) believes, "If you can see it that way, you can handle almost anything with calm and grace" (p. 113). The privilege that we have as school leaders comes with the obligation to ourselves to do what it takes to keep us mentally and physically healthy, and that starts with our self-awareness.

To maintain an appropriate balance of exertion and exhilaration, whether at school or on a mountain trail, it's necessary to summon the necessary tools to manage yourself and the various demands you'll face. You will also require trusted reinforcement. In the mountains, it's never a good idea to trek alone. You will benefit from guides, a map, a compass, and fellow hikers who are with you from start to finish. Similarly, principals benefit from a guiding and supportive network, as well as what I call a *super ally* (which I'll explain later) to help you stay centered on the job.

About This Book

Think of this book as your backpack filled with tips and tools to help you on your journey to increasing your self-awareness and effectiveness as a school leader. Each chapter is broken down into five tips, and the tips feature a variety of models, paradigms, strategies, inventories, activities, and surveys you can use to help you on the journey. Some of these instruments are

Introduction 3

interactive worksheets or templates, some require a few art supplies, and others require taking surveys online or simply engaging in some intentional thinking.

Every journey starts with the question, Where do I want to go? This may sound like a simple question, but you will not reach your destination without the proper map. The destination here is successful school leadership, so to begin the journey, chapter 1, "Mapping Your Route," includes tips and tools for organization, setting goals, decision making, finding your purpose, and analyzing your personality type and traits.

Just as with backpacking, each trek along the journey of effective school leadership requires different tools depending on the immediate need and circumstance. For instance, you don't need crampons in Guatemala, but you must have them to climb the ice fields and glaciers in Greenland. Likewise, you may need to use a priority diagram tool for triaging your pressing tasks when the more traditional to-do (and get-done) list becomes too hectic and overwhelming. Therefore, feel free to pick and choose which tools to use based on whatever circumstances you're facing at any particular time. The way you use them is also up to you. They shouldn't turn into a chore. For example, when you do choose to use a tool, you might fill out one line and come back days or weeks later to add to it. There are reproducible versions of many of these tools at the end of each chapter.

Once your route is mapped, you can ask yourself, "What do I need to pack for this journey?" This question is all about anticipating your needs and being prepared. Therefore, chapter 2, "Packing Your Bag," includes tips and tools for putting safety first, knowing the laws, promoting your strengths, creating a network, and studying your boss.

As with backpacking, situational awareness as a school leader is key to your survival. You must continuously ask yourself, "Am I aware of what is happening right now?" Do I have the tools I need to effectively handle situations I encounter along the way? Chapter 3, "Navigating the Trail," offers tips and tools for staying calm, keeping your balance, listening carefully, expressing yourself, and knowing your limits.

Reflection and recharging are essential parts of your journey; you will continually pack and unpack your bag. As you unpack your bag each day, ask yourself what you handled well, what you could have done differently in a particular situation, and how you are going to recharge for the next day. You will want to give additional thought to whether you were able to summon the necessary tools to manage yourself and your responsibilities. As you repack for the next day, assess which tools should remain in the pack and which ones, if any, should be added or set aside. Therefore, chapter 4, "Unpacking Your Bag," includes tips and tools for giving yourself a break, reflecting on your experiences, laughing about the experience, recharging for whatever lies ahead, and celebrating your accomplishments.

Now, let's take a hike!

CHAPTER 1
Mapping Your Route

Maps are important visual representations that point us in the direction we want to go. Without a map, we have little orientation of where we are versus where we want to end up. Case in point: after a spectacular day of skiing in Italy, my friends and I had to make our way back to Switzerland. We figured Switzerland was just "over there," so all we'd have to do was go to the top of the mountain we were on and take a left. We took a left and skied right into a dead end, a rope marking the ski area boundary. After several tense minutes of skiing in a steep, unauthorized area of the mountain, we arrived in Switzerland. Had any of the five of us consulted the neatly folded ski map we each had in our pocket, we would have seen that there was a gondola from Italy that would have taken us right to the Swiss border, saving us a lot of stress. We could have easily avoided that dead end if we'd just taken a moment to use a map.

Principals need maps just as badly. Although we might not need physical paper maps, we need mental maps to guide us on our professional journey toward more effective school leadership by setting us on a particular course. Mental maps help us understand our environment and how to interact with the elements within it.

As a principal, you have multiple elements within your environment that you are juggling at all times. In order to help you keep the balls in the air, the five tips in this chapter offer a series of mental maps in the form of models for organization, setting goals, making decisions, and finding your purpose, as well as surveys and instruments to help you "psych up" by learning more about your work styles and personality traits as they pertain to school leadership.

Tip 1: Get Organized

My backpack has lots of pockets, zippers, and compartments, and even my random-thinking brain needs to know where my gear is packed. If it starts to rain, I would prefer not to have to pull everything out of my pack to find my raincoat. If I need moleskin for a blister, gloves, or a warm hat, I need to know where I have stored them so that I don't have to spill the entire pack contents out all over the trail. Similarly, in my office, I have my laptop, desktop, drawers, file cabinets, and closets overflowing with stuff, and I need to know where the important documents, folders, and manuals are in the event I need to retrieve something specific at a moment's notice. Being organized is key to leading hikes and leading schools.

Principals have more to do in a day than they can possibly accomplish. Between district meetings, principal meetings, staff meetings, team meetings, individualized education plan (IEP) meetings, committee meetings, parent-teacher association (PTA) meetings, conferences, teacher observations and evaluations, as well as all of the ad hoc parent, student, and teacher meetings that you need to squeeze into your workday, it's difficult to find the time to get everything accomplished. While you probably have a to-do list sitting on your desk, you need to be able to prioritize those tasks and activities efficiently and mindfully and make the most of your time, energy, and talents. If everything is a priority, nothing is a priority. As Stephen R. Covey (2021) states, "The key is not to prioritize what's on your schedule, but to schedule your priorities." Covey first wrote these words in 1989, and they remain as true in 2021 when he tweeted them again. Sometimes you may feel that your list of priorities should be horizontal, because everything seems equally important and it's hard to determine what should be done first. How do you determine what actually rises to the top? Deadlines are one indication, but more than deadlines matter when organizing tasks. With so many tasks, prioritizing them can become just another task if you don't have a system. Graphing your tasks and projects is an excellent way to help organize and visualize where your priorities lie. It can also illustrate which tasks you would be better off delegating. This tip provides a tool to help prioritize all of those tasks, a spreadsheet to help you decide which tasks to delegate, and a reflection tool to determine your mind style and personal productivity style, both of which can help you organize your work individually and with others.

Tool: Priority Score Worksheet

There are many ways to organize different tasks. One that I favor is the action priority matrix. The idea is based on the work of Covey (1989), and examples and templates abound on the internet; a good one is available online (visit https://bit.ly/3Okr2li). Most of the time, we scribble down the daily to-do list and then try to accomplish it all without giving much thought to the true importance of each task and to what we need to do first. The matrix helps you choose the activities you should prioritize and the ones you should avoid if you want to make the most of your time and opportunities. The principle behind using the matrix is that you score each activity that you need to complete on two scales: (1) the impact the activity will have on the school and (2) the effort involved in completing the activity. Each task is scored on a scale from 1 to 10, 1 being little effort and less impact, and 10 being major effort and impact.

The matrix offers four types of priorities.

1. **Quick wins:** High impact with low effort. These activities give you a good return with relatively little effort. They're the ones that are the easiest to cross off your list.

2. **Major projects:** Require high impact and high effort. They take a long time to complete

and can crowd out the other activities in the matrix. Major projects require more delegation of tasks in order to complete them in due time.

3. **Fill-ins:** Low-impact, low-effort tasks. These tasks are easily delegated.
4. **Thankless tasks:** Low impact but high effort. These activities monopolize your time and end up giving low returns. These are the tasks to tackle when there are few projects ahead on the priority matrix.

Think of the quick wins as easy hikes with little or no elevation change that keep you moving without taxing your time and energy, as opposed to major projects that require more gear, more time, and more energy. You probably won't feel like you've accomplished as much with a quick win as a major project, but you can't devote the necessary time to that major project if you haven't knocked off a few of those quick wins.

Prioritizing tasks in this way is useful because school leaders rarely have time to complete all of the tasks and projects on their to-do lists. As a school leader, you need to choose tasks and projects intelligently, spending more time on the high-value activities that keep operations moving smoothly. You can also delegate or remove tasks that contribute little to school operations.

Similar to the action priority matrix, another model I've found useful weighs your passion for the task against the value of your contribution. Take a look at the tasks on your to-do list. You will be passionate about some of them and wince at others. If you find you have very little passion for a particular task, and the value of your individual contribution is low, then delegate the task. An example of that for me is Title I documentation. I have absolutely no passion for uploading documents into different file folders online. Title I funding contributes to the school's budget, but it does not require much contribution on my part, so I delegate that task.

If you have low passion for the task but you feel your contribution is valuable, then you'll have to tolerate doing it. There are going to be aspects of the principal job that you won't like. For these, you really have to weigh what you feel your value of contribution is and either form a team to tackle the tasks together or grin and do it.

Finally, if you have a high passion for the task or project and feel you have a high-value contribution, then it becomes a priority. Ideally, you want to focus your efforts, talents, and time on tasks and projects that you are passionate about and highly value. I am passionate about and highly value teacher observations and reflection dialogues, so those always rise to the top of the list. Although I don't have a great passion for working on the budget, my value of contribution is high. Therefore, I have to place the budget worksheet near the top of my list as well.

One other tool to help you decide on which tasks to prioritize and which to delegate is the Eisenhower matrix. President Dwight D. Eisenhower led the construction of the Interstate Highway System, created NASA, signed civil rights legislation into law, ended the Korean War, and added Alaska and Hawaii as the forty-ninth and fiftieth states, to name a few of his actions. Eisenhower invented this matrix to help him decide on what to prioritize:

> He understood the fundamental difference between the Urgent and the Important. In a 1954 speech, Eisenhower quoted an unnamed university president who said, "I have two kinds of problems, the urgent and the important. The urgent are not important, and the important are never urgent. (Todoist, n.d.)

The matrix has four quadrants to help visualize tasks in terms of their urgency and importance, with those that are both urgent and important in the upper left. In the upper right are tasks that are not urgent but nonetheless are important. These activities or tasks don't have a rigid timeline but bring you closer to your goals. The lower left quadrant is for items that are not important but need to be done. These are the tasks that don't require your time and effort, which we usually refer to as busywork. These are the tasks you delegate. And finally, the lower right quadrant is for distractions that lure you away from your work. I compare them to spur trails that, while perhaps entertaining, are ultimately a time suck—better to delete them.

Incorporating the notion of time sensitivity along with effort, impact, passion, and contribution ratings, the priority score worksheet (figure 1.1) illustrates where your priorities lie, which tasks can get done quickly and easily, and which tasks should probably be delegated. For the following example, I took a typical to-do list and assigned numbers from 1 to 10 for each task depending on the effort it would take to complete, the impact it will have on the school, the passion I have for completing the task, the importance of my contribution, and the urgency and importance. To determine whether I would do it myself or delegate it, I also classified each task by the four priorities I outlined near the start of this section.

Task	Effort	Impact	Passion	Contribution	Urgency	Importance	Do it or delegate it?
Work on master schedule	10	10	1	5	3	10	Major project but no passion, so delegate
Sign payroll	3	10	2	8	10	10	Quick win: Little effort, but large impact and contribution so just get it done and off the list
Meet with student council	5	7	9	9	2	7	Quick win: Not a lot of effort but means a lot to the students—schedule an hour to meet
Type up weekly bulletin	6	9	6	10	7	9	Major project: High impact and contribution; it's a priority
Lead all-school assembly	5	10	10	10	5	10	Quick win: Little effort but high passion and large impact and contribution; schedule it
Update the website	4	10	2	3	2	8	Fill-in: Not a lot of effort, no passion, low contribution; delegate
Send parent email	2	4	2	9	10	10	Fill-in: Low effort but impacts parents; get it done and off the list
Teacher observation	9	9	10	10	8	10	Major project: High passion, effort, impact, and contribution; top priority
Input Title I documentation	8	10	1	4	2	9	Thankless task: No passion, low contribution, but high impact; delegate
Prepare staff meeting agenda	8	8	8	6	9	10	Quick win: Fairly high effort, impact, and passion; get my part done and delegate to the others on the agenda
Review behavior referrals	6	3	1	6	6	9	Thankless task: Very low passion but need the data; delegate the referrals and then get the data
Review budget	8	9	3	10	3	10	Major project: Low passion, but high impact and contribution; priority
Compose parent newsletter	8	8	7	10	6	9	Quick win: One of those things I have to do; fit it in and get it done

Figure 1.1: Priority score worksheet.

Visit **go.SolutionTree.com/leadership** *for a free reproducible version of this figure.*

Working through this scoring process provides a helpful way to see how to handle various tasks and can offer more utility than a simple to-do list. If you're struggling to separate out the most important tasks, averaging the scores or using simple graphic organizers like Venn diagrams, quadrants, or grids with X and Y axes can help visualize which tasks to take on and which ones to delegate.

Once you have your scores, look at your deadlines (that urgency) and rank your priorities. In this example, the teacher observation, budget report, staff meeting agenda, and parent newsletter would take precedence. However, when you consider the urgency, there may be a few other tasks near the top, like that parent email. Get those done and off the list so that you can concentrate your efforts on those major projects.

Tool: Share the Load Spreadsheet

The previous tool is useful for making sense of your various tasks, and perhaps it helped you decide it's time to delegate additional tasks. Using a spreadsheet that illustrates who does what can help you figure out what to delegate and to whom it should be delegated. Tzippi Moss (2020), author of *Angels and Tahina*, a memoir of her journey hiking the Israel Trail, comments, "We each carry not just an outer pack, but an inner one as well. And traveling light results in shedding weight not only physically, but metaphorically" (p. 65). You need to keep your pack as light as possible whether hiking or prioritizing your priorities, and you shed weight when you know how and when to delegate certain tasks.

Having charted your to-do list using the matrices in the previous section, you have undoubtedly come up with some tasks that are low on your priority list. You need to let go of them. Jesse Sostrin (2017), author of *The Manager's Dilemma: Beyond the Job Description*, states, "One of the most difficult transitions for leaders to make is the shift from *doing* to *leading*." While you might want to be seen as a doer, someone who is involved in the daily work, rather than someone who just hands off tasks, there are just too many tasks and complex projects for you to accomplish in a timely manner. Delegating tasks is a necessary element of the job. Delegating is not shirking your responsibility; it's empowering others to take on particular responsibilities as well.

To keep those balls in the air, Sostrin (2017) explains that you need to be less involved and more essential. This goes back to looking at the matrices just discussed and determining the impact and passion of each task or project. The higher the impact and passion, the more essential it is for you to be involved. The lower the impact and passion, the less you need to be involved and the more likely it is that those tasks are delegated. When delegating tasks to a coworker, acknowledge their importance and strengths and explain why they are qualified to do the job. That gives them the confidence to complete the task and gives you the time to work on a project that is far more essential. And of course, when the job is complete, a small gift, such as a chocolate bar with a note of appreciation, is greatly valued.

To monitor staff involvement in activities, tasks, and events, I maintain what I call the *share the load spreadsheet*. I enter every staff member's name in the first column and the activity, task, or event for which each is responsible in the columns to the right. There are staff members with activities, tasks, and events in multiple cells, while there are others who would never have entries if not for being "voluntold." Sharing the load is important because it keeps those who regularly volunteer from getting burned out and resenting those who do not carry their weight. There will always be those who do more, but there should be a minimum for which each person is responsible.

Once you have delegated a task, activity, or event to a staff member, use a spreadsheet program like Microsoft Excel or Google Sheets to keep track (see figure 1.2, page 10, for an example with staff names omitted). Breaking down tasks by staff member will not only help you decide who is best to handle various tasks but also help you keep track of who is doing what. A share the load spreadsheet is not designed to share with staff. It is your private document to help you balance staff contribution and delegated tasks.

Position	Staff Name	Responsibility 1	Responsibility 2	Responsibility 3
Grade 7 Language Arts		Honor roll breakfasts	Essay contests	
Grade 7 Mathematics		Junior varsity sports	Master schedule	
Grade 7 Science		Parent-teacher association (PTA)	Science fair	
Grade 7 Social Studies		History day	Ski club	
Grade 8 Language Arts		Master schedule	Poetry slam	Technology support
Grade 8 Mathematics		Mathematics team	Varsity sports	
Grade 8 Science		Science fair		
Grade 8 Social Studies		History day	Geography bee	
Instrumental Music		Band concerts	Orchestra concerts	
Physical Education		Eighth-grade leadership program	Intramural sports	
Vocal Music		Choir concerts	Play productions	
Social Worker		Positive behavioral interventions and supports (PBIS) chair	Attendance	
Counselor		Master schedule	Course registration	Transition to high school (spring)

Figure 1.2: Share the load spreadsheet example.

Tool: Thinking and Productivity Styles Reflection

Sometimes, in order to get organized, it's helpful to look within to better understand how you think. How do your thinking and productivity styles impact your work and how you work with those around you? My office clerk commented that I was like a ping-pong ball, whizzing from one side of the table to the other, because I was always shifting my attention from one task to the next. I replied that if I couldn't ping-pong between tasks, then I would not be well suited for my job. I understood my own thinking and productivity styles and how to use them to stay organized, but to her, it looked at bit random. One day I had us both complete a mind styles survey. Anthony Gregorc (1982), widely recognized for his work in learning styles, developed the mind styles model, which provides an organized way to understand how the mind works. When we looked at the results, we could clearly see the differences in our mind styles. Based on our answers, she was heavily concrete-sequential, while I was heavily abstract-random. And thank goodness I had a clerk who was concrete-sequential! This survey gave context to our styles of thinking and productivity. Once she understood that we had very different work styles, it was easy to see how we complemented each other in ways that allowed us to organize and complete all the necessary tasks as a team.

There are many different styles of thinking and productivity. Whether you finish tasks in a particular sequence or ping-pong back and forth between different tasks, whether you color-code your lists, or whether you're someone who prefers to work alone or with a team, knowing your personal style is useful in helping you manage yourself with regard to work completion.

My clerk and I reflected two of the four types of thinking styles, which include (1) concrete-sequential (my office clerk), (2) abstract-random (me), (3) concrete-random, and (4) abstract-sequential (Gregorc, 1982). If you are more sequential, you are more likely to follow a step-by-step process in a logical sequence. If you are more random in nature, you act more likely to stop and start activities or projects at will, depending on what you deem important at the moment. Concrete individuals deal with things that exist in the physical world, using their senses to learn new concepts, while abstract individuals prefer the ideal world, using reason and intuition to deal with ideas and concepts (Wille, 2004).

While the mind styles model in particular and the notion of learning styles as teaching tools in general have faced criticism (Cuevas, 2015; Reio & Wiswell, 2006), Gregorc (2020) maintains that using mind styles can be important to self-understanding: "There is nothing more fulfilling than to realize that you are somebody [and] your mental design has meaning." Essentially, you can use the information from these surveys to further your perspective on yourself and others while still understanding the limits of what such surveys can really tell you. People are complicated, so knowing their preferences and tendencies can only take you so far.

As my clerk and I discovered, the combinations of our strongest perception and ordering abilities were, in a sense, polar opposites. She, as a concrete-sequential thinker, works best with order, logical sequence, predictability, and facts in a structured environment. As an abstract-random thinker, I prefer listening to others to gather data and focusing on the issues at hand. That trait of focusing on the issues at hand is what makes me look like that whizzing ping-pong ball. When an issue arises, I quickly switch from what I was doing to the new issue.

This also means that I have to think about with whom I am working and to whom I am writing or speaking. There are situations where I have to compensate for being random. I've had to teach myself to intentionally think logically and sequentially when writing and speaking so that my audience doesn't get confused or frustrated. It can definitely be a detriment if I don't think about how my thinking style affects others. If people get confused or frustrated by lack of order in my communication, I've handed them every reason to tune me out.

Understanding how you prefer to work helps you to form teams that complement your thinking style. To learn more about how your mind works, you can take a thinking styles assessment online at www.incredibleart.org/files/p-test.htm for $1.99, or review the following summaries and decide which combination of strengths and talents define how you work best (Anderson, n.d.; Gregorc, 1982).

- **Concrete-sequential:** You tend to like order, predictability, logical sequence, and following directions. You really like having a schedule or agenda to follow.
- **Concrete-random:** You are more likely to experiment, take risks, and solve problems independently. You really like having concrete examples.
- **Abstract-sequential:** You like your points to be heard, you analyze situations before making a decision, and you tend to apply logic. You really like being able to work alone.
- **Abstract-random:** You listen to others, you prefer group harmony, and you have healthy relationships with others. You really like to focus on the issues at hand.

Once you understand your preferred thinking style, it's beneficial to discover the thinking styles of your staff and coworkers. Have them take the assessment or have them self-assess by looking at Gregorc's chart online (Anderson, n.d.) or at the preceding descriptions.

Both thinking and productivity styles reflect how we prefer to process information, solve problems, and complete tasks. While Gregorc (1982, 2020) explains our preferences with mind styles, Carson Tate (2015b), author of *Work Simply*, explains our preferences with productivity styles. Tate (2015b) illustrates one of the most widely used models to explain cognitive styles of human thinking and behavior. The whole-brain model, developed by Ned Herrmann in 1979, was designed to illustrate how the brain perceives and processes information (Herrmann, 1996). The model uses four quadrants, each representing the unique way "we perceive, comprehend, manage, communicate, and use information, all of which impact our productivity at work and in life" (Tate, 2015b, pp. 27–28).

The four productivity styles include the following (Tate, 2015b).

1. **Prioritizer:** Logical, analytical, fact-based, critical, and realistic thinking
2. **Planner:** Organized, sequential, planned, and detailed thinking
3. **Arranger:** Supportive, expressive, and emotional thinking
4. **Visualizer:** Holistic, intuitive, integrating, and synthesizing thinking

Tate (2015a) developed a measurement tool called the productivity style assessment, based on Herrmann's work. It is a quick assessment to help you understand your own style of productivity. This assessment gives you an instant report of your personal style of productivity, along with the characteristics of that style. There are twenty-eight questions in this assessment, focusing on how you prioritize your tasks, how you manage your time regarding tasks and projects, and how you prefer to work on those tasks and projects (Tate, 2015a). You can take this quick assessment at https://bit.ly/41zNVp9, and once you submit your answers, you will receive your dominant productivity style along with an explanation of the characteristics of your style.

When I took the assessment, my dominant productivity style was *arranger*, which Tate (2015a) describes like this:

> They encourage teamwork to maximize output, and they make decisions intuitively as events unfold. They block off time to complete work but excel at partnering with others to get it done. They communicate effectively, which helps them build and lead project teams. They tend to maintain visual lists, often using color.

When I think about these characteristics in terms of how I work as a principal, I prefer to work with teams who are passionate and excited about the focus of the task. I usually schedule a block of time to work on the task or project, but if the team is available to work at a different time, I do my best to make it happen when it's most convenient for the team. As for maintaining visual lists using color, my office is papered wall to wall with color-coded sticky notes. I may not be able to locate the note immediately (it's that random trait), but I will know what color I am looking for.

Jamie Birt (2022), a career coach, identifies a similar list of four productivity styles.

1. **Logical:** Drivers, doers, data-oriented
2. **Detail-oriented:** Sequential, organized, detailed-oriented
3. **Supportive:** Expressive, value collaboration, build relationships
4. **Idea-oriented:** Pioneers, leaders, big-picture thinkers

There are a variety of quick assessments you can take to determine your personal productivity style. They may not use the exact same style names and groups of traits that Tate (2015a, 2015b) or Birt (2022) use, but they all provide insight into your personal style. Here are an additional few you can try.

- https://hbr.org./2015/01/assessment-whats-your-personal-productivity-style
- www.indeed.com/career-advice/career-development/working-styles
- www.scienceofpeople.com/work-style

These models and others like them can help you understand your own productivity style and can help you form effective teams based on other members' productivity styles. Once you understand your own productivity style, it helps to have those who complement your style working with you to complete tasks and projects. You need the planners who are super organized to keep the team on track. You need the prioritizers to have the facts and logic, and you need the visualizers who can synthesize and pull it all together. And, of course, you'll need an arranger like me, the cheerleader, who encourages the teamwork and ensures that the project gets done.

Once others on your staff define their preferred thinking and productivity styles, use figure 1.3 to note their characteristics. To determine each one's style, you may ask if they would be willing to take one of the assessments or have them reflect on the traits of the different models and have each self-determine which they feel fits them most accurately.

Team Member	Thinking Style	Productivity Style
Staff A	Very concrete, needs a lot of advance notice with regard to change	Visualizer, idea-oriented; sees the big picture
Staff B	More random and flexible. Can ask for something at the last minute	Prioritizer, logical; data driven
Staff C	Very sequential, needs to see the steps involved	Arranger, supportive; gets everyone involved
Staff D	Sequential, likes things to be in a certain order	Planner, detail-oriented; organizes the details

Figure 1.3: Thinking and productivity styles reflection.

*Visit **go.SolutionTree.com/leadership** for a free reproducible version of this figure.*

Communicating your work style is as important as understanding it. My clerk did not truly understand my work style until we took that assessment and discussed the results. We learned that we had different productivity styles, but we realized that together, we were able to get everything done. Having teams of members with different productivity styles will allow for more specialization and project success. For example, if you are not detail oriented, explain to coworkers that you see the big picture but really need a team of people who will focus on the details. When you are vulnerable about a particular area of strength, others will welcome the opportunity to put their strengths to work.

I learned from that snowstorm in Switzerland that I need to be organized when I take extended hikes. If I don't know where the bear spray is and I find that I need it, well, that's a problem. To avoid preventable problems both on the trail and in the office, knowing how to organize, prioritize, and delegate your unending list of tasks will allow you to complete the important tasks and projects in a timely and less-stressful manner. And now that you understand your thinking and productivity styles, you will find that you work more effectively with teams to accomplish those tasks and projects.

Tip 2: Set Goals

If your goal is to successfully reach the summit, you have to know the route, which is meticulously planned out prior to setting foot on the trail. In between the trailhead and the summit is a process with steps that need to be taken to reach the summit. Similarly, in the role of a principal, if you want to succeed, you have to set goals. According to Harvey Mackay (2022), writing for the *Minneapolis Star Tribune*, "Goals serve as a stimulus to life. They help us focus, and they remind us what we're working toward. Without goals, there is no purpose, and without purpose, there will be no significant accomplishments." And Edwin A. Locke and Gary P. Latham (2019), drawing on fifty years of research, show that setting clear goals leads to better performance.

Goals give you focus and direction; they give you a reason to get things done. When you have a goal, you will have some type of plan to lead to that goal. When you and your team achieve a goal, it gives everyone a sense of accomplishment and competence to move forward with additional aspirations and goals. When setting goals, you have to carefully craft them so that you can ultimately achieve what you set out to accomplish. If you don't achieve a particular goal, you can recraft that goal or take a different approach. This tip offers tools for developing SMART goals, reflecting on the *why* behind each goal, and keeping track of progress on goals.

Tool: SMART Goal Template

Brainstorming your goals should start with asking yourself a few questions: How do I set reasonable goals for myself? Where am I right now with what I want to do? How much training will I need to attain my goals? Do I need to spend an extraordinary amount of time learning new skills in order to achieve my goals? Will attaining my goals be expensive in terms of funding, time, and resources? You want to exert effort toward achieving your goals, but you do not want to exhaust your time and resources to no avail.

Start with a SMART goal, a time-tested best-practice method for setting goals. SMART goals were first outlined by George T. Doran in a 1981 issue of *Management Review*, described as having a meaningful effect by being measurable and attainable. The concept has become widely popular in education (Conzemius & O'Neill, 2014). SMART is an acronym for *specific, measurable, attainable, relevant,* and *time bound*. In some SMART goal definitions, R refers to realistic or results oriented (Conzemius & O'Neill, 2014). In effect, you can put all of the R-words together to form a goal that is results oriented, realistic, and relevant to your life. Principals and their leadership teams usually have schoolwide goals written into a yearly plan, typically aligned with strategies and interventions for continuous improvement. However, setting your own personal and professional goals gives you your own purpose and focus.

Locke and Latham's (2019) extensive research into goal setting and task performance led to five key principles for successful goal setting that align with and support the thinking behind SMART goals. These principles include the following.

1. **Commitment:** The degree to which you are attached to your goal and the determination to reach it
2. **Clarity:** The degree to which your goals are clear, specific, and unambiguous
3. **Challenge:** The degree of the goal's difficulty. The goal must be challenging yet attainable.
4. **Complexity:** The degree of the goal's demands. Keep your goals realistic in both skill level and time frame.
5. **Feedback:** The degree to which you monitor your progress. Immediate feedback helps to determine your progress and the degree to which the goal is being met.

I'm not setting a goal to climb Mount Everest. It's not anywhere on any list. I know it's not achievable, and I'm not going to exert the effort and expense to try to conquer that mountain. There are plenty of other mountains I can climb that allow me to breathe without supplemental oxygen and allow me to stay fairly warm in the process. Mount Snowdon in Wales was a challenge, but it was achievable with the perfect balance of exertion and exhilaration. Finding that balance of exertion toward achieving the goal and exhilaration of attaining it is key to feeling a sense of accomplishment without undue stress.

A SMART goal starts with a specific *action-oriented* statement of what you intend to accomplish. Goals should be stated using precise terms, not vague ones, and should be quantified as much as possible. You can set professional SMART goals as well as personal SMART goals. Ask yourself what you are willing to work toward accomplishing. If your goal is to work out at the gym five days a week, that might be a bit lofty given a principal's school or family schedule. Twice a week might be more reasonable and attainable over time. But if five is your goal, hey, go for it. In any case, write down your goal and keep it somewhere in sight.

Once you have written down your specific goal, you must find a way to *measure* your progress and provide evidence that proves whether or not you have achieved your goal. You need to have some type of device to measure your progress. If your goal is to work out at the gym twice a week, that is easy to measure and will provide evidence as to whether or not you are achieving the goal.

It's important that your goal is *attainable* and possible to achieve within a specified time constraint. If you find that your goal is not attainable in that time frame, you will need to adjust the goal itself or the time frame.

Your goal also needs to be *realistic and relevant* to your values, purpose, and abilities. If the goal is not relevant to what you want to accomplish in the immediate future, there will be no motivation or urgency to work on it. While your goal may be challenging, it should not be impossible to attain. When you fail to reach a goal, you lose motivation to set additional goals.

Lastly, your SMART goal needs to be bound by a realistic *time frame*. If your time frame is too short, you will be under undue stress to achieve it. If your time frame is too far in the future, you may be less likely to find the motivation or urgency to pursue it.

In figure 1.4, I provide a sample of a professional and personal SMART goal. A reproducible version is available on page 33.

	Goal	Professional	Personal
S	Specific	Visit five classrooms, record observations, and provide feedback by the end of each week.	Invest 10 percent of every paycheck into my portfolio.
M	Measurable	Track data regarding classroom visits and observations, and provide feedback.	Review portfolio and track investments.
A	Attainable	Given my daily schedule, it is realistic to visit five classrooms per week, record observations, and provide feedback.	Given my expenses, I can afford to invest 10 percent of every paycheck.
R	Relevant, realistic	Providing feedback to teachers regarding classroom instruction is a priority.	Investing a certain amount of money each month is a sound financial responsibility.
T	Time bound or timely	Complete twenty classroom observations by the end of the month.	Invest 10 percent of each paycheck biweekly for nine months.

Figure 1.4: SMART goal template.

 Tool: The Why of My Goal Process

Beyond thinking through attributes of your goals, reflecting on *why* you are setting a particular goal is essential to achieving them consistently. *Harvard Business Review* writers Rakshitha Arni Ravishankar and Kelsey Alpaio (2022) outline five ways to set more achievable goals. They advise connecting every goal you write to why you are challenging yourself to achieve that goal. As in decision making, you have to be able to articulate *why* you have chosen to pursue a particular goal. Their five steps are the following.

1. Answer the question of *why*. Ask yourself, "Why am I setting this goal?"

2. Break your goal down into manageable pieces or steps.

3. Set a deadline, and then increase the time by 25 percent so that you don't abandon your goal if you don't make the first deadline. You can even add intermittent deadlines to help keep yourself on track.

4. Instead of getting hung up on improvement, focus on what you can continue doing that will be productive toward your goal.

5. Don't spend too much time thinking about missed goals or failures in the past. Remember what worked and what didn't work, and stay optimistic.

The tool in figure 1.5 (page 16) provides a way to map out each goal according to these steps. A reproducible version is available on page 34.

Why	My goal is to observe five classrooms per week so that I can provide feedback regarding classroom instruction to each teacher the following week.
Steps	First, I will observe each class. Then I will type up my notes. Finally, I will meet with each teacher to provide feedback the following week.
Deadline	I would like to attain my goal by the end of each week, but will accept a deadline of the following Monday.
Focus	I will continue to make sure my calendar allows for five classroom observations per week.
Progress monitoring	If I am unable to observe five classrooms in a given week, I will prioritize the ones I feel I need to observe the most so that I can provide the necessary feedback in a timely manner.

Source: Adapted from Ravishankar & Alpaio, 2022.
Figure 1.5: The why of my goal process.

 **Tool: Progress Report**

Even if you've clarified and thought through your goals, in the end, you still need to hit your deadlines. What is the best way to hold yourself accountable and keep to those deadlines? Author Kristi DePaul (2022) explains that a major factor for missing a deadline is what is known as the planning fallacy. The *planning fallacy*, she says, is that "our perceptions of our available time, our abilities, and any roadblocks we may hit are greatly skewed" (DePaul, 2022). We tend to be overly optimistic about the ease of attaining a goal. We don't factor in the extra time we had to spend on a behavior incident, how exhausted we are at the end of the day, or an impromptu administration meeting. And with all the interruptions we have every day, it's hard to remain on any one task for any length of time.

Markus K. Brunnermeier, Filippos Papakonstantinou, and Jonathan A. Parker (2008) studied the planning fallacy and found that people underestimate the amount of time something will take to achieve and thus tend to postpone working on that task or goal. The planning fallacy leads you to have to cram in the end because you have far more than you originally anticipated. (Remember your college days?)

So how do you overcome the planning fallacy? DePaul (2022) offers these three steps to keep you from falling into the college days of cramming.

1. **Take an outside view:** Your view may be distorted, so ask others how much time it might take to achieve your goal. You can also research what you are expecting to accomplish to see what time frames are advised.

2. **Commit early and publicly:** Start right away and talk to people about your plans. Gather the resources and supplies you need to achieve your goal and have them at hand. Use a calendar to keep track of your progress.

3. **Add in some buffer time:** Just as Ravishankar and Alpaio (2022) advise, this is that 25 percent increase in time to allow for those interfering factors that you can't control.

Goals can easily get lost in the sheer magnitude of your job. So how do you keep your goals on the front burner? Mackay (2005, 2022), author of *Swim With the Sharks Without Being Eaten Alive*, claims that one of the most effective incentives to succeed in holding yourself to your goals is to talk about your goals with others. Talking to friends, family, coworkers, and bosses about your aspirations and goals puts pressure on yourself to achieve them. He also advises keeping goals front and center where you can actually see them. This negates the out-of-sight, out-of-mind situation and forces you to question your progress.

Gail Matthews (2020), a psychology professor at Dominican University of California who studies goal achievement, finds that people who write down their goals and share their progress with others are significantly more likely to achieve their goals. Acknowledging your progress is important for holding yourself to your goals. Even the smallest steps toward attaining a goal should be recognized and appreciated. Don't dwell on what you haven't accomplished; celebrate what you have achieved so far.

To avoid the planning fallacy and capitalize on some of the advice shared in this section, each week, review your goal, who you shared it with that week, and your progress toward achieving it. The progress report in figure 1.6 provides an example. A reproducible version is available on page 35. Finish the report with the steps you will take toward achieving your goal in the next week.

Your goals don't have to be complicated or rigorous. They need to be relevant and important to you. You don't need to climb Mt. Everest. A smaller mountain will provide you with the motivation to succeed. As Mackay (2005) iterates, "A goal is a dream with a deadline" (p. 57). When you write down your goal and monitor the progress, you will find the exhilaration of success outpaces the exertion of getting there.

My Goal	Observe five classrooms per week so that I can provide feedback regarding classroom instruction.
Who I Shared It With This Week	The five teachers I intend to observe and my secretary
My Progress	I was able to observe in five classrooms but was only able to meet with four of them the following week.
Next Steps	Reduce the number of observations per week to four so that teachers receive timely feedback the following week.

Figure 1.6: Progress report.

Tip 3: Make a Decision

You come to where two trails intersect, and you need to make a decision. Which trail do I take? One trail may be steeper, the other longer, one may require a river crossing, and one of them may bring you right back to where you started. Having a map on the trail helps you decide which one to take. In the principal's office, there isn't one map to guide your decision; however, there are tools you can use to help you decide which route to take, given your situation.

Principals make hundreds of decisions every day. The degree of complexity, severity, priority, time at hand, and number of people affected all factor into any decision you ultimately make. In many cases, you will be working with a leadership team or focus group to work toward a decision. Whatever the decision, and regardless of how it was made, you are ultimately responsible for the outcome. Decision making is the art of inquiry: asking the right questions in order to get the data and evidence you need to make that crucial decision. Decisions have to be grounded with purpose and integrity. As principals, we have to think critically about our options, and we have to be able to explain why we are making certain decisions. There's a delicate balance of compliance with policies and regulations versus challenging the status quo. We need to navigate that spectrum and understand our reasons and rationales for our judgment. To assist you in arriving at timely decisions, this tip offers tools for ascertaining the why behind decisions (the two-tine litmus test and starting with the why), considering the impact of concerns and influence, finding the root causes of problems to improve decision making (the fishbone diagram), and avoiding the pitfalls of bad decisions.

Tool: Two-Tine Litmus Test

Why are you making the decision you're making? You have to be able to articulate your reasons for making decisions. Making decisions based on vague thoughts like "Just 'cause I thought it would be a good idea" isn't good enough. This is especially important as a school leader. Simon Sinek (2009), author of *Start With Why*, explains that when people know why you are proposing an idea, you are inspiring them to act along with you. As a principal, if you are able to inspire people, you give them a sense of belonging, and you create a following of people who act because they are inspired, not because they are cajoled or manipulated.

I found that starting with a simple approach works well when making a decision in the office. I ask myself two questions: (1) "Is it good for students?" and (2) "Is it good for the school?" This is what I call the *two-tine litmus test*. Figure 1.7 offers a way to visualize the two-tine litmus test.

Some decisions can be made directly based on the litmus test. These decisions usually do not involve systemic change or a lot of money. These decisions are more procedural or managerial in nature. Other decisions that involve a greater degree of change or money can begin with the litmus test. If a decision passes the litmus test and more evidence and rationalization for change and funding are necessary, there are additional tools. While this test is simple in nature, it's not just a yes-or-no prospect. Of course, if the answer is *no*, the test is done. If the answer is *yes*, then you need to be able to articulate why the answer is yes.

As an example, I had to make a decision regarding whether to continue our prekindergarten program. We were able to fund this program for one year through Title I funding, but after that first year, we no longer had the funds for a viable program. I didn't want to lose that program, as I believed it was an excellent means of preparing students for kindergarten. I suggested to school district administrators that, to continue this program, I could charge tuition, charging enough to provide scholarships for families who could not afford to pay the fee. I was told I could not charge tuition, but I could charge a fee through the community education program. However, district leaders articulated two caveats: (1) if I did not cover my expenses, those dollars would be subtracted from my general education budget, and (2) there would be no curricular support from the early childhood education department.

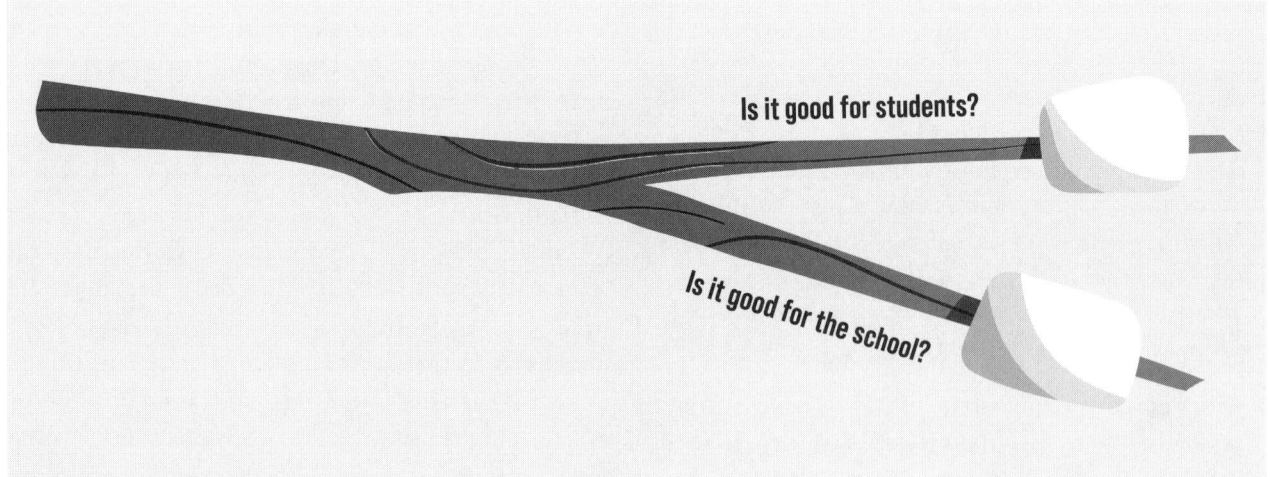

Figure 1.7: Two-tine litmus test.

My decision-making process began with the two-tine litmus test. I could easily answer the first question of whether the program was good for students. Yes, because it is a high-quality program that prepares students for success in kindergarten and beyond. I could also easily answer the second question of whether it was good for the school. Yes, because it would allow us to maintain a program that is in high demand, and it would boost a lagging kindergarten enrollment. While it is easy to stop at the answer of *yes*, what is more important are answers to the questions of *why* it is good for students and *why* it is good for the school.

I could easily see that it would be a sound decision to continue the program; however, I would have to rely on an outside funding source, as we did not have the budget for this program to continue. Outside funding is more complex and involves a financial risk that would affect the entire school budget. Therefore, I needed to use other decision-making tools to proceed with this decision.

Tool: Start With the Why Process

The litmus test helped me arrive at the why in general terms—why it was good for students and why it was good for the school. We had a quality program that would prepare students for school success and boost our kindergarten enrollment the following year. However, families needed to know why they should enroll in a public-school program for which they would have to pay a fee when there were fully funded options within the school district.

Simon Sinek (2009) explains that "people don't buy WHAT you do, they buy WHY you do it" (p. 41). His mantra pertains to both products and services. Sinek's (2009) concept of the *Golden Circle* imagines three concentric circles that suggest a process for the questions we ask, starting in the middle with *why*, then moving outward to *how* and finally to the outermost circle for *what*. He believes that to inspire people to buy into your decision, they need to know *why* you are making that decision.

The why in my example was not just the prekindergarten program; it was our belief in providing a quality learning environment that would prepare students for school success in kindergarten and beyond. We also believed that when families experienced school success in prekindergarten, they would be more inclined to remain at the school for subsequent years, creating a more stable enrollment. But of course, it is not enough just to decide why you make a certain decision; you have to back it up with *how* you will make this decision happen. To make this program a reality, I had to fund it in an unconventional way, asking families to pay a fee for this public school program when there were other prekindergarten programs in the school district that were fully funded.

Using Sinek's (2009) Golden Circle, I started in the middle with the reason why I wanted to continue providing a prekindergarten program. I then moved out toward how I could continue it, explaining that I would charge each family a fee for the program based on the fixed costs plus the scholarship funds. The fee would be reasonably priced based on covering our costs, including scholarships, and on what I found private four-year-old programs to cost. Once I could explain why I wanted the program and how I was going to fund it, I could begin selling the what—the actual program.

Tool: Concern and Influence Organizer

Once you understand your *why* of a particular situation, you can begin to look at the *how* and *what*: What about this situation can you control and how can you influence it? What do you need to consider when making the decision?

Many of our decisions come with a myriad of conditions we can't control, and when you start to focus and fret over the things out of your control, you do nothing but waste time and energy. Stephen R. Covey's (1989) model of the circles of concern and influence emphasizes how you can think positively about the things you can influence rather than negatively on the things you cannot control. This model allows you to visually look at what school issues are of concern and what aspects of the issues you can influence and control.

The aim of the circles of concern and influence model is to help you take responsibility for your work concerns and thus be more proactive, productive, and happier. The idea is to expend your energy on the things you can influence, even if you can't control them. When you focus on the things you can influence, you expand your knowledge and experience, thus increasing your circle of influence. Proactive people channel their energy in the circle of influence. They focus and work on the things they can actually do something about. They look at the situation with a positive mindset, which causes their circle of influence to enlarge. In contrast, reactive people focus on the circle of concern: the circumstances over which they have no control. The negative energy causes the circle of influence to shrink in relation to the circle of concern. Choosing your responses to circumstances can powerfully affect your ability to influence your circumstances.

You can use this model to help you and your team look at areas of concern. You will realize you have more power than you think over things that feel out of your control. Circles of concern and influence are a great tool for resilience. If anyone feels out of control, you can question all of the aspects where they feel that lack of control and see if they can have more agency regarding them.

For the things they simply can't control, get them to stop worrying about them. You can't affect government policy or the weather—so either pack what you need to get through the ordeal or just put those things aside and park them for a while.

Let's go back to the decision regarding whether or not to continue the prekindergarten program. I certainly could not afford to lose any money from my school budget, so to help with my decision, I used the circles of concern and influence to guide my thinking. The concern and influence organizer in figure 1.8 helps get them on paper. First, I listed my concerns, those areas that I could not control. I could not control the fact that I did not have the school funds to continue the program, I could not control the fact that I would lack district support for the program, nor could I control that there were no precedents to follow. I then listed those aspects that I could influence: the prekindergarten curriculum, the cost of the program, the classroom space, and the fact that I could provide scholarships for families who qualified for educational benefits by adjusting the cost per pupil. A reproducible version is available on page 36.

Covey (1989) explains that "proactive people focus their efforts in the Circle of Influence. They work on the things they can do something about" (p. 90). I set up the model (figure 1.9) in the manner of a proactive, growth mindset with the circle of influence larger than the circle of concern to visualize concentrating my energy on the things I could influence.

I decided to charge the fee and risk the financial aspects and lack of district support. It was a wise decision; as the program flourished, I was able to sustain the scholarships and not lose any school funds, and the school enrollment began to increase. Two years later, the legislature approved prekindergarten programs in public schools, and we were already three years ahead with a successful program.

Concern	Influence
Funding	Program curriculum
Lack of district support	Cost per pupil
No precedents to follow	Classroom space
	Provide scholarships

Source: Adapted from Covey, 1989.

Figure 1.8: Concern and influence organizer.

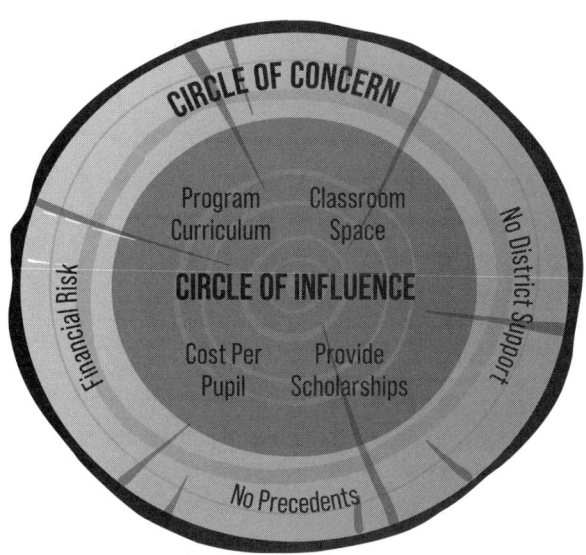

Source: Adapted with permission from The 7 Habits of Highly Effective People, *Stephen R. Covey, 1989.*
Figure 1.9: Circles of concern and influence example.

 **Tool: Fishbone Diagram**

Sometimes making a decision relies on understanding the root cause of the problem. *Root-cause analysis* is a process that helps teams identify underlying factors or causes of a problem or an event for which the team needs to make decisions requiring corrective action. Prior to making a decision, understanding the contributing factors of why a program, event, or policy is not meeting student needs can help the team develop strategies for improvement.

The fishbone diagram, originally developed by Kaoru Ishikawa (1968), a pioneer of modern management, is a tool that allows you to do a deep dive into your stated problem to get a better understanding of what systems may be causing the problem. Visualizing the causes enables the team to engage in a deeper dialogue as you make decisions for improvement. Using the fishbone diagram can help identify root causes rather than just symptoms. The fishbone diagram continues to be widely used for root-cause analysis (Creighton, 2022). To choose a template that fits your needs, you can find an array of choices by searching *fishbone diagram templates*.

To use the fishbone diagram, follow these steps.

1. Agree on the problem statement, and write it in the box at the far right. Be as specific as possible about the problem.

2. Agree on major categories or themes as causes of the problem. Write these on the large bones extending from the spine.

3. Brainstorm the possible causes of the problem. Ask questions about each major category and write those causes on the smaller bones extending from each major category.

In figure 1.10 (page 22), I demonstrate how we have used the fishbone diagram to look at underperforming standardized mathematics scores. The example I used in figure 1.10 is the situation of students underperforming on standardized mathematics tests. To understand why our students were not performing at a level proficient with the grade level, we did a root-cause analysis using the fishbone diagram. We stated our problem in the form of a question: Why are our students underperforming on standardized mathematics tests? We then arrived at four major areas that could hold the answers to our question: (1) curriculum, (2) teacher preparation, (3) testing procedures, and (4) student preparation. We then brainstormed the factors or causes that could be contributing to the problem. Were we covering all the standards using the current mathematics curriculum? Did teachers know which standards needed to be mastered? Did students have the necessary practice to gain test-taking strategies and skills? These were all possible causes to the effect of the test scores. After we analyzed the root causes, we made decisions regarding the areas in which to start our corrective actions.

Once the team has analyzed some root causes, it will help you make subsequent decisions to improve the situation. In this case, some decisions may involve altering the curriculum or possibly just adjusting the sequence or pacing. Teachers may need more professional learning or the students may have had insufficient practice and lack some of the necessary testing strategies. By asking questions and engaging in dialogue to learn from team members, decisions may become clearer and solutions will begin to evolve.

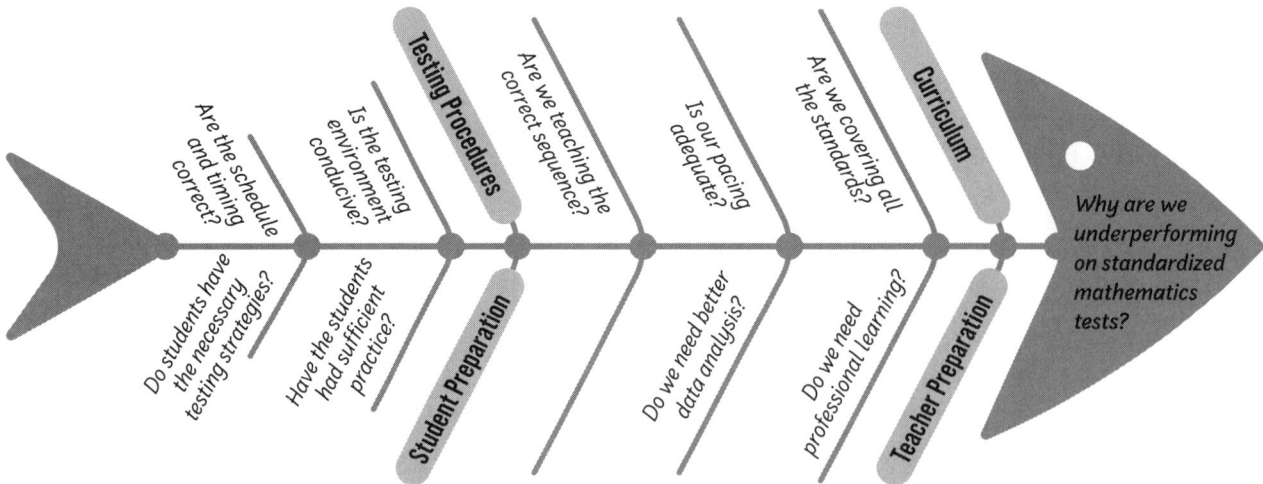

Source: Adapted from Ishikawa, 1968.
Figure 1.10: Fishbone diagram.

 Tool: Heuristics

On a backpacking trip in northern Minnesota, my hiking companion Jackie and I came to a bridge that had been washed out and had to decide how best to get across the stream. We had several options. We could just wade across in our boots, take our boots off and wade barefoot, or change into another pair of footwear. I opted for wading across in my boots as it was too rocky and muddy for bare feet, and I really wanted to have a dry pair of shoes at the end of the day for when I was done hiking. That turned out to be a poor decision. My boots became waterlogged, and we had miles to go before we camped. They were so heavy that my feet became bruised and sore for the rest of the trip.

As a school leader, with all the many decisions you make every day, you are bound to run into pitfalls. Whether it is making a major curricular or financial decision to deciding what to have for lunch, there will be times when you make a wrong or bad decision. So how do you minimize the risk of making a bad decision?

Kendra Cherry (2022d), author and educational consultant, offers several tips on how to avoid the pitfalls of making a bad decision. One of her tips is using *heuristics*, which are mental rules or shortcuts that allow you to make decisions quickly by simplifying things so that you don't spend enormous amounts of time analyzing every detail (Cherry, 2022b, 2022d).

These mental shortcuts are useful for quick decision making. For example, should I go to Arby's for lunch today or just get a lunch in the cafeteria? Pros: I really want a roast beef sandwich, fries, and a diet soda. Cons: I don't have time to drive over there and wait in the drive-through, I'll end up consuming more fat, calories, and caffeine than I should, and chances are, it will get cold before I eat it because something will require my attention as soon as I get back. The thought of eating something other than a school lunch is extremely tempting, but what's holding me back from that fast-food lunch is the time it takes to get there and back. The cons really outweigh my desire for fast food. My mental shortcut plays up the advantages of the school lunch.

Heuristics can be helpful if you use these shortcuts wisely. The key is to recognize when your mental shortcuts are leading to good decisions and when they reinforce biased thinking. If you recognize pitfalls, such as *optimism bias*, which is "our tendency to overestimate the likelihood of experiencing good events while underestimating the likelihood of experiencing bad events" (Cherry, 2022d), you can avoid those shortcuts that lead to poor decision making. In the previous hiking example, I was sure I could cross that stream without getting much water in my boots. I was far too optimistic about my chances of getting across while keeping water out of my boots. If I had been able to recognize the optimism bias that led me to that decision, my feet would have thanked me.

Other factors that can contribute to making bad decisions include automatic thinking (engaging in actions on autopilot), multitasking (trying to keep those balls in the air without giving yourself a break), and decision fatigue (an overload of decision making that leads to stress and fatigue; Cherry, 2022d). Heuristics can contribute to or help you avoid these pitfalls.

While there is evidence that this tool can lead to sound decision making (Marewski & Gigerenzer, 2012), it can also backfire. This tool is a thinking exercise—as you move through your day, what mental shortcuts do you find yourself using? Reinforce the ones that are helpful, and eliminate the ones that are not.

Some decisions in the wilderness can result literally in either life or death. Most of your decisions won't be quite that dire, but some can have serious consequences. Careful thought processes and use of models, charts, and diagrams can help you make decisions visually as well as mentally. When the decisions involve greater risk, eliminate distractions, use appropriate models, consider all your options, consult your team or outside sources, and when fatigue sets in, take a break.

Tip 4: Know Your Purpose

Supreme Court Justice Ruth Bader Ginsburg knew what she was fighting for: justice and human rights, especially with regard to how they impacted women. Her mantra, "Fight for the things that you care about, but do it in a way that will lead others to join you" (as quoted by Vagianos, 2015), is what a principal needs to consider when making decisions, setting goals, and every other aspect of leading a school.

What are your beliefs, values, and goals? What is your purpose? While there are instruments to identify your strengths and personality type (see tip 5, page 28), you also have to dig deep within yourself to find an identity that is truly your own. This deep self-awareness helps you understand where to find the sources of your inner strengths that allow you to stay true to your belief system. You have to achieve a delicate balance between satisfying your inner self and the environment in which you live and work. When life seems like it's all uphill, like the last few steps up a steep incline, when you are breathless and lightheaded, you have to push your limits to get to your destination. Sometimes the job will feel like you're continuously heading toward fifteen thousand feet, and you will have to dig deeper to find meaning and purpose in order to stay true to yourself.

Psychologist Steven Hayes (n.d.) explains that values are your chosen qualities of being and doing. Values, he says, are not goals; they are "enduring, ongoing guides to living" (Hayes, n.d.). Your values tell you where to exert your energy and focus as well as where your motivation lies. Being a principal is important in my life, and my values, beliefs, and goals all comprise my life as a principal, not to mention my life as the person writing this book. Think about your values, your beliefs, and your purpose as you utilize some of the inventories in this section to gain deeper self-awareness. The tools for this tip include finding your *ikigai*, or purpose for getting up in the morning, a values grid for determining which values are most important to you, and a reflection tool to help strive for balance among four archetypes.

Tool: Your Ikigai

Ikigai is an Okinawan word loosely translated as the purpose for which you wake up in the morning (Gaines, 2020). It's what motivates you to live your life. Ken Mogi (2018), author of *Awakening Your Ikigai: How the Japanese Wake Up to Joy and Purpose Every Day*, is a neuroscientist based in Tokyo who lectures on concepts such as ikigai and the brain. He describes ikigai as the Japanese word for describing the pleasures and meaning of life, from "small, everyday things to big goals and achievements" (Mogi, 2018, p. 6). Ikigai, Mogi (2018) says, "gives your life a purpose and the grit to carry on" (p. 13).

Ikigai, in a way, is the antithesis of Western culture. It's not the grand goals and accomplishments; as Mogi (2018) explains, it's the small things that make your day, as small as a good cup of coffee in the morning. Happiness is fleeting moments. Mogi contends that we tend to get too preoccupied with our big goals, and we lose the small moments of happiness: "It's what's enjoyed by you" (as quoted by Kemp, 2020).

There are five pillars of ikigai, which are not mutually exclusive and have no inherent order or hierarchy (Kemp, 2020; Mogi, 2018).

1. **Starting small:** This pillar is about paying attention to the process of working toward goals and appreciating the smaller moments.

2. **Releasing yourself:** Releasing yourself, Mogi explains, is about finding happiness through acceptance of your own way of engaging with life (Kemp, 2020).

3. **Harmony and sustainability:** This pillar applies to your relationship with nature and how your actions might impact others.

4. **The joy of small things:** Indulging in small pleasures releases dopamine in the brain. This pillar is about intentionally finding happiness in things like a cup of coffee or a run before work, those little things you do for yourself.

5. **Being in the here and now:** Be intentional about valuing the present, a state of mind that should not be dismissed because it might seem childlike; it can release you to be free and creative.

Figure 1.11 illustrates examples of my ikigai, what motivates me to do the things that bring me joy in life. I find purpose in writing, freedom in skiing, protecting nature, and seeing joy in others.

Ikigai Pillars	Example
Pillar 1: Starting small	When I began writing this book, I had to look at the small steps I needed to complete each tip, tool, and chapter. The end product was a long journey from the start of the trek, but taking care of the details along the way allowed me to achieve my goal of a published book.
Pillar 2: Releasing yourself	I've learned over the years to accept my strengths and limitations. I've also accepted that they change over time. The black diamonds I could once ski do not beckon me anymore. I am far more content cruising the easier slopes and truly enjoying the ride.
Pillar 3: Harmony and sustainability	When hiking, whatever we pack in, we pack out. We never leave anything behind. It's called leave no trace. When we find a bit of trail trash, we add it to our packs, as well as the coveted trail treasure we'll occasionally come across. Living with harmony and sustainability encourages us to leave no trace in other aspects of our lives as well.
Pillar 4: The joy of small things	Every Friday morning started with treats in the staff lounge. Everyone gathered in the lounge to partake in the week's smorgasbord. People started the day on Friday in good spirits (that wonderful sugar high). You could hear and feel the joy of starting the day together with good food.
Pillar 5: Being in the here and now	As a child, I always wanted to be a rock star. Playing the drums in a rock band as an adult brings out my inner child, allowing me to be creative and expressive, generating the much-needed diversion from the stress of a day in the wilderness.

Source: Adapted from Mogi, 2018.

Figure 1.11: Your ikigai.

Visit **go.SolutionTree.com/leadership** for a free reproducible version of this figure.

 Tool: Values Organizer

Your values are about what you're willing to fight for. Brené Brown (2018), author of *Dare to Lead*, believes in "living into our values" (p. 186), meaning we don't just practice them, we truly walk our talk. Brown (2018) says, "We are clear about what we believe and hold important, and we take care that our intentions, words, thoughts, and behaviors align with those beliefs" (p. 186). In order to live into our values, we have to be able to name our values.

Brown (2018) identifies over one hundred values (visit https://bit.ly/3y2SkUg for a list). You can reduce that list down to the number of core values of your choice. Once you have those values listed, try to whittle the list down; Brown (2018) specifies three, but I found that five was a comfortable number. It's not a simple task, but once you start really reflecting and delving into your values, the ones that are nearest and dearest to you will emerge.

When I did this exercise, I looked at Brown's (2018) list and pared my list down to twenty-five values that I felt represented those most dear to me. I then whittled those twenty-five down to five that I felt encompassed the other values in the list.

1. **Belonging** (compassion, cooperation, fun, and humor)
2. **Growth** (achievement, wisdom, perseverance, open-mindedness, making a difference, and learning)
3. **Inclusion** (diversity, equality, and power)
4. **Respect** (kindness, integrity, and trust)
5. **Well-being** (safety, health, spirituality, and wealth)

We need to define these values, Brown (2018) says, because "daring leaders who live into their values are never silent about hard things" (p. 194). Knowing your values and what you stand for allows you to have the difficult, courageous conversations that are necessary as a school leader. You might not know what you will encounter on any given day, but knowing which values on which you stand firm gives you the support you need to confront the difficult, tense situations you may find yourself facing.

As your top values emerge, Brown (2018) poses three questions of each value that ask you to reflect on behaviors that support your value, behaviors that are outside your value, and an example of when you were fully living into your value. So ask yourself: "(1) Does this define me? (2) Is this who I am at my best? and (3) Is this a filter that I use to make hard decisions?" (Brown, 2018, p. 190). These values are the ones you lean on to make your decisions and set your goals.

Once you have identified your values, you can do a quick self-check to see how close you truly are to living into your values. Draw or visualize a mountain range with one of your values at the peak of each mountain (see figure 1.12 for an example). Place yourself at the elevation closest to where you believe you are in living into that value. If you are close to the summit, you stand firm on that value and truly live into it. And if you're closer to the base of the mountain, it's time to lace up those metaphorical hiking boots and be intentional about getting closer to what's important to you. The reproducible version on page 37 provides a template to try this exercise for yourself.

Figure 1.12: Values organizer.

Tool: Four Archetypes Reflection

Finding your inner self requires you to go even deeper than just acknowledging your values. Discovering your inner self requires a high level of reflection and self-awareness. Your outer self is visible to those around you. To those in my inner circle, I am defined by some as my career choice—a principal. Others identify me foremost by my relationship with them—as their mother, daughter, sister, or friend. And still others identify me by my talents and hobbies—as a tennis player, drummer, hiking afficionado, or skier. What is much less visible, and in many cases, invisible, is my inner self. When looking for this elusive aspect of yourself, it helps to consider what sets you apart.

To give some context to understanding your inner self, Angeles Arrien (1993) illustrates four archetypes that comprise what she calls the four-fold way. Arrien was a Basque-American cultural anthropologist who studied Indigenous cultures. In a YouTube video she recorded shortly before her death in 2014, called *Connecting to the Wilderness Within*, she explains, "There is something that every Indigenous culture has in common. There's a deep connection to nature and a deep connection to storytelling" (Borges, 2019).

The four archetypes include the following (Arrien, 1993).

1. **The way of the warrior:** Being present, which allows you to access the human resources of power, presence, and communication

2. **The way of the healer:** Paying attention to what has heart and meaning, which allows you to open up to the human resources of love, gratitude, acknowledgment, and validation

3. **The way of the visionary:** Telling the truth without blame or judgment, which allows you to maintain your authenticity and develops your inner vision and intuition

4. **The way of the teacher:** Being open to outcomes and not attached, which allows you to recover human resources of wisdom and objectivity

When I read Arrien's (1993) book *The Four-Fold Way* for the first time, I was well into my stint as a middle school principal and living a tense and intense existence. Many changes were imposed on the school, and, with the stress I was experiencing, some of my spirit was being quashed. I felt like I was on a trail in a wilderness with which I was quite unfamiliar. Arrien (1993) believed it is important to stay present to what is, so, rather than grasping for what I wanted things to be like, I had to work with and in the present.

When I studied the attributes of each archetype, I had to accept that I most closely identified with the warrior, even though, at heart, I wanted to believe I more closely identified with the teacher. But when I read her reflection questions asking where in my life I stopped dancing and singing, I realized it was when major changes that occurred at the middle school created that tense, stressful work situation. Arrien (1993) explains that when we stop dancing and singing, we begin to experience soul loss or loss of spirit, and dancing is the warrior's way to retrieve those parts of the self that are lost or unremembered. This coincided with a poem I had written as a self-reflection that illustrated the power of dancing and how it *can* lift the soul. In other words, I was out of balance and needed to explore ways I could restore that balance and spirit in order to reverse my perception of my work situation.

When All Else Fails, Dance!

'Twas the day before winter break
   when all was a flutter

I went down to the art room
   with all the clutter.

I found students in ugly sweaters clad

How could I possibly ever be mad?

They were watching this video
   all in amaze,

This dance, dance, dance video—
   it's all the craze.

So, I started to dance with the teens
   on that day,

And all of my cares just melted away.

If felt so great to really let loose,

Who cared if all the cameras
were on my caboose?

We shouted with joy as our arms
and legs flailed,

It was hard to think of all the things
that had failed.

So, I thought, from now on,
when things pile up,

Stress sets in and runneth over
thy cup,

Take yourself up on that wonderful chance

To move it and shake it,
just let loose and dance!

Arrien (1993) demonstrates that virtually all shamanic traditions draw on the power of those four archetypes in order to live in harmony and balance with our environment and with our own inner nature. She explains how Indigenous peoples consider it vitally important for us to be balanced in those four areas: leading, healing, visioning, and teaching. For many of us, though, she says, this balance is far from reality. Most of us tend to lean more toward one area, while leaving others relatively undeveloped. You can reflect on which archetype you are most closely aligned and where you might be out of balance.

To help organize my thoughts about each archetype, I created a simple reflection tool (see figure 1.13) that outlines the four archetypes and the traits of each. As I reflected more about my inner self and the balance that was lacking, I realized the teacher was there all the time, but it was being protected by the warrior. While deep down I know I was still the teacher, the warrior was necessary to provide me the resilience I needed to find my purpose in leading that middle school.

Warrior: Presence—Power and communication	Healer: Heart and meaning—Love, gratitude, acknowledgment, and validation
Reflection:	Reflection:
I needed to be present in the current situation. I could not dwell on the past. My job was now to work through the change and stay positive.	*The stress was affecting others, so I had to acknowledge that while the changes were difficult, we still had the one thing that could not be shaken, and that was our commitment to teaching all kids.*
Visionary: Truth telling without blame and judgment—Authenticity, inner vision, and intuition	Teacher: Openness to outcomes and unattached—Wisdom and objectivity
Reflection:	Reflection:
While I could definitely find others to blame for creating the situation I was facing, doing so would not help me lead the school through the changes. I had to find the inner strength to continue to power through the experience.	*I bowed to the time-honored Serenity Prayer—I had to acknowledge that I must accept the things I cannot change, have the courage to change the things I could, and have the wisdom to know the difference.*

Source: Adapted from Arrien, 1993.

Figure 1.13: Four archetypes reflection.

Visit **go.SolutionTree.com/leadership** *for a free reproducible version of this figure.*

Tip 5: Psych Yourself Up

If you wonder why you get along well with certain staff and not so well with others, or why certain teachers work well with some folks and not as well with others, it is probably due to personality. Personality has a lot to do with how we work with one another, much like the thinking and productivity styles addressed in tip 1 (page 6). All of these tools help you maintain a diverse, well-functioning ecosystem. As a school leader, you are going to encounter different types of personalities, and your ability to adapt your personality style to support those around you will help you succeed in building those important relationships.

The American Psychological Association (APA, n.d.a) defines *personality* as "individual differences in characteristic patterns of thinking, feeling, and behaving." We all have our own preferences as to how we work, whether we prefer to work independently, with one or two others, or with a large team. Knowing your personality type allows you to be more observant of the personality traits around you. In some cases, you may have to adapt your style to others in order to achieve particular goals and avoid unnecessary conflict. For your staff to work well with limited conflict, it is beneficial to understand your psychological type preferences so that you can be most efficient, effective, and comfortable with your own self (Perrine, 2019).

Tool: Personality and Temperament Self-Reflection Chart

There are numerous assessments that are designed to reveal your personality type and temperament that offer a good starting point, first to self-assess and then, eventually, to gather data about your staff. One of the most widely used is the time-tested Myers-Briggs Type Indicator. Myers-Briggs was developed in the 1940s by Isabel Briggs Myers and her mother Katharine Briggs, based on the work of Carl Jung's theory of psychological type and with the goal of making personality type theory accessible (Myers & Briggs Foundation, n.d.).

While it has received justified criticism throughout the years, the questionnaire continues to be updated, and research is ongoing (Gordon, 2020). The instrument expresses personality types as four-letter codes. For example, I am an ENFP (extraversion, intuition, feeling, perceiving). I have taken the survey multiple times over several years, and it always reveals the same type.

According to the Myers-Briggs inventory, as an ENFP, I am enthusiastic and imaginative. I see life as full of possibilities, and I'm spontaneous and flexible. I can make connections between events and information rather quickly and can confidently proceed based on the patterns I see. I do like affirmation from others and readily give others appreciation and support (Myers & Briggs Foundation, n.d.).

The idea behind knowing about your personality type is not to define yourself in stone but to understand yourself and your tendencies as well as to appreciate the differences between people with whom you work (or live). Some evidence suggests a possible neurological basis for personality type; that is, people's neural networks are a foundation for their cognitive, emotional, and behavioral patterns (Nardi, 2011). The Myers-Briggs does not measure ability, traits, or the character of people; it sorts preferences for what you most often perceive and how you tend to reach conclusions and come to decisions. There is no "right" personality type for a principal; they are all equal, nor do people exist at the extreme ends of each spectrum. Many people have tendencies in both directions of a type, and while there are some types that are more common than others for people in leadership positions, no one personality type makes or breaks a principal, an educator, or anyone else. You can take the Myers-Briggs online at www.mbtionline.com. The Myers-Briggs test costs $50 to take online; however, as a free alternative, you can take the TypeFinder Personality Test (https://bit.ly/3HFbMdU), which is based on the Myers-Briggs.

Another popular personality test is called the Big Five, or the five-factor model of personality, which grew out of decades of personality trait research. Lewis R. Goldberg (1990), a prominent researcher in the field of personality psychology, identifies five primary factors of personality.

1. **Openness:** Characteristics such as imagination and insight
2. **Conscientiousness:** Thoughtfulness, good impulse control, goal-directed behaviors
3. **Extraversion:** Excitability, sociability, talkativeness, assertiveness, and high level of emotional expression
4. **Agreeableness:** Trust, altruism, kindness, affection, other prosocial behaviors
5. **Neuroticism:** Sadness, moodiness, and emotional instability

Notice that the first letters of the five form the acronym OCEAN. The Big Five factors are very broad and encompass many other traits and characteristics into one cohesive factor. For example, the factor of agreeableness includes traits like generosity, amiability, and warmth (on the positive side) and aggressiveness and temper (on the negative side). All of these traits and characteristics, along with many more, make up the broader factor of agreeableness (Ackerman, 2017).

Each of these five personality factors represents a range between two extremes, and you lie somewhere on the continuum. For example, you will fall somewhere between extroversion and introversion, and your trait will be described as your degree of extroversion, regardless of how strong you are on the continuum. You can take the Big Five Inventory online (visit https://bit.ly/2ERqAEJ).

When you finish the online test, you will receive a results summary of your Big Five personality traits. The summary gives you a percentile score between 1 and 100. My inventory gives me the following results.

1. **Openness (59):** I am fairly open to new experiences.
2. **Conscientiousness (15):** I am impulsive and disorganized.
3. **Extraversion (74):** I am outgoing and social.
4. **Agreeableness (71):** I am friendly and optimistic.
5. **Neuroticism (87):** I am emotionally stable.

What I concluded from this assessment is that I am a social, friendly, outgoing person who is usually open to new experiences, but I tend to be impulsive and disorganized. It's a pretty accurate assessment. I was a bit surprised that I scored as low as I did on the C (conscientiousness), but I believe I scored fairly low on that trait not because I'm not conscientious about getting things done but because of the way I get things done. As I already noted, I'm quite random and tend to swing my focus from one thing to another. Also, my office is always a cluttered mess with books, papers, and sticky notes everywhere. I get things done but in a more random, cluttered manner. So, as I reflect on this analysis, I should probably neaten my workspace a bit so as not to appear so disorganized.

The third tool that I like to use is called the temperament sorter. Educational psychologist David Keirsey (1998), based on years of research, identified four basic temperaments, each with its own unique qualities, shortcomings, strengths, and challenges. The model was validated by further research (Kelly & Jugovic, 2001) and continues to factor into research on personality evaluations (Lima & de Castro, 2019; Robbins & Ross, 2020). He sorts them into four categories based on the temperaments.

1. **Artisan:** Artisans make up 30 percent of the population. They tend to be adaptable, daring, enticing, excited, impulsive, optimistic, persuasive, playful, and tactful.
2. **Guardian:** Guardians make up 45 percent of the population. They tend to be cautious, concerned, dependable, detailed, factual, law-abiding, logistical, and steady.
3. **Idealist:** Idealists make up 15 percent of the population. They tend to be authentic, diplomatic, empathetic, imaginative, intuitive, kindhearted, relational, romantic, and sensitive.
4. **Rational:** Rationals make up 10 percent of the population. They tend to be calm, curious, independent, ingenious, innovative, logical, pragmatic, strategic, and systemic.

The temperament sorter is a tool that you can use to learn about the attitudes, values, and talents of yourself and your staff. By identifying one's temperament, you are able to better understand an individual's personal needs, contributions to the workplace, and the roles each plays in society.

Visit www.keirsey.com to take the Keirsey Temperament Sorter. You will find out what your temperament is, and you can also learn about the needs, contributions, and roles of your staff. Knowing what each individual's temperament is allows you to understand why certain people behave as they do, and what you can do to build capacity of individuals and teams.

One thing to keep in mind when analyzing your personality traits is that, in some cases, your personality traits can work against you:

> When considering what it takes to succeed at work, we often focus on innate strengths: high intelligence, the ability to learn, the ambition to achieve, and the social skills to develop strong relationships. But these characteristics always coexist with weaknesses—aspects of personality that might seem innocuous or even advantageous in some circumstances but that when left unchecked can wreak havoc on careers and organizations. (Chamorro-Premuzic, 2017)

According to psychologist Tomas Chamorro-Premuzic (2017), drawing from the work of Robert Hogan and Joyce Hogan (2001), leaders tend to do a poorer job at assessing the dark side of their traits than they do their positive aspects of their traits, and most leaders have at least three of the dark side of their traits. For example, one of my traits is that I'm excitable. As Chamorro-Premuzic (2017) explains, that works in my favor in that it helps me display passion and enthusiasm to coworkers, but on the flip side, it can also make me volatile and unpredictable.

These traits each have an upside and a downside. Figure 1.14 gives examples of those upsides and downsides as explained by Chamorro-Premuzic (2017). I related the characteristics of the four temperaments to Hogan and Hogan's (2001) traits to illustrate the possible downsides of particular traits.

Trait	🎧 Upside	⏻ Downside
Cautious (Guardian)	Careful, precise	Indecisive, risk-averse
Excitable (Artisan)	Passionate, enthusiastic	Volatile, prone to outbursts
Leisurely (Rational)	Relaxed, easy-going	Passive-aggressive, driven by personal agenda
Reserved (Rational)	Calm under pressure	Uncommunicative, insensitive
Skeptical (Idealist)	Politically astute, hard to fool	Mistrustful, quarrelsome
Bold (Artisan)	Assertive, filled with conviction	Arrogant, grandiose
Colorful (Artisan)	Entertaining, expressive	Socially obtuse
Imaginative (Idealist)	Creative, visionary	Subject to wacky ideas, constant change
Mischievous (Artisan)	Risk-tolerant, charmingly persuasive	Impulsive, manipulative
Diligent (Guardian)	Hard working, holds high standards	Perfectionistic, micromanaging
Dutiful (Guardian)	Compliant, loyal	Submissive, conflict-averse

Source: Adapted from Chamorro-Premuzic, 2017.
Figure 1.14: The upsides and downsides to personality traits.

The Keirsey Temperament Sorter, like the Myers-Briggs Type Indicator and the Big Five model, is a helpful way to bring your own personality to the forefront and reflect on what you have learned. To help you can use figure 1.15 to keep track of your results and reflect on them.

As you fill in your personality traits in figure 1.15, reflect on how they work in your favor as well as how they might work against you.

Myers-Briggs Personality Type	Big Five Traits	Keirsey Temperament
ENFP (Extrovert, Intuitive, Feeling, Perceptive)	Optimistic, outgoing, open to new experiences	Artisan (adaptable, daring, enticing, excited, impulsive, optimistic, persuasive, playful, and tactful)
How might your personality traits work in your favor?		
As an artisan, I am passionate, assertive, and expressive.		
How might your personality traits work against you?		
As an artisan, I need to be aware of being a bit volatile, arrogant, and impulsive when teaming with coworkers and colleagues.		

Figure 1.15: Personality and temperament self-reflection chart.

Visit **go.SolutionTree.com/leadership** *for a free reproducible version of this figure.*

Tool: The Big Picture (Staff Chart)

Besides doing your own reflection, I've found it helpful to ask staff members to take the assessments as well. This is a great tool to help make sure people are well suited to working together on teams and assigned tasks. To keep your staff fresh and enthusiastic about taking these personality tests, don't give them all at once. You want accurate results, so put adequate time between each inventory. That way, they are more eager to engage in doing the inventory and don't suffer from test fatigue, which could alter results.

Now that you and your staff are completely "psyched up," you can add the temperaments to a master list, even including thinking and productivity styles, and have the big picture of your staff's personality traits. This allows you to put all the pieces together and have a bird's-eye view of your professional learning community (PLC). For example, my entry would look like figure 1.16. The reproducible version on page 38 includes space for more staff members.

Name	Thinking Style	Productivity Style	Myers-Briggs Personality Type	Big Five Traits	Keirsey Temperament
Nancy Flynn	Abstract Random	Arranger	ENFP	Optimistic, outgoing, open to new experiences	Artisan

Figure 1.16: The big picture (staff chart).

When the chart is completely filled in, share it with your staff and explain why it is important to understand and acknowledge the traits and strengths each person brings to the table.

 ## Summary and What's Next

Your mental map is set. You are now super organized, have set some goals, and are prepared to make decisions; you've discovered your purpose and completely psychoanalyzed yourself. You are now ready to pack your bag. To begin, slide that mental map into the side pocket for easy access.

Loading your pack is an art and a science. It definitely matters what's packed at the bottom, the middle, and the top. When heading to the mountains, I meticulously pack what I need for that particular trip, wear sturdy hiking boots, and make sure I have a reliable map and compass. Those are the things I can control. What I can't control are the weather, the terrain, wild animals, and the behavior of other hikers. While I can't control those things, I can be mentally and physically prepared for those types of encounters.

Having a safety plan, not just for the school but for yourself, is critical. There is a need for both physical safety and psychological safety. Chapter 2 looks at physical and psychological safety and offers tools to help you feel safe in your job. By knowing the laws, knowing your strengths, understanding your boss, and creating a solid, reliable network of colleagues, you are providing the safety net that you need to be successful as a principal. It's hard to survive in the wilderness without a medical kit, food, water, and the other necessary tools and supplies for survival. It's the same for the office. Pack yourself with knowledge of how to access those plans, laws, strengths, and colleagues if and when a storm hits.

SMART Goal Template

	Goal	Professional	Personal
S	Specific		
M	Measurable		
A	Attainable		
R	Relevant, Realistic		
T	Time bound		

The Why of My Goal Process

Why	My goal is to _____ so that I can _____
Steps	First, I will _____ Then, I will _____ Finally, I will _____
Deadline	I would like to attain my goal by _____ but will accept a deadline of _____
Focus	I will continue to _____
Progress monitoring	If I am unable to _____ I will prioritize _____

Source: Adapted from Ravishankar, R., & Alpaio, K. (2022, August 30). 5 ways to set more achievable goals. *Accessed at https://hbr.org/2022/08/5-ways-to-set-more-achievable-goals on October 21, 2022.*

The Principal's Backpack © 2024 Solution Tree Press • SolutionTree.com
Visit **go.SolutionTree.com/leadership** to download this free reproducible.

Progress Report

My Goal	
Who I Shared It With This Week	
My Progress	
Next Steps	

Concern and Influence Organizer

Concern	Influence

Source: Adapted from Covey, S. R. (1989). The 7 habits of highly effective people: Powerful lessons in personal change. New York: Simon & Schuster.

The Principal's Backpack © 2024 Solution Tree Press • SolutionTree.com
Visit **go.SolutionTree.com/leadership** to download this free reproducible.

The Big Picture (Staff Chart)

Staff Member	Thinking Style	Productivity Style	Myers-Briggs Personality Type	Big Five Traits	Keirsey Temperament

CHAPTER 2

Packing Your Bag

Packing your bag for any trip, be it on a trail, a plane, or in your car, you can carry just so much without making the trip miserable. I know that thirty pounds is the limit for my pack when I'm on the trail, so I have to be deliberate about what I pack so that I have what I need to survive as well as some things I need to enjoy the trip. We all have some extras that we carry even though they add a bit more weight. When backpacking, I really like having my camp chair at the end of the day, and a small pillow makes for a much better night's sleep. My friend Jackie must pack her coffee press, as it's the only way she can start her day.

Packing your principal backpack needs to be just as deliberate. There are essential items that you need for survival, and then there are the ones that you want to have to keep the job enjoyable. This chapter focuses on five essential tips you need to survive the job. Those tips include putting safety first, knowing the laws, discovering your strengths, creating a network, and studying your boss. There are a few things that can derail your journey. If you don't have a good safety plan and know what to do in an emergency, or if you don't have a good understanding of the basic laws and policies that pertain to your leadership position, you can put others besides just yourself in harm's way.

Having a network is crucial, as you can't do this job alone, and knowing as much as you can about your working relationship with your boss will keep you sailing even if the water gets a little choppy.

Tip 6: Put Safety First

"Good grief: I had to call the ECC again! Shots fired (7–10) and they hit 3 staff cars and the building by my office! No one was hurt. I had a lockout. Then dismissal happened. Holy s——t I'm tired." This is a real text I received from a colleague in her first month on the job as an elementary principal in an urban school district. A bit of a trial by (gun)fire.

In the wilderness or in the school, physical and psychological safety are top priorities. While psychological safety can be more difficult to define or quantify (see page 43), *physical safety* means ensuring that the environment is free from hazards, meaning anything that can bring physical harm to anyone in the school building or its environs. Physical hazards can be seen, smelled, or heard, and are usually rectified by the appropriate staff or other professionals. Many times, for example, you'll hear someone say that it smells like gas down that hall or there's water leaking in the cafeteria. You go and investigate the smell or the leak and contact those who can fix them. While some hazards are larger in scope than others, such as gunshots, you can usually keep people safe by cordoning off the area or evacuating students and staff. Even if you've heard innumerable times by the same teacher that he smells gas in the hall (and you can't smell a thing), you still have to check each and every report of a physical hazard immediately and document the event with details of who, what, where, when, and how it was rectified from start to finish.

Physical hazards also include student and adult behavior either within or outside of the school. Shots are fired in the community, a loaded gun is brought to school, a student throws a chair over the railing from the second floor. Keeping everyone safe can be a stressful part of the job, as most of the time, the hazards we deal with are spontaneous. But having some tools ready to go can help you ensure that you're ready to respond. This tip includes tools for keeping track of emergency procedures, role-playing scenarios, recalling the resources available from the U.S. Department of Homeland Security, and assessing psychological safety.

 Tool: Emergency Procedures One-Pager

Are you ready for anything? As I listened to the news on the day after a first grader shot and badly wounded his teacher in his classroom in Newport News, Virginia, I heard the superintendent of the local school district remark, "Who would have thought a first grader would bring a gun to school and shoot his teacher?" (Holt, 2023). Sadly, we all need to think about it, and you need to think about how you would deal with something even as tragic as this incident. Luckily, the second grader who brought the loaded gun to my school did not pull the trigger. But these and other types of emergencies can and do happen, and preparation is key.

You likely have a school safety plan on your shelf or in your file cabinet. My school safety manual is rather lengthy, as it includes absolutely anything that could go wrong. It is hard to remember all the details in that manual, but having a *one-pager* that succinctly outlines what to do and who to call takes a little of the stress off finding the information when the cortisol is flowing.

Once you've noted the most important procedures and information from your school safety plan, you can add them to your one-pager, which acts as a quick reference to turn to when something unexpected happens. Figure 2.1 is a sample of an emergency procedures one-pager. A reproducible version is available on page 65. Put the emergencies in alphabetical order so that you can find the one you're looking for quickly. Keep it to one page, share it with your safety or crisis team, and have it readily available. If possible, memorize the information for the ones you feel you have a greater chance of experiencing.

Emergency	What to Do First	Who to Call	Phone Number	Safe Haven for Evacuation	Safety Team Member	Radio Channel or Extension	Door Number
Assault	Lockout	Emergency Communications Center (ECC)	XXX-XXXX		Crisis Team	X	X
Bomb threat	Pull fire alarm and evacuate	911		Community Center	Crisis Team		
Fire	Pull fire alarm and evacuate	911		Community Center			
Gas	All-school announcement and evacuate	ECC	XXX-XXXX	Community Center	Engineer	X	X
Serious medical	Lockout	911			Nurse	X	X
Severe weather	All-school announcement and move everyone to a safe location in the school	X	X	X	Crisis Team	NOAA Weather Service and local news and weather media	X
Shots fired	Lockdown	ECC	XXX-XXXX		Crisis Team	X	X
Weapon	Seize the weapon, if possible. If not possible, lockdown	ECC if weapon is seized; 911 if not	XXX-XXXX		Crisis Team	X	X

Figure 2.1: Emergency procedures one-pager example.

To help determine what to include in a one-pager, I find it helpful to use information from the School Superintendents Association (AASA, n.d.), which created a comprehensive School Safety and Crisis Planning toolkit. This toolkit includes what to do before, during, and after a crisis; offers resources and guidance for administrators; and includes a school safety and crisis hotline. Many principals don't continually think about what to do before a crisis hits, but being proactive mitigates the effects of the crisis. For example, before a crisis hits, ask yourself these questions (AASA, n.d.).

- Do I have a detailed safety plan in place, and do I know exactly where it is?
- Does my safety team know exactly where it is?
- Do I have certain individuals identified as a safety or crisis team?
- Do I have all the names and numbers of people I need to contact immediately, and where can they be located for immediate access?
- Do I have a safe place to which I can evacuate the entire school, if necessary?
- Do all staff know the drill procedures and escape routes?

Look through your school safety manual and note the important emergency procedures, what to do first, and whom to call for immediate help. Make sure evacuation routes are updated and highly visible in every room, and the room number is clearly posted on the evacuation route. This is especially important in the event there is a substitute teacher or volunteer in the room. Also, check to see that all of your exterior doors are numbered on the outside and the inside. If you need to direct emergency services to a particular area of the school, you need to know what door is closest to the situation. Memorize the door numbers of the major exterior doors so that wherever you are in the building, you can direct personnel to the correct location.

Have AASA's (n.d.) questions answered before the school year begins. Put safety first! Once a crisis hits, *stay calm*, and follow protocol (AASA, n.d.). Staying calm in an emergency is vital. If you're in a panic, try not to look like it. Take some deep breaths and keep your head clear. I once had an administrative intern who would race to the site of an incident. Racing to a site only encouraged students to race there as well, which hindered any interventions. While you want to get there as quickly as possible, don't draw attention to yourself as visually concerned or panicked. Take one or two members of your safety or crisis team with you, but you don't want everyone else to know that you are heading toward a disturbance. You'll get there a few seconds later, but you won't have half the school body trailing you (or worse, getting there before you).

Tool: Role-Playing Scenarios

As I write and update my school safety plan year after year, I run scenarios through my head and role-play how I would handle particular situations. I always ask myself, "What would I do first?" I think about how an emergency or crisis might play out and how I would handle it, who I would call, and what staff would assist me. I also involve my staff members, so that everyone has a good handle on what to do when the real thing happens. I use scenarios of assaultive behavior of both students and adults, fire, gas, and medical emergencies. I have seen most of the situations listed in my one-pager, and I'm sure you have seen (or will see) more than your share as well. Being prepared is crucial. Emergencies and crises are well beyond your control, but how you deal with them is totally within it. Thinking through the scenarios in an organized way with your team is an important tool to be prepared.

Imagine you have a crisis situation such as a suspicious intruder, weapon, fire, gas leak, or other perilous situation that requires your immediate and full attention. Play the situation out in your mind. Knowing what you might do in a certain situation will help you stay calm and keep everybody safe. While rehearsing different scenarios, think about your strengths, your circle of influence, and your network and critical friends whom might have experienced a crisis. Also think about who you would need to inform and in what order. Rehearse finding the procedures for your crisis on your one-pager and in your safety plan and mentally go through the steps.

Figure 2.2 illustrates examples of scenarios you can role-play by yourself and with your crisis or safety team. Use your emergency procedures one-pager to guide your actions as you role-play. Put the situation in a particular part of the school and see if you can recall the door number closest to the situation.

Scenario	Role-play: Have you rehearsed this scenario, and would you know what to do if faced with this situation?
Active shooter	☐ Yes ☐ No
Assaultive behavior—student on staff	☐ Yes ☐ No
Assaultive behavior—student on student	☐ Yes ☐ No
Bomb threat	☐ Yes ☐ No
Death of a student or staff member	☐ Yes ☐ No
Fire in the cafeteria during lunch	☐ Yes ☐ No
Hazardous materials	☐ Yes ☐ No
Medical emergency, staff	☐ Yes ☐ No
Medical emergency, student	☐ Yes ☐ No
Outside disturbance	☐ Yes ☐ No
Weapon (possession)	☐ Yes ☐ No

Figure 2.2: Role-playing scenarios.

*Visit **go.SolutionTree.com/leadership** for a free reproducible version of this figure.*

Tool: U.S. Homeland Security Website

If you would like additional information for safety protocols, an excellent resource for school safety procedures and protocols is the U.S. Department of Homeland Security website (www.schoolsafety.gov), which has tools to learn about efforts you can take or research about the right safety resources for your school. These resources include bullying and cyberbullying, cybersecurity, emergency planning, infectious diseases and public health, mental health, school climate, violence, and threat assessment. The website is quite extensive and even has a state search tool for each individual U.S. state so that you can research your state's school safety programs and regional contacts from federal agencies. The International School Safety Institute (https://internationalschoolsafety.org) also offers guidelines for becoming a safer school.

Tool: Psychological Safety Assessment

Psychological safety is not as easy to discern or correct as physical safety. Amy C. Edmondson and Zhike Lei (2014), experts in organizational behavior and learning, define *psychological safety* as a work environment in which it is safe to take risks to speak up, challenge ideas, and where you are comfortable expressing yourself. When staff members feel psychologically safe, they have a perception of being able to take such risks in the work environment. The presence of or lack of psychological safety also helps explain why and how people in the organization share information and knowledge.

Psychological safety is rarely addressed in school safety plans. To successfully manage yourself, you will need to calculate and determine your own psychological safety. Do the organizational conditions exist for you to safely speak up, challenge ideas, and suggest solutions? How do you determine that safety? And as principal, you must ensure you also address the psychological safety of your entire building. You want to be able to set the conditions for your staff to feel safe to speak up, challenge ideas, and suggest solutions.

To assess the degree of psychological safety in your environment, Edmondson (2004), who pioneered work on this topic, offers seven questions that you can ask yourself to determine whether ideal safety conditions exist. These questions can help you assess your safety in leading your school and working with your supervisor. Figure 2.3 is a chart that you can use to record your own evidence for the answer to each question.

Question	Yes or No	Reasons or Evidence
If I make a mistake, do other team members hold it against me?	No	No, as long as I acknowledge the mistake and take responsibility for repairing any damage.
Are other principals able to bring up problems and tough issues?	Yes	They can bring them up, but there is not always resolution.
Does my supervisor sometimes reject others for being different?	No	My supervisor does not reject others for being different but may reject others' decisions for being different from the status quo.
It is safe for me to take risks?	Yes	I took the risk of maintaining the preK program when it was advised that we relinquish it, and it proved to be a risk worth taking.
It is difficult to ask other district staff members for help?	Yes	I perceive them as busy with other issues, so I usually turn to my colleagues for help unless the issue requires district intervention.
Would my supervisor deliberately act in a way that undermines my efforts?	No	My supervisor wins when I win.
Does my supervisor value and utilize my unique skills and talents?	Yes	My supervisor knows where my strengths lie.

Source: Adapted from Edmondson, 2004.

Figure 2.3: Psychological safety assessment chart.

*Visit **go.SolutionTree.com/leadership** for a free reproducible version of this figure.*

Some of these questions may take some time, research, and testing to determine. You can use these questions to survey your staff as well to see how psychologically safe they feel among other staff members and administrators. When giving a survey of this nature, it's very important to maintain the staff's anonymity to preserve their psychological safety and the legitimacy of the answers. As principal, you want to create the conditions for psychological safety for your staff, so you need to know which conditions exist and which areas of psychological safety need some work.

Unlike physical hazards like a water leak or the smell of gas, you're not going to have staff running to you to let you know about the fact that they don't feel it's safe for them to take a risk. Therefore, questions such as Edmondson's (2004) work in two ways: (1) for you to assess your psychological safety for managing up, and (2) for you to assess the staff's psychological safety under your leadership. You should use all seven when assessing your own psychological safety, but leave question 2 off the staff's assessment. For example, for staff, you can use question 1 so that it reflects how a staff member feels with regard to psychological safety in the building. You can use questions 3 and 4, substituting the word *principal* for *supervisor*, and take out the word *district* in question 5. Both versions are available online. If you find that the majority of staff feel that it's not safe to take a risk, you are going to have to dig deeper and find the reasons why they don't feel safe taking a risk. You'll need to ask more questions and accept the feedback.

The key to psychological safety is getting all of your staff members to feel safe and comfortable at work. When Google studied teamwork, its data "indicated that psychological safety, more than anything else, was critical to making a team work" (Duhigg, 2016). People need to feel comfortable enough to share their thoughts, comments, and ideas without feeling embarrassed or shamed.

Once you have assessed the psychological safety of your school, the natural follow-up question is how to improve it. Connor Brooke (2016), author of the article "How to Build Psychological Safety on Your Team," offers the following tips you can use to promote psychological safety in your workplace.

- **Be inclusive:** Make sure everyone feels important; listen to all voices.
- **Encourage failure:** Allow people to feel comfortable making a mistake.
- **Ask a lot of questions:** Get people thinking and talking together.
- **Remove the fear:** Make sure everyone is safe to speak up.
- **Establish accountability:** Make sure that everyone is working toward the same goal or purpose.
- **Admit your own mistakes:** Be a role model for letting others know it's OK to make a mistake.
- **Be available:** Let everyone know you are available to help and that they should not be afraid to come to you with questions or concerns.

Check the pulse of psychological safety on a regular basis to confirm whether or not the safety exists. It may exist for some members and not for others. If there are certain members who never speak up or contribute to discussions, privately ask them why they are reticent. If you sense it is a matter of feeling safe, inquire about what aspects of the environment they feel are not safe, and then work to rectify the situation.

When it comes to both physical safety and psychological safety, it is unrealistic for you to be able to consider and list every possible emergency or incident, because some things you just don't see coming. However, being prepared for most emergencies will keep you centered and prepared for the ones that blindside you. Have safety or crisis team meetings on a regular basis to prepare, and always meet as a team to debrief when there is an event. If you need additional support in a crisis, there are usually crisis personnel, such as counselors and social workers, in your district who specialize in trauma and can assist you and your team, school, and community through a crisis. Always reach out to others for support in a time of crisis. It's also important to reach out to others when you need advice to improve your conditions for psychological safety as well as in times of crisis. Securing support is the definition of self-management, especially in times of stressful events.

Tip 7: Know the Laws

National parks in every country have laws, rules, regulations, or warnings that you must obey. When setting off on a trail in any park in any country, you must read and obey the signs. One of my favorite signs is in the Grand Canyon. It has a special note to the young, strong, and invincible, the last line of which reads: "NO KIDDING, DO NOT attempt to hike from the rim to the river and back without being prepared to possibly suffer the following: permanent brain damage; cardiac arrest; death." And just in case you're thinking of hiking the Julian Alps in Slovenia in high heels, there's a sign warning against that, too.

Knowing the rules, laws, and regulations is important as well. Jo Ann Krueger, my school law professor at the University of New Mexico, started the course by saying, "My job is to keep you out of the headlines and off the six o'clock news" (personal communication, January, 1999). There are things that will happen during your tenure as a principal that you can't control, and then there are things you definitely can control. Knowing the laws and policies—both federal and local—will help keep you out of the trouble you can control. This tip offers tools for keeping track of the most important laws and a quick reference guide for the many laws, policies, and procedures you need to know as a principal.

Tool: Web Resources for Laws

Your district will have all the local policies on its website, and you can find U.S. state and national laws and policies related to other topics such as special education, immigration, human rights, and any others on which you need further clarification on the internet, the websites of which are in table 2.1 for those in the United States and in table 2.2 for several countries outside of the United States.

There are fundamental differences between laws and policies. Laws are formal documents that are enforceable. They are administered through the judiciary, established to bring about equality in society. Laws are applied in a state for all citizens of the state, and such laws are subject to formal amendments (Chukwuemeka, 2022). Policies, on the other hand, are more informal documents and act more as guides. They are usually made in the name of citizens of a society, such as a school district, to achieve certain goals which will benefit them (Chukwuemeka, 2022). School districts in the same state may have different policies, but they all must adhere to the same laws. Therefore, it is important to know the laws in general, and the policies that govern your district.

Table 2.1: Web Resources for Laws in the United States

Law	Topic	Website
Special Education	IDEA (Individuals With Disabilities Education Act)	https://sites.ed.gov/idea/about-idea
Immigration	U.S. Citizenship and Immigration Services	www.uscis.gov/laws-and-policy
Human Rights	Universal Declaration of Human Rights	www.ohchr.org
Search and Seizure	Fourth Amendment to the U.S. Constitution	www.govinfo.gov

Table 2.2: Web Resources for Laws Outside of the United States

Category	Country	Website
Education Law and Policy	Canada	www.schooladvocacy.ca/left_level3/law_policy.html
Education Policy	Australia	www.oecd.org/education/highlightsaustralia.htm
Statutory Policies for Schools	United Kingdom	https://bit.ly/3yHf24q

Tool: Law and Policy Reference Guide

How well do you know the local laws, policies, and procedures, and do you know where to look to learn more? This knowledge can keep *you* out of the news. The loaded gun incident I alluded to earlier is a perfect example of how knowing the district's policy and following the appropriate procedures makes a huge difference. The incident at the school ended up in the news—I didn't. The local news report that night emphasized how the school's procedures were followed and that they worked (Haavik, 2019) rather than a much more tragic outcome. If I hadn't known what to do or hadn't followed protocol, I could have been the subject of the news story along with the seven-year-old with the gun. Not that anyone wants to see a seven-year-old with a gun on the news, but no principal wants to be in the headlines for something that could have been avoided, again, by being prepared for anything and everything.

Figure 2.4 outlines categories for many of the laws and policies of which you should have basic knowledge. This list is not exhaustive, but it contains those that are likely to be most pertinent to day-to-day life as a school leader. For each category, read up on the law or policy, and next to each entry, enter the location of where you can find the full description. The reproducible version on page 66 provides space for this. This could be an internet link to the district or federal site for full disclosure of the law or policy or the page number where you would find it in your district's principal handbook or school handbook. Keep the reference guide handy or affix it to the cover of your safety manual.

Knowing the laws and policies definitely helps, but many incidents happen without warning or control, and staying emotionally calm and collected keeps the stress more at the acute level and allows you to think with a level head. I've seen headlines such as "Principal extorts money from PTA." If you mismanage money, get involved in subordinate relationships, or engage in anything related to illicit drugs, it could cost you your career. At the end of the day, always use your common sense (remember that Grand Canyon sign).

A	Athletics
	Alternative education
	Attendance and truancy

| B | Behavior and discipline |
| | Bullying prevention |

| C | Communications |
| | Contracts |

| D | Data privacy |
| | Digital literacy |

E	Equal rights
	Equity
	Extracurricular activities

| F | Field trips |
| | Funding |

| G | Gender equity |
| | Grants |

| H | Human resources |
| | Human rights |

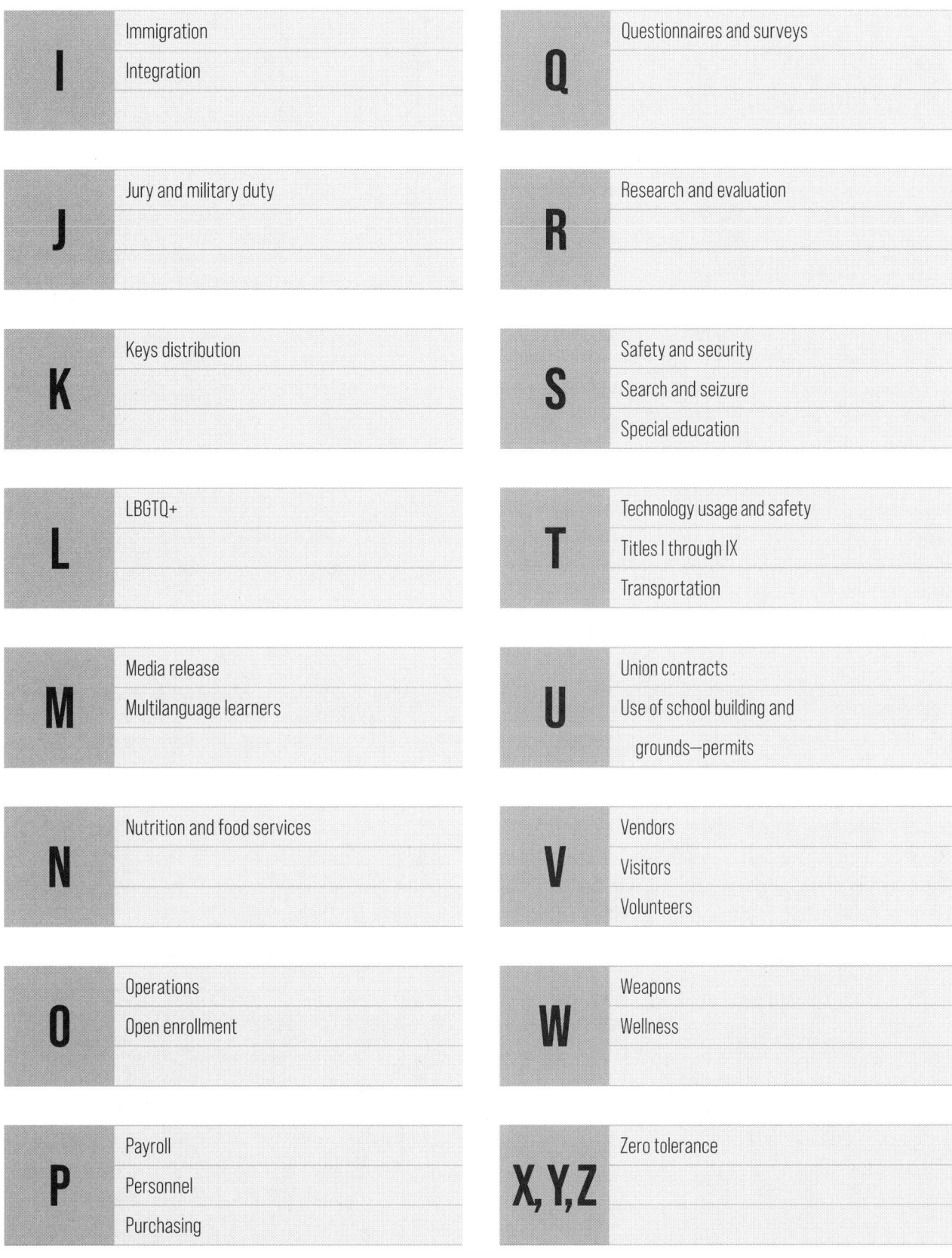

Figure 2.4: Law and policy reference guide.

Tip 8: Discover Your Strengths

In tennis, my forehand is stronger than my backhand, and in golf, my drives are much more accurate than my putts. It's pretty easy to name your strengths as they relate to sports and hobbies, but they are not as easy to name when it comes to the job. If you were interviewing for a leadership position and the interviewer asked you to highlight your strengths, could you articulate them? If you were to ask your boss to write you a letter of recommendation, what would she say were your qualities as a school leader?

While you may not easily be able to name your talents and strengths, all principals have them stowed somewhere in their packs. Your strengths need to be stowed near the top of your pack so that you can find them easily without having to dig through everything in order to use them. Like the thinking and productivity styles and personality trait tools from tip 5 (page 28), the tools in this section will help you self-evaluate to determine your own attributes and opportunities. The difference between strengths and personality profiles is that strengths are those activities that you do well and have a natural passion and ability for, while personality traits reflect your strongest patterns of thought, feeling, or behavior (Meier, n.d.).

As a principal, not only is it beneficial for you to use your talents and strengths, but you will want to call on others who have talents and strengths where you do not. If you are like me, you tend to be more aware of your weaknesses than you are of your strengths, which is why it is important to keep a concrete list of your strengths handy. Peter Drucker (2008), author of *Managing Oneself*, says the only way to really discover your strengths is through feedback analysis. He maintains that while most people think they know what they are good at, they are usually wrong. As with my ability to articulate my shortfalls, Drucker (2008) agrees that more often than not, people know what they are not good at. While weaknesses are opportunities for improvement, your strengths offer firmer ground on which to build your career. This tip offers tools to self-evaluate your strengths and to organize the strengths you discover from using strengths assessments.

Tool: Strengths Self-Evaluation

A good start for learning about your strengths is to engage in self-evaluation. This gives you the opportunity to reflect on what you already know about yourself, which you can later compare and contrast to what you find out using other tools. We find out a lot about ourselves through assessments that are analyzed for us. But this section's tool allows you to fill in the blanks without anyone else analyzing or scoring your answers. The results are all yours. So, before taking an online strengths test, and there are many to choose from, start with this self-evaluation. This reflection exercise asks you to think about the things you're good at, compliments you have received, challenges you've overcome, your values, and things that make you unique. These are attributes you likely use constantly, but you may take them for granted (Therapist Aid, 2021).

When I interview candidates for a position at the school, I always ask them about a unique quality that they bring to the team. Most candidates answer with phrases such as *loves kids*, *good team player*, or *good listener*. However, I'm always looking for that truly unique characteristic, so if you can't articulate one at the moment, reflect on it and write it down. Figure 2.5 provides an example of some prompts you can use. A reproducible version is available on page 69. After you have filled in the self-evaluation, try two online tools (StrengthsFinder and High 5) in the next section and use the organizer to triangulate all of the results regarding your qualities, your talents, and your strengths.

What am I good at in my job as a principal?

What professional challenges have I overcome?

What makes me unique in my capacity as a principal?

What compliments have I received, from either my own staff or other principals?

How have I helped or made others happy at work?

What do I value the most in my professional life?

Source: Adapted from Therapist Aid, 2021.
Figure 2.5: Strengths self-evaluation.

Tool: Strengths Assessments Organizer

Now that you've had a chance to reflect on your own, I recommend using other resources to give you more context on your strengths. Marcus Buckingham and Donald O. Clifton (2001), authors of *Now, Discover Your Strengths*, define *talent* as "any recurring pattern of thought, feeling, or behavior that can be productively applied" (p. 48). They explain that it is impossible to build a strength without underlying talent and that talents are the most important raw material for strength building.

Talents are based on your brain's synaptic connections, and by identifying your most powerful talents, along with the skills and knowledge you pick up along the way, you will build your strengths. Talents are, in a way, a magnetic pull that keeps you coming back to that activity, path, or pursuit over and over. Elite artists, musicians, athletes, and scholars all have talent, but they also hone their skills and continue learning throughout their lives.

Your strengths are a combination of your talents, knowledge, and skills. Once you identify your talents and add your knowledge and skills, you can build on your strengths. Strengths, according to Buckingham and Clifton (2001), are "consistent near perfect performance in any activity" (p. 25). They believe that for an activity to be a strength, you must be able to do it consistently and derive some intrinsic satisfaction from that activity. When thinking of an activity that you believe is a strength, ask yourself, "Do I enjoy the activity? And, can I continue to do the activity happily and successfully?" If you can answer yes to these two questions, that activity is probably one of your strengths.

Buckingham and Clifton (2001) also point out that you will excel only by maximizing your strengths, not by fixing your weaknesses. As author and researcher Tom Rath (2007) puts it, "People have several times more potential for growth when they invest energy in developing their strengths instead of correcting their deficiencies" (p. i). While being aware of your weaknesses is certainly useful, the point is that playing to your strengths might be a better way to keep you out of professional potholes than getting hung up on where you don't excel.

According to behavioral scientist Nicole Celestine (2019), "Our strengths reflect inherent potentials that can help us achieve goals across our personal and professional lives." Therefore, she says, it is worth the time and effort to take a few of these assessments. As Drucker (2008) says, you need that feedback.

One way to discover your themes of talent is to take the popular online test called StrengthsFinder. The test was developed in 1999 by Donald O. Clifton, considered the father of strengths-based psychology. Clifton, Rath, and a team of scientists at Gallup created the online StrengthsFinder assessment. Research continually validates the efficacy of discovering strengths using StrengthsFinder and other tools (Miglianico, Dubreuil, Miquelon, Bakker, & Martin-Krumm, 2020). While the full assessment is fee-based, High 5 Test offers a free alternative (https://high5test.com/strengthsfinder-free).

Based on Gallup's forty-year study of human strengths, Clifton and Rath created a language of the thirty-four most common talents and developed the Clifton StrengthsFinder to help people discover and articulate their talents (Buckingham & Clifton, 2001). Figure 2.6 (page 50) provides a list of each talent and a short description.

The StrengthsFinder test allows people to identify their top five themes of talent, ranging alphabetically from *achiever* to *woo*. The test helps you understand how each of your top five areas of talent plays out as strengths in your life. Rath (2007) maintains that when people have the opportunity to focus on their strengths every day, they are "six times as likely to be engaged in their jobs and more than three times as likely to report having an excellent quality of life in general" (p. iii).

When I took the StrengthsFinder, I came up with the following as my top five in alphabetical order.

- **Activator:** I want to start and get it done.
- **Arranger:** I will manage variables to get the job done.
- **Futurist:** I see visions of what could be.
- **Inclusiveness:** I want everyone to feel part of the group.
- **Maximizer:** I want the biggest bang for my buck.

Achiever You are driven.	**Connectedness** You believe things happen for a reason.	**Harmony** You look for areas of agreement.	**Relator** You are pulled toward people.
Activator You are ready to start.	**Context** You look back to understand the present.	**Ideation** You are fascinated by ideas.	**Responsibility** You take ownership for what you commit to.
Adaptability You live in the moment.	**Deliberative** You are careful and vigilant.	**Inclusiveness** You want people to feel part of the group.	**Restorative** You love to solve problems.
Analytical You like to see proof.	**Developer** You see the potential in others.	**Individualization** You focus on individuals' differences.	**Self-Assurance** You have faith in your strengths.
Arranger You like to conduct.	**Discipline** You need order and predictability.	**Input** You are inquisitive.	**Significance** You want to be recognized.
Belief Your core values are enduring.	**Empathy** You sense the emotions of others.	**Intellection** You like to think.	**Strategic** You can sort through clutter and find the best route.
Command You like to take charge.	**Fairness** You are aware of balance.	**Learner** You love to learn.	**Woo** You enjoy the challenge of meeting new people.
Communication You like to speak and write.	**Focus** You need a clear destination.	**Maximizer** You measure in terms of excellence.	
Competition You compare yourself to others.	**Futuristic** You are fascinated by the future.	**Positivity** You are generous with praise.	

Source: Adapted from Buckingham & Clifton, 2001.
Figure 2.6: Thirty-four talents.

Having these listed out like this was a big step toward using these talents to capitalize on my strengths.

Another assessment is the High 5 strengths test, which is rooted in the principles of positive psychology (https://high5test.com). This one is free, though there are further insights available for a fee. This assessment is composed of 120 statements that ask you to specify your answer regarding how you feel about that statement along a continuum from totally disagree to totally agree. Once you have completed the assessment, you receive a report of where your strengths lie.

When I take the High 5 strengths test, I receive the following results.

- **Philomath:** I love learning, explore many interests, follow new paths, and acquire as much knowledge as possible.
- **Catalyst:** I love to get things started and can create momentum in stagnant environments. I have a hard time waiting and wasting time when I could be moving forward.
- **Coach:** I love discovering the potential in people and supporting others' personal growth.
- **Winner:** Competition is essential for me.
- **Self-believer:** I'm independent and self-sufficient and inspire others with my confidence and certainty.

These are only two of the many strengths assessments out there. They've been helpful for me, but if you are interested in branching out to more, Celestine (2019) has compiled a list of nine (https://positivepsychology.com/strength-finding-tests) that you can use right away.

You may now be thinking that is all well and good, but how do you analyze your results? While some of the tools offer such insights for a price, another alternative I have found helpful is something called the strengths wheel, of which there are several variations. Originally developed by positive psychology expert and coach Matt Driver (2011), the strengths wheel offers a way to plot your strengths in a visual way and place them into a particular context (in your case, most likely the school setting). This is a useful way to optimize how you use your strengths.

I used a template available at https://bit.ly/3ZY2Fh5 to create my own strengths wheel. In short, the idea is to indicate to what extent you currently use each strength and how much scope there is to use the strength more. The larger the gap between your current use and the scope for using it more, the more potential you have to use your strength more. If you have already "maxed out" your use, the wheel can also help you see that. From that, you can create a visual representation that provides some helpful insight.

For example, when I plotted all my strengths from the High 5 strengths test, I found that my current use of my strength of *winner* was higher than my scope for using it more; that is, I feel I overuse that strength. I've been competing in sports all my life, but I'd rather appear more cooperative than competitive in the work setting. Therefore, I have to monitor myself on that winner aspect of my leadership. It is the same with the catalyst. While I love to get things done, I have to find the patience to work with those who have a different work productivity style and not be so eager to move on when others may not be ready to do so.

When you plot your own wheel, ask yourself which strengths you could allow yourself to use more and which strengths leave little or no room for growth. You can come back to the strengths wheel over time and replot your strengths as you begin to use certain strengths to a greater or lesser degree.

To help you keep track of all this information, I designed a simple chart (see figure 2.7, page 52) where you can record your results from any strengths assessments you take, reflect on any insights you might have gained from tools like the strengths wheel, and consider how best to use your strengths in your work as a school leader. A reproducible version is available on page 70.

All principals have different sets of talents and strengths, and there is no prescribed set that is more exemplary of a school leader than others. How you leverage your strengths is what really matters. James Brook and Paul Brewerton (2016), authors of *Optimize Your Strengths*, explain that truly outstanding leaders don't just know their strengths, they *stretch* their strengths. They look for ways to improve and take

StrengthsFinder Top Five	High 5 Strengths	Other Results
• Activator • Arranger • Futurist • Inclusiveness • Maximizer	• Philomath • Catalyst • Coach • Winner • Self-believer	

Insights From the Strengths Wheel

I feel I overuse the "winner" strength. I've been competing in sports all my life, but I'd rather appear more cooperative than competitive in the work setting. Therefore, I have to monitor myself on that winner aspect of my leadership. It is the same with the catalyst. While I love to get things done, I have to find the patience to work with those who have a different work productivity style and not be so eager to move on when others may not be ready to do so.

How to Use My Strengths Going Forward

As an activator and arranger, I get things started and I get things done, but I must be cognizant of the pace at which others are working. I adhere to the mantra, the more the merrier, and am concerned about including all who want to join in. This is good in theory, just don't let it get so large that it becomes unmanageable and detrimental to fulfilling goals. Keep the competition low key (except on the court or field).

Figure 2.7: Strengths assessments organizer.

advantage of new opportunities and use their strengths to move beyond their comfort zones. Successful leaders, they say, "have a true understanding of and ability to leverage their 'leadership edge' (their unique strengths, abilities, and skills) to influence and inspire others to achieve extraordinary results" (Brook & Brewerton, 2016, p. 26). They also assert, "Effective leaders remain mindful of their strengths to boost their confidence, resourcefulness and energy to overcome performance blockers. They tap into the talents of those around them, using their strengths to compensate for any areas of weakness" (Brook & Brewerton, 2016, p. 23).

As you discover your strengths, use them to set your goals, work productively with colleagues and staff, and leverage them while looking for new and innovative ways to boost your leadership roles.

Tip 9: Create a Network

Effective leaders have very powerful networks. As a principal, you need to be highly selective in choosing a network of people who will support you, energize you, and help you grow professionally. You need people with diverse perspectives who are comfortable giving and receiving feedback, are easily contacted, and are committed to working with you. Rob Cross and Robert J. Thomas (2011), drawing on fifteen years of collected data from their research, write in the *Harvard Business Review* that there are seven critical kinds of connections you want to have.

1. People who provide information, ideas, or expertise
2. People who offer mentoring
3. People who give you feedback
4. People who lend personal support
5. People who increase your sense of purpose
6. People who promote work-life balance
7. People who energize you and you enjoy being with

Cross and Thomas (2011) also emphasize that forming a close network with as many of these types as possible is more important than just knowing a lot of people.

This tip includes tools to help you build a powerful and effective network that includes all of these types of connections so that you always know who to call for support. The tip includes advice for hiring a coach, finding a super ally, identifying your critical friends, and joining a professional organization.

 Tool: Hire a Coach

Sometimes you just need to have someone who will listen, provide support, and offer advice as you navigate the trail. The best career decision I ever made as a principal was to hire a professional coach who was not affiliated with the school district in which I was working. Think about it. The best tennis players in the world have coaches. Each top player has their own coach who travels with them constantly. Why would the number one player in the world need a coach? To continuously improve. To stay on top. To have constant feedback and advice. Those who are driven to be the best are those who seek advice and feedback. They are lifelong learners who never say, "I know it all." They say, "I want to know more."

A coach is an essential person in your network. Working with a coach is the epitome of professional learning. Meeting bimonthly with my coach allows me to discuss issues or concerns that would be difficult to discuss with someone in-district. We have explored models, surveys, and inventories, many of which appear in this book. He has taught me to deeply reflect, reframe perspectives, and look at issues through different and, sometimes, opposing lenses. In fact, I would never have been able to write this book without our coaching conversations. Coaching sessions are sacred time for me. There are no interruptions, no phone calls, no emails, and no texts. I never open my laptop; I have only my journal and my number 9–leaded mechanical pencil at the table during our sessions. Coaching sessions should never be interrupted unless there is a dire emergency or situation. Most of the time, I schedule my coaching sessions outside of school hours—usually early in the morning—so that I will not be interrupted.

The best way to find a good coach is to ask colleagues, university professors, and members of professional organizations for referrals. You can even schedule trial sessions with coaches until you find the one you feel is the best fit. Finding a good coach may take some time and more than one of these trial sessions. You will want to consider whether you prefer a coach who is an employee of your own district or one who has no connections to the district. There are pros and cons to both, and it depends on whether you are comfortable discussing issues or concerns you are facing with someone who has other connections within the district. A coach is someone whom you can trust unconditionally, so be particular in whom you ultimately hire.

Remember, the best fit is not the one who always agrees with you; it's the one that makes you think differently and deeply about your practice. As you search for a coach who will meet all your needs, you can use the coaching referral and contact log in figure 2.8 (page 54).

Some school districts provide principals and assistant principals with professional learning funds that they can use to further their growth as school leaders. While these funds also need to cover memberships in local and national professional organizations, budgeting for professional growth through coaching is also a worthwhile way to allocate the funds. If your district does not have specific funds for principal professional growth, check to see if there are general staff development funds available in the school or district budget. If there are no school or district funds available, hiring a coach may have to be an out-of-pocket cost. Costs vary, so you may have to do a little research for one that fits your needs and your budget.

Name	Referred by	Contact Info	Contacted Date	Coaching Session Date	Cost

Figure 2.8: Coaching referral and contact log.

*Visit **go.SolutionTree.com/leadership** for a free reproducible version of this figure.*

Once you schedule your coaching sessions, you will want to come prepared with topics for discussion. Before each session, think about what goals you are currently working on or those you would like to begin to work on, decisions you may have made or need to make, strategies and interventions you have tried or would like to try, a particular learning focus, and any data you have collected or would like your coach to collect. Being prepared for your coaching sessions will make your sessions far more productive and successful. Figure 2.9 lists topics for coaching discussions with space to record coaching session outcomes. It is by no means exhaustive, and you can add ones that are pertinent to your coaching sessions; the reproducible version on page 71 provides space for this.

Date:	Coach:
Topics for Discussion	**Coaching Feedback**
Goals: What am I working on? What do I want to begin working on?	
Decisions: Have I made decisions, or do I need to make some decisions that I would like to discuss?	
Interventions or strategies: Have I tried new interventions or strategies for which I would like feedback?	
Learning focus: Is there a particular focus or issue that I would like to discuss?	
Data: Do I have data I would like to discuss and analyze?	

Figure 2.9: Questions to prepare for being coached.

Tool: Find a Super Ally

While you will usually have scheduled sessions with your coach, you also need colleagues who you can call on at the spur of the moment, when you need immediate advice, or when you just want to run an idea by someone else. That's where your super ally and your critical friends come in.

I have what I call my super ally, the one colleague whom I know I can genuinely trust to ask any question, run any idea by, complain about my supervisor, or discuss any aspect of school life, personal life—anything, at any time. A super ally is a gift. This is a person you truly trust and who has that same trust in you. Trust is the single greatest factor when confiding in your super ally because the last thing you want is for your business to become everyone else's business. A super ally lifts you up, makes you laugh, and can find that sliver of sunshine amid the storm. I always know who I'm gonna call.

Your super ally understands the pressures of your job, and is that one person you can call, text, or email for any reason. And while your super ally is as busy at their school as you are at yours, they return those calls, texts, or emails immediately or as soon as possible. And, of course, it's mutual. You do the same for them. Trust is the number one essential element of a super ally. But how do you really know who you can trust? In *Dare to Lead*, Brown (2018) identifies seven behaviors that make up the backbone of trust. She calls it BRAVING, and it's an acronym for those seven behaviors that define trust:

- **Boundaries:** We always respect each other's boundaries
- **Reliability:** We do what we say we're going to do, and don't promise to do something we can't deliver
- **Accountability:** We own our mistakes and learn from each other
- **Vault:** We keep the information truly between ourselves
- **Integrity:** We choose courage over comfort and practice our values
- **Nonjudgment:** We can ask each other for what we need and talk about how we feel without judgment
- **Generosity:** You are generous with words and actions of others (Brown, 2018, pp. 225-227)

It's not easy to just go out and find yourself a super ally. Building trust takes time and experience. You have to determine how safe you feel exposing your areas of vulnerability with another colleague. You can also refer back to Edmondson's (2004) psychological safety questions from tip 6 (page 40) to help determine the level of safety you have with your colleagues, and like any situation, test the waters first. There are definitely colleagues who may look like super allies on the outside but are focused on personal gain on the inside. Beware, but try to find at least one super ally.

Tool: Critical Friends Process Worksheet

While it's beneficial to have a coach and a super ally, principals also benefit from having a cadre of critical friends. Arthur L. Costa and Bena Kallick (1993), cofounders of the Institute for Habits of Mind, define a *critical friend* as:

> a trusted person who asks provocative questions, provides data to be examined through another lens, and offers critique of a person's work as a friend. A critical friend takes the time to fully understand the context of the work presented and the outcomes that the person or group is working toward. The friend is an advocate for the success of that work.

Critical friends are useful to have in various focus groups. I have been a member of several different critical friends groups over the years. I have been part of what we call the *singleton* group, education leaders who delve into issues that revolve around being the sole administrator. I've been in a critical friends group of principals that belong to the same school district area and to one that pertained directly to our International Baccalaureate school status. You can create your critical friends group for any situation that will offer you advice and support. One of the major features of a critical friends group is that the group can provide feedback to each other on any topic on which a member needs advice. Research has found the critical friends concept is beneficial for action research by educators at all levels to improve their practice (Noor & Shafee, 2021).

There is an actual process for critical friends groups interested in discussing topics and providing feedback in a systematic manner. Developed in 1994 by the Annenberg Institute for School Reform at Brown University and rooted in K–12 education, the model was designed to examine curricula and outcomes of student performance to improve classroom instruction (Pennsylvania Adult Education Resources, 2017). The model uses a set of guiding questions on which group members offer feedback to those seeking assistance and advice. The purpose of the critical friends process is to engage in self-directed, autonomous professional learning (Pennsylvania Adult Education Resources, 2017).

While the protocol is a trademarked, branded product currently facilitated by the National School Reform Faculty (https://nsrfharmony.org), its basic tenets can be useful for groups of like-minded principals who need dedicated time and structure to promote collaborative professional learning among principals on an ongoing basis. It focuses on developing collegial relationships and encouraging reflective practice. You will want your critical friends group to comprise colleagues who trust each other and can provide honest feedback that may sometimes be difficult to hear. You want your friends to push you past your comfort zone in order to realize the change you are seeking. Summon the courage to have difficult conversations, experience vulnerability and discomfort, and be willing to heed the advice.

Critical friends groups are usually limited to between four and six members; smaller groups allow time for a feedback cycle of all members consisting of four steps: (1) principals state problems they currently face, (2) the rest of the group asks questions to analyze the situation, (3) the group discusses and provides feedback, and (4) presenting principals respond to feedback (Hatfield, n.d.). The feedback can be warm, consisting of supportive, appreciative statements; cool, which offers different ways to think about the problem; or hard, which challenges and extends the presenter's thinking or raises concerns (Hatfield, n.d.). The group can repeat this cycle for every member who needs it.

Schedule a set time, preferably once a month, to meet either in person, which is preferable, or virtually via Zoom, Teams, or any other synchronous screen method. Have the problem or issue that you want to share with your colleagues prepared in advance, along with any pertinent data and information you would like to share as well.

There are three roles that group members will assume during a critical friends session (Hatfield, n.d.).

1. **Facilitator:** The facilitator reviews the process with the group members, sets the time limits, and manages the time. This should take about three minutes. He, she, or they participate in the discussion but make sure all voices are heard. The facilitator takes about five minutes at the end of the session to lead the debriefing process.

2. **Presenter:** After presenting the problem for about five minutes, the presenter should sit back and take notes during the discussion while listening carefully to ensure he, she, or they can respond effectively. It is best to avoid eye contact during the discussion. After the feedback is presented, the presenter should spend about five minutes responding specifically to feedback.

3. **Discussants:** The discussants use the bulk of the time in the middle of the session. For five minutes after the presenter has shared the topic and context of the discussion, they ask any necessary clarifying questions. Then, for about twelve minutes, discussants address the issue brought up by the presenter and give feedback that is both positive and critical. While some of the feedback will be critical in nature, discussants should give all feedback in a supportive manner.

You can decide how many times you want to cycle through the process during a critical friends session. It takes about thirty-five minutes for each cycle, so with four people in the group, it would take a little over two hours for everyone to have the role of presenter. It's important for the facilitator to monitor the time carefully because getting off track regarding the purpose of the meeting may mean that not all presenters have an opportunity to share. Use the template in figure 2.10 to facilitate this process. A reproducible version is available on page 72.

Date: 4/5/23

Critical Friends Session

Presenter: *Member A*

Facilitator: *Member B*

Discussants: *Members B, C, and D*

Presenter's Issue	Clarifying Questions	Feedback
I can't find time to attend collaborative meetings, which makes it difficult for me to monitor student achievement on a regular basis in my school's PLC.	*1. When are the collaborative meetings usually scheduled—before, during, or after school?* *2. Are the days and times consistent from week to week, or do they change frequently?* *3. What is actually keeping you from attending collaborative meetings?*	*Get organized! Look at your tasks and use a priority matrix to prioritize team meeting attendance.* *Make sure the meetings are scheduled on your calendar and delegate tasks that might keep you from attending.* *Tell the staff you will be attending their collaborative meetings, as it will help you keep your word.*

Source: Adapted from Appleby, 1998.
Figure 2.10: Critical friends process worksheet.

Tool: Join a Professional Organization

To cast a wider network, joining a professional organization can offer a wide range of opportunities for professional growth. This can help you feel a larger sense of belonging. By joining professional organizations, you can connect with colleagues and experts outside of your own district, state, and country.

Joining a professional organization is critical in keeping up with the latest knowledge and best practices locally, regionally, and globally. It helps you to stay abreast of current issues in education and offers opportunities for personal advancement in leadership. Organizations offer conferences, seminars, webinars, and professional journals with articles related to all aspects of a principal's job. Along with obtaining more knowledge, you can usually obtain credits you need for relicensure. Some professional organizations, such as the National Association of Elementary School Principals and the National Association of Secondary School Principals, offer additional benefits, including legal services and professional liability coverage for job protection defense.

Professional organizations come in all shapes and sizes at the local, national, and international levels. Joining an organization gives you access to professional learning, resources and materials, as well as networking and prospective job opportunities. Some of the nationally known professional organizations that offer information, professional development, and experts in the field of school administration include the following.

- **AASA:** School Superintendents Association (www.aasa.org)
- **ASCD:** Association for Supervision and Curriculum Development (www.ascd.org)
- **CoSN:** Consortium for School Networking (www.cosn.org)
- **NAESP:** National Association of Elementary School Principals (www.naesp.org)
- **NASSP:** National Association of Secondary School Principals (www.nassp.org)
- **NEA:** National Education Association (www.nea.org)

There are local chapters of AASA, NAESP, and NASSP in every state. Professional organizations that cater to specific areas of education include:

- **ILA:** International Literacy Association (www.literacyworldwide.org)
- **ISTE:** International Society for Technology in Education (www.iste.org)
- **NAEA:** National Art Education Association (www.arteducators.org)
- **NBEA:** National Business Education Association (www.nbea.org)
- **NCSS:** National Council for the Social Studies (www.ncss.org)
- **NCTE:** National Council of Teachers of English (www.ncte.org)
- **NCTM:** National Council of Teachers of Mathematics (www.nctm.org)

You cannot do this job alone. You need a network that is both local and global. The burnout rate for principals is on the rise. According to a nationally representative RAND Corporation survey of 1,540 principals conducted in January of 2022, researchers found that 48 percent of principals said they were burned out (Steiner et al., 2022). To combat burnout and to keep a positive mindset regarding the demanding job of a principal, you need to rely on coaches, colleagues, organizations, family, and friends for advice, support, love, and entertainment.

Tip 10: Study Your Boss

When hiking, your guide helps you make the best decisions regarding routes and trails, knows how far the next water source is, and reminds you to stop, eat, and rest along the way. You also help your guide by staying hydrated, eating properly, and pacing yourself to stave off fatigue. If you fall victim to dehydration and fatigue, you impact the group's ability to forge on.

Likewise, with your superiors, it's much to your advantage to work together for the good of the entire system. If you're not in good favor with your supervisor, it impacts your school's ability to move forward. This tip is your guide to managing up, which, if done successfully, will allow you to obtain the best possible outcomes for both you and your supervisor. The tools include putting your boss under a (metaphorical) microscope, a contributions chart to ensure you are ready to highlight your accomplishments, and the four Ds process to help manage disagreements.

Tool: My Boss Under a Microscope Organizer

The first question to ask is what you need to know about your boss. In her article "What Everyone Should Know About Managing Up," Dana Rousmaniere (2015) maintains that the most important skill to master is figuring out how to be a genuine source of help to your supervisor. Rousmaniere (2015) says, "Managing up doesn't mean sucking up. It means being the most effective employee you can be." Being an effective principal is the best path to a healthy relationship with your boss and "begins and ends with you doing your job, and doing it well" (Rousmaniere, 2015).

Whitney Johnson (2014), an influential management thinker, agrees that as a principal, you must be very clear about the job that you were hired to do—and do it. Johnson (2014) adds to always make sure you understand what your *boss* was hired to do. Almost everything we do in education points directly to improving student achievement. While that is your charge at the school level, that is also your supervisor's job at the district level. Find out specifically what your supervisor's academic goals are, not just for your school but for the district, so that you can work together toward the specific objectives. When principals meet objectives, it contributes to district leaders meeting their objectives, as they have agendas based on their bosses' expectations.

When deciding when to involve your supervisor in a matter, decide if the matter really is urgent. You don't want to get into a situation of crying wolf. Supervisors most likely have several principals who report directly to them, so making the most of their time is very important. When involving your supervisor, if the matter is not a drop-everything-and-attend-to-this-matter situation, then clearly communicate that at the beginning of the message, be it phone or email. Tell your supervisor that it's not urgent, but you would like some advice or reassurance regarding a decision or whatever the matter. That creates the opportunity for your supervisor to look into the matter, gather more information for you, and attend to other matters that do meet the urgent criteria. John J. Gabarro and John P. Kotter (1993), in a classic *Harvard Business Review* article, say supervisors "don't have unlimited time, encyclopedic knowledge, or extrasensory perception; nor are they evil enemies. They have their own pressures and concerns that are sometimes at odds with the wishes of the subordinate—and often with good reason" (p. 154). This is why it is vital that you discern between urgent matters that require immediate assistance and those that can wait.

While not every principal-supervisor relationship is harmonious, it is important to keep in mind that the supervisory relationship involves mutual dependence. Both need each other to achieve success. Gabarro and Kotter (1993) agree that "at a minimum, you need to appreciate your boss's goals and pressures, his or her strengths and weaknesses" (p. 152). They maintain that in order to get the resources, the information, the advice, or the permission you need, it always falls to who has the power or leverage, and that is your supervisor. Gabarro and Kotter (1993) stress, "To fail to make that relationship one of mutual respect and understanding is to miss a major factor in being effective" (p. 156).

Business researchers Marcello Russo, Gabriele Morandin, and Massimo Bergami (2021) offer three steps for building a good relationship with your boss. First, envision what you want your relationship with your boss to look like. Do this by "visualizing your future self—your hopes, wishes, aspirations and fears associated with who you want to be at work" (Russo et al., 2021). They also advise that you make an action plan, where you find opportunities to work with your boss on tasks or projects. Lastly, they encourage you to monitor your relationship (Russo et al., 2021). Figure out what is working in the relationship with your boss and acknowledge your challenges.

In order to gain an understanding of your boss, you need to ask a few questions. For one, you should find out your boss's preferred style of communication for receiving information, whether it is an email, a text, or a phone call. I once spent ample time crafting an email to my boss detailing a situation I was facing at school. I needed a quick reply, and I got one immediately—a three-word email replying, "Use bullet points." With that response, I stored that communication style in my head and always keep the facts short and to the (bullet) point. Understanding your boss's communication preferences will save you time and the frustration of having to resend the email, whether in bullet points or any other style, especially if you need advice quickly. Ask about the best time to consult your boss with information other than that which needs an immediate response.

Steve Arneson (2014), author of *What Your Boss Really Wants From You*, explains that if you really want to understand your boss and understand what drives his, her, or their behavior, you have to study your boss. He sets forth ten questions that are designed to offer you awareness into your boss's behavior or mindset. You can get the answers to these questions either by asking your boss directly, by talking with your colleagues, or by paying close attention to your immediate environment. The ten questions involve areas of management style, leadership brand, relationships, and primary motivation. Studying your boss's management style is essential to operating within your boss's preferred work style.

Arneson's (2014) first five questions focus on management style.

1. **When and how is your boss most approachable?** Determine if you need an appointment, the preferred method of communication, and any subjects that are just not up for debate.

2. **What is your boss's preferred management style?** Recognize your boss's decision-making style, and figure out how much information and lead time are necessary to make a decision. Look for the best time to offer new ideas.

3. **What behaviors does your boss reward?** Pay attention to how your supervisor rewards or punishes certain behaviors, and note what happens to other principals in certain situations.

4. **What is your boss trying to accomplish in this role?** Try to figure out your boss's mission and goals.

5. **What is your boss worried about?** Make sure you are not one of your boss's stressors. Pay attention to demeanor, moods, and body language to determine the best time to approach your boss with a situation or new idea.

Question 6 is about what Arneson (2014) calls your boss's leadership brand.

6. **What is your boss's reputation in the school district?** Listen to what other people say about your supervisor. Try to get an overall balanced perception of his, her, or their reputation through studying and observing in order to get a more accurate picture.

Questions 7–9 revolve around relationships (Arneson, 2014).

7. **Whom does your boss respect?** "If you pay attention to what he respects in others, you will have a good idea of what he wants to see in you" (Arneson, 2014, p. 35). Make a list of those qualities your boss respects and you will find yourself more successful in managing up.

8. **Where does your boss have influence?** Take a look at the track records of your district leader and consider what the successes and failures look like.

9. **What is your boss's relationship like with his, her, or their boss?** Listen to what your boss says about working for others and watch their interactions, because understanding that relationship will help you understand more about your boss's behavior, motives, goals, and expectations.

Lastly, question 10 is about your boss's primary motivation (Arneson, 2014).

10. **What is your boss's primary motivation?** Motives are powered by wealth, recognition, awards, job advancement, or just job security. Figuring out that primary motivation is essential to managing up.

As you learn more about your boss, use the chart in figure 2.11 to record your findings. This is a particularly delicate tool, and you might only want to fill out a line or two here and there as needed, coming back to it later to add further insights. Keep it handy but out of sight.

Tool: Contributions Chart

Another question to ask is whether your boss actually knows about your accomplishments. This goes back to knowing your strengths. Using your strengths to build a working relationship with your boss is a plus. Does your boss recognize your strengths? Promoting your skills and talents with your supervisor takes a bit of skill in itself. If you were to ask your boss to write you a letter of recommendation, what would he, she, or they say about you? What would your boss highlight? It's not enough for you to know about your boss; it's also important for your boss to know about you. How do you convey your strengths, achievements, and successes to your boss without coming across as threatening, egotistical, or smarmy? If you know your reputation, you can probably figure out what your boss would consider your strengths.

According to Arneson (2014), by analyzing yourself through your supervisor's eyes, you complete the cycle of assessment you started by analyzing your supervisor. To do this, you have to reflect honestly on your strengths, achievements, and successes, as well as the areas in which you need to improve. This means burying your ego and building an impartial view of how your supervisor really sees you. If you have a yearly evaluation with your supervisor, take the emotion out of the evaluation and read it for what it's really worth. Even if you do not agree with how you're evaluated in certain areas,

Understanding My Boss	Your Evidence
Management Style	
Best time to approach	
Best approach to meeting or speaking	
Preferred method of communication	
Subjects not open to debate	
Decision-making style	
Rewarded behaviors	
Goals	
Worries or stress	
Leadership Brand	
Reputation	
Relationships	
Respect	
Influence and success	
Managing up	
Primary Motivation	
Motives	

Source: Adapted from Arneson, 2014.

Figure 2.11: My boss under a microscope organizer.

Visit **go.SolutionTree.com/leadership** *for a free reproducible version of this figure.*

that evaluation is how your boss sees it. If you want to manage up effectively, you will demonstrate that you are working on those particular areas. You can also look for what skills and talents your boss values about you and continue to promote those as you improve in other areas.

Sharon Florentine (2016) of *CIO* offers tips for improving your self-promotion skills. One thing she advises is not to assume your boss knows exactly what you do. While your boss knows you are a principal, think about what makes your work stand out. Are you concentrating on a particular area of student achievement, community building, or partnerships? Whatever it is, let it be known. And while informing others about your work, be cognizant of crossing the line of articulating your value with bragging. Share your accomplishments on social media, blogs, and within your professional organization, but do it without the air of superiority that could work against you. Keep a list of your accomplishments handy so, if asked, you can readily call them to mind and discuss them without looking like you're conjuring something up. One way to do this is to keep a journal—either handwritten or computer generated—so you can refer to it easily. Also, keep a current résumé handy. This helps allow you to adopt what Florentine (2016) calls an *accomplishment mindset and narrative.*

To consolidate a few of the worksheets you may have already completed, add your goals, strengths, and skills to a chart like the example in figure 2.12 (page 62), along with your accomplishments, areas of focus, and areas for growth. When you have the opportunity to meet with your boss, review this chart in advance of your meeting and make sure you highlight what you contribute to the school and to the district.

Goals:	Skills:
Continue studying and implementing culturally responsive teaching, focusing on helping students become independent learners. Ensure rigor in instruction and giving students the opportunity to engage in productive struggles that grow their brainpower and allow them to attain the stamina they need to attack and solve problems independently.	Listening and communication
Strengths:	**Areas of focus:**
Activator, catalyst, coach	Create a culturally responsive environment where diversity is valued and all students and adults thrive and achieve at high levels.
Accomplishments:	**Areas for growth:**
I created a structure and framework to ensure a high-functioning site equity team.	Seek opportunities to engage in cross racial conversations about diversity and culture and how they impact student achievement.

Figure 2.12: Contributions chart.

Visit **go.SolutionTree.com/leadership** *for a free reproducible version of this figure.*

Tool: Four Ds Process Worksheet

If you've ever seen the movie *The Devil Wears Prada* (Frankel, 2006), you've seen the epitome of the boss from hell abusing her positional power. Of course, it's a comedy-drama film, but sometimes reality can mimic that sort of fiction. Some of you can probably say, "I've been there," in some of the scenes in that movie. There is a definite absence of psychological safety in that workplace. You may not be in a situation that dire, but there will be times when you don't agree with your boss or when your boss is making things difficult for you.

I would never have climbed Wanupichu in Peru without first climbing mountains on a smaller scale. Similarly, you don't want to go head-to-head with your supervisor without testing the waters. To determine the psychological safety of working with your supervisor, try asking for small, more incidental things; ask your colleagues how they fared when challenging an idea; or think about how you promote your unique skills and talents with your supervisor.

When contemplating communicating any displeasure, "pick your whines," says David D. Perlmutter (2007), writing for *The Chronicle of Higher Education*. Perlmutter (2007) explains that "gaining a reputation as a malcontent will not enhance your career." You need to take legitimate concerns and grievances to your supervisor, but keep in mind the relative importance of the problem or concern. Take into account how many times you have complained about a certain issue or situation or made certain requests, and determine whether you should really pursue it or give it a rest. Just remember, it's not always just about you and your concerns. If it's truly a concern that affects more than just you, then it's probably worth mentioning—at least once. Depending on the feedback on the concern, take the lead of the supervisor. If he, she, or they are not as concerned as you are, leave it alone. If it is still a concern for you in the future and enough time has elapsed, bring it up again, acknowledging and referencing the feedback you received from the initial communication.

In our increasingly complex world, where issues do not always have an immediate answer, the need for individuals to think together to arrive at a solution becomes a necessity. In many cases, your supervisor may not have an answer for one or more of your queries. This will necessitate your ability to balance advocacy with inquiry. *Advocacy* is explicitly telling your supervisor what you want or need, while *inquiry* is asking for a particular want or need.

Rick Ross and Charlotte Roberts (1994), authors of "Balancing Inquiry and Advocacy," offer protocols for improving both advocacy and inquiry. Protocols for improved advocacy involve making your thinking process visible and publicly testing your conclusions and assumptions. Protocols for improved inquiry involve asking others to make their thinking process visible and comparing your assumptions to theirs. If you are facing a point of view with which you disagree, again inquire about what led the person to that view and make sure you truly understand their view. Once you understand their view, raise your concerns again and state what is leading you to have those concerns.

If you are truly at an impasse with your boss about a particular issue, you have to accept the position of impasse and look for information that will allow people to move forward. Ask for and seek data or logic that might change their views and continue to look for avenues of change. However, sometimes doing this may be difficult or uncomfortable because the lack of psychological safety is too great.

Everyone hopes to have a boss who is supportive and makes it possible to succeed at the job. But in some cases, your supervisor will not be so supportive and make it much harder for you to succeed at your job. When your answers to Edmondson's (2004) questions reveal that the degree of safety of working with your supervisor seems low, Katherine Crowley and Kathi Elster (2010), authors of *Working for You Isn't Working for Me*, offer some advice for handling those difficult boss-employee relationships. They identify several boss behaviors that leave those on the receiving end feeling angry, manipulated, defeated, and with a general lack of control. Some examples of these behaviors include bosses who send mixed messages, constantly find fault or change priorities, micromanage, take credit for other people's work, blur the lines of responsibility, and are incapable of making decisions. People with bosses who behave badly employ coping mechanisms such as avoidance, self-doubt, sulking, bad-mouthing, confrontation, retaliation, or shutting out their boss.

Crowley and Elster (2010) offer a four-step process to dealing with those difficult boss-employee relationships. This is a four-step process that can help you take back your power. Each D stands for a specific set of actions that can help you improve your relationship with your supervisor. The Four Ds model can also help you navigate a situation in a way that protects your psychological safety.

1. **Detect:** In this stage, you realize that you are in a toxic relationship and understand how it is affecting you.

2. **Detach:** When you detach, you accept that you are not going to change your boss's behavior and you start looking for ways to take back your power. Focus on what you can control—your own energy, self-esteem, and confidence.

3. **Depersonalize:** By depersonalizing, you are taking your boss's behavior less personally and discovering ways to get what you need in the workplace.

4. **Deal:** This means devising a plan of protection to manage the relationship with your supervisor and creating a strategy for moving forward. The goal is to convert your relationship with your supervisor from intolerable to acceptable.

I designed figure 2.13 (page 64) as a guide through this process and a way to record your thoughts on each step. The following example provides ideas about what to record in the Your Actions column. This worksheet is best kept private unless you are discussing the situation with your coach, super ally, or critical friends.

Four Ds Process	Situation	Response	Your Actions	Outcome
Detect	You are in a toxic relationship with your boss.	Acknowledge the situation.	I am at this point in the relationship: *Don't rock the boat. Know your limits [see tip 15, page 96].*	
Detach	You are not going to change your boss's behavior.	Take charge of the things you can control.	I can control the following: *My responses and the tone of my responses. Know what voice to use [see tip 14, page 91].*	
Depersonalize	You are affected emotionally.	Don't take your boss's behavior personally. Look for ways to get what you need and reflect on what you bring to the relationship.	I can bring the following to the relationship: *I can bring calm rationale and data to support it. Use mindfulness techniques [see tip 11, page 76].*	
Deal	This is reality.	Devise a plan of protection to manage the relationship and a strategy to move forward.	This is what I need to do: *Stay calm and focus on what is in my circle of influence [see tip 3, page 17].*	

Source: Adapted from Crowley & Elster, 2010.

Figure 2.13: Four Ds process worksheet.

Visit **go.SolutionTree.com/leadership** for a free reproducible version of this figure.

Summary and What's Next

Everyone works for someone else, unless of course, you're in some other line of work and you are the sole employee. As a school leader, you have to be able to both manage yourself and manage up. You must first know yourself. You must know the laws and policies that impact you daily, keep safety first, and use your network to create the working environment that works for everyone—including your boss. Yes, it's a huge, complex, and sometimes overwhelming job, and to help you navigate it all in as sane a manner as possible, chapter 3 provides tips and tools on how to keep your stress levels at bay by staying calm, keeping your balance, listening, speaking, and acknowledging your limitations.

Emergency Procedures One-Pager

Emergency	What to Do First	Who to Call	Phone Number	Safe Haven for Evacuation	Safety Team Member	Radio Channel or Extension	Door Number

The Principal's Backpack © 2024 Solution Tree Press • SolutionTree.com
Visit **go.SolutionTree.com/leadership** to download this free reproducible.

Law and Policy Reference Guide

A	
Athletics	
Alternative education	
Attendance and truancy	

E	
Equal rights	
Equity	
Extracurricular activities	

B	
Behavior and discipline	
Bullying prevention	

F	
Field trips	
Funding	

C	
Communications	
Contracts	

G	
Gender equity	
Grants	

D	
Data privacy	
Digital literacy	

H	
Human resources	
Human rights	

I	Immigration
	Integration

M	Media release
	Multilanguage learners

J	Jury and military duty

N	Nutrition and food services

K	Keys distribution

O	Operations
	Open enrollment

L	LBGTQ+

P	Payroll
	Personnel
	Purchasing

| Q | Questionnaires and surveys | | U | Union contracts |
| | | | | Use of school building and grounds—permits |

R	Research and evaluation		V	Vendors
				Visitors
				Volunteers

S	Safety and security		W	Weapons
	Search and seizure			Wellness
	Special education			

T	Technology usage and safety		X, Y, Z	Zero tolerance
	Titles I through IX			
	Transportation			

The Principal's Backpack © 2024 Solution Tree Press • SolutionTree.com
Visit **go.SolutionTree.com/leadership** to download this free reproducible.

Strengths Self-Evaluation

What am I good at in my job as a principal?	What compliments have I received, from either my own staff or other principals?

What professional challenges have I overcome?	How have I helped or made others happy at work?

What makes me unique in my capacity as a principal?	What do I value the most in my professional life?

Source: Adapted from Therapist Aid. (2021). My strengths and qualities. Accessed at www.therapistaid.com/therapy-worksheet/my-strengths-and-qualities on November 22, 2022.

Strengths Assessments Organizer

StrengthsFinder Top Five	High 5 Strengths	Other Results

Insights From the Strengths Wheel

How to Use My Strengths Going Forward

Questions to Prepare for Being Coached

Date:	Coach:
Topics for Discussion	**Coaching Feedback**
Goals: What am I working on? What do I want to begin working on?	
Decisions: Have I made decisions, or do I need to make some decisions that I would like to discuss?	
Interventions or strategies: Have I tried new interventions or strategies for which I would like feedback?	
Learning focus: Is there a particular focus or issue that I would like to discuss?	
Data: Do I have data I would like to discuss and analyze?	

Critical Friends Process Worksheet

Instructions: Use one worksheet per cycle.

Date:

Critical Friends Session

Presenter:

Facilitator:

Discussants:

Presenter's Issue	Clarifying Questions	Feedback

Source: Adapted from Appleby, J. (1998). Becoming critical friends: Reflections of an NSRF coach. Providence, RI: Annenberg Institute for School Reform at Brown University.

CHAPTER 3
Navigating the Trail

Navigating the trail means moving in the direction you have chosen and mapped out: your focus. Most hiking trails are marked with blazes. For example, the trails in the Swiss Alps are marked with red and white blazes painted on rocks and trees. Blazes show you the direction of the *main trail* and let you know you're on the right path. Along the main trail, there are *spur trails* that lure you off the main trail for scenic overlooks, shortcuts, or campgrounds. As principals, we all get lured off the main trail for a myriad of reasons, but always keep the main trail in sight. That's the direction you have chosen, and it's where you need to keep your focus, unless you come to an impasse and have to re-map your route. It's very easy to get turned around and disoriented when you leave the main trail. If you become completely absorbed with the spur trail, you may end up completely lost and may not find the main trail again for some time. This is where stress starts to set in.

Now that you have mapped your route and have packed your bag in chapters 1 and 2, you're ready to step out on the trail. This entails being ready for any and every situation you encounter. And regardless of the situation, keeping your stress levels low and manageable, even in a crisis, is vital to thinking clearly and making sound decisions. The tools in this chapter provide some ways to help with that, but before getting to them, it's important to understand the effects of stress.

According to a longevity survey of principals in Australia conducted by Philip Riley (2015) of the Institute for Positive Psychology and Education:

> Citing mounting demands, a lack of time and little support, principals are struggling to meet the requirements of the job. Principals are the victims of stress at a rate 1.7 times higher than the population in general. And things are only getting worse. Findings show that school leaders' thoughts of self-harm and poor quality-of-life concerns were double that of previous years. (as cited in Fischetti & Imig, 2015)

The survey also finds that the number one stress factor for principals is the "sheer quantity of work" (Riley, 2015). Just take a look at the job descriptions posted for principal positions, and they look positively exhaustive. Results from the same survey two years later reveal that over half of principals worked fifty-six hours a week or more, with 27 percent working up to sixty-five hours per week (Riley, 2018). Education reporter Natasha Robinson (2018) summarizes the results: principals showed "higher levels of burnout than the general population, [had] twice as much difficulty sleeping as a result of stress and were at higher risk of depression."

Al, my friend and fellow principal, is an example of how this chronic stress can affect lives. At one time, he had four children under the age of six and was working over fifty hours a week in a challenging school. Exertion got the best of him. The exhilaration was gone, and survival became the name of the game. Deep depression set in, and Al was looking for a way out—not just out of the principal position, but a way out of life. He actually had a plan. Luckily, Al had a support network and was able to get the help he needed to climb back out. He's now an assistant principal, and while the job is still challenging, he is able to balance his family life with his work responsibilities. Al currently maintains a website called *The Depression Files*. His blog and podcast (https://thedepressionfiles.com) offer a lot of information regarding mental health.

The onset of the COVID-19 pandemic exacerbated these stresses, according to a RAND research report (Woo & Steiner, 2022). Using data gathered following the 2020–2021 school year from principals in the United States, researchers found that 80 percent of secondary school principals experienced frequent job-related stress during that school year. In particular, the researchers find that female principals, principals of color, and principals of high-poverty schools are likely to experience constant stress (Woo & Steiner, 2022). More than a quarter of educators, including principals, experience symptoms of depression (Will, 2022).

The term *stress* has been used since the early 1900s to define different types of situations that cause a physiological and psychological change. The American Institute of Stress (n.d.) offers a definition of stress as "a condition or feeling experienced when a person perceives that demands exceed the personal and social resources the individual is able to mobilize."

Stress can be beneficial in that it motivates us to succeed in completing tasks and can actually boost brain power by stimulating the production of *neurotrophins*, brain chemicals that strengthen the connections between neurons in the brain (Curley, 2019; Lindberg, 2019; MacMillan, 2022). The clinical term for positive stress is *eustress*—the exhilaration. We need a certain amount of eustress in our lives to function. Clinical psychiatrist Michael Genovese explains, "Eustress helps us stay motivated, work toward goals, and feel good about life" (Lindberg, 2019).

However, most of the time, when we refer to stress, especially when we relate it to the principal job, we're talking about the harmful stress: *distress*—the exertion. This is the stress that leads to unhealthy eating and sleeping habits, lack of energy or desire to exercise, and less involvement in personal activities after school, all of which can wreak havoc on your body in the form of headaches to high blood pressure (American Institute of Stress, n.d.). In your line of work as a principal, your stressors may tend to be more emotional and psychological than physical, or you may find yourself with more physical ailments. Regardless, long-term stress is harmful and can be very serious (American Psychological Association, 2018).

When your body senses stress, your adrenal glands release cortisol into your bloodstream. *Cortisol* is a hormone that increases your heart rate and blood pressure (Mawri, 2022). While this response can help in some situations, constant stress can cause the release of too much cortisol, which can contribute to higher levels of blood sugar, weight gain, immune system suppression, digestive problems, and even heart disease (Mawri, 2022).

Managing stress can be complicated and confusing because there are different types, including acute stress, episodic acute stress, and chronic stress (American Institute of Stress, n.d.). Each type of stress has its own characteristics, symptoms, duration, and treatment approaches. Knowing your signs of stress and seeking solutions can help you relieve them before they control you. There will always be times of stress on the job: deadlines, crises, conflict, endless paperwork, and many, many more. Understand the different types of stress and be aware of what type you are under at any given time. Table 3.1 breaks down each type.

The notion that the job of a principal can be quite stressful is well documented, so what you need to navigate the trails are tools that help you understand stress and stay ahead of it, a figurative compass to direct you in a healthy, balanced direction. This chapter provides five tips and tools to stay calm, maintain your balance, listen, express yourself, and understand your limits.

Table 3.1: Stress Types and What They Can Lead To

Type	What It Is	Symptoms and Possible Outcomes
Acute stress	Demands and pressures of the recent past, present, and near future: · Deadlines · Arguments · Violence · Receiving bad news	· Anger or irritability · Anxiety · Headaches and body pains · Gastrointestinal issues · Rapid heartbeat, dizziness, shortness of breath, and even chest pain
Episodic acute stress	Frequent instances of acute stress leading to constant worry and exhaustion	· Frequent headaches or migraines · Hypertension · Chest pain · Heart disease · Clinical depression
Chronic stress	Grinding stress over the course of years, often caused by life problems outside of our control: · Poverty · War · Racism · Trauma	· Chronic and acute, serious illnesses · Suicidal ideation · Stroke and heart attack

Source: Adapted from American Institute of Stress, n.d.; American Psychological Association, 2018.

Tip 11: Stay Calm

We hear it all the time: keep calm and carry on. As a school leader, you must remain calm regardless of what storm is brewing around you. People look to you for reassurance and support, and while you may be raging inside, you are cool and collected on the outside. When the tension in the school rises, yours needs to sink. It's not easy to remain calm in the midst of a storm, but by keeping your body calm and your stress under control, you can make important decisions with a clear head.

You will always encounter some stress, but remaining calm and utilizing appropriate strategies will help keep your stress levels manageable. So, whether it's a student or staff member pushing your buttons or an all-out fight in the cafeteria, you need to be the model of calm, rational behavior and thinking. As discussed in tip 6 (page 40), while you might want to run to where there is a disturbance somewhere in the building, unless it is truly a matter of life and death, resist that urge and walk as calmly as possible so as to not cause unnecessary anxiety on the part of staff and students. Don't draw attention to a fight or any other type of disturbance. Stay calm and try to de-escalate and move the disturbance from others' view as quickly as possible. Staying calm helps you think rationally rather than impulsively and keeps others from panicking. In the wilderness, rationally using knowledge can save your life: you need to know what creatures to run from and in which cases you want to remain as still as possible. When encountering a wolf, bobcat, bear, or mountain lion, the first survival tip is to stop, remain calm, and move very slowly so as not to excite the animal. On the other hand, if you see a moose, run.

Similarly, in a school, being able to manage your emotions and remain calm is essential to your performance. Stress is a necessary emotion, as our brains are not wired to respond and take action unless we feel some level of emotional arousal, and experts say that performance peaks with moderate levels of stress (Curley, 2019). As long as the stress is not sustained over a long period of time, it can improve production. There are plenty of ways to help reduce the inevitable stress of the principal's job and keep it at manageable levels.

You may think that healthy habits are some of the easier tools to utilize from your pack, but stress makes it all too easy to fall into habits like eating on the run, drinking too much caffeine, finding little time for your hobbies, and tossing and turning all night. You are likely already well aware of the negative effects of these and other common habits and how they end up making stress even worse. But how do you actually become a more stress-resistant person to keep yourself more balanced?

Bessel van der Kolk, founder of Trauma Research Foundation and prolific researcher and author on trauma and post-traumatic stress disorder, outlines traits found among stress-resistant people (van Dernoot Lipsky, 2009). He maintains that stress-resistant people have a sense of personal control. They perceive a connection between their own actions and how they feel; they believe in their own capacity to influence the course of their lives (van Dernoot Lipsky, 2009). Stress-resistant people are also usually in pursuit of personally meaningful tasks. They are present and engaged in their lives, and this helps them to be active, instead of passive, during challenging times. They engage in healthy lifestyle choices by generally avoiding known dietary stimulants of refined white sugar, caffeine, and nicotine. Instead, they seek out multiple periods of hard exercise each week and find time each day for a period of relaxation (van Dernoot Lipsky, 2009).

The International Sports Sciences Association (ISSA, 2021) also weighs in on the habits of stress-resistant people. To become more stress resistant, ISSA (2021) recommends daily mindfulness practice that keeps you present in the moment. Meditation and deep breathing exercises allow you to calm your mind and focus on the present. ISSA (2021) also recommends scheduling activities that increase your happiness (see tip 18, page 118, for more on this subject). The more activities you have that you enjoy doing, the easier it will be to face adversity when it comes your way. And of course, physical activity and a good network of support are critical to fighting stress.

Laura van Dernoot Lipsky (2009), author of *Trauma Stewardship*, reminds us that our health requires daily maintenance. At times, we feel that as principals we have greater capabilities than we really do, and thus, we don't attend to our personal health as immediately as we should. As van Dernoot Lipsky (2009) points out, "When we realize the degree to which we can determine our focus, we may also open to the possibility that we have more options about how we structure our lives and work than we may have thought" (p. 180).

Consider, for example, that while you may need your morning coffee or that noon Diet Coke, caffeine stimulates the release of adrenaline into your body (BWell Health Promotion, n.d.). Adrenaline, which along with cortisol, is the source of the fight-or-flight response, can induce you to find a quick, impulsive response rather than a rational, thought-out response (American Institute of Stress, n.d.). The adrenaline is necessary when encountering a bear on the trail, but not always when dealing with school issues.

Sleep is another element essential to low stress that's within your control. Your emotional regulation and ability to focus are both reduced when you are sleep deprived (National Heart, Lung, and Blood Institute, 2022). Sleep deprivation also interferes with hormonal regulation, including stress hormones (Vinall, 2021). So, when you are tempted to stay up late to finish a project, think twice about what the lack of sleep will mean for the next day's events.

It's especially important during the workday to find time to relax and unwind. When trekking, I never get to the top of the mountain or the next lodge without periods of rest. I rest, relax, and nourish my body along the way. And once at my destination, I need a good meal, a good local beer, and a good night's sleep to be ready for the next day's adventure. It's the same for the work week. It's difficult to face any type of challenge when exhausted and sleep deprived.

Keep the tools for promoting good physical and mental health in one of those outer pockets of your pack so that you can tap into them at a moment's notice. Keeping your stress at bay will promote better health, and better health will allow you to manage yourself and all of your responsibilities. This tip includes tools for engaging in mindfulness techniques, listening to binaural beats, and practicing office yoga poses, which can all contribute to helping you stay calm and achieve a level of equanimity that is required to handle all the stress of the job.

Tool: Mindfulness Techniques Organizer

Mindfulness techniques have been studied since 1982, when professor of medicine Jon Kabat-Zinn (1990) first introduced his mindfulness-based stress-reduction program, which help his clients learn how to build their capacity to respond to stress, pain, and chronic illness (Mindful Staff, 2022). Mindful Staff (2022) defines *mindfulness* as "the basic human ability to be fully present, aware of where we are and what we're doing, and not overly reactive or overwhelmed by what's going on around us." Kathy Flaminio, school social worker and founder of MoveMindfully, recommends three mindfulness techniques: (1) breathing, (2) movement, and (3) rest (MoveMindfullyConnect, 2021).

Breathing

The practice of mindfulness begins with noticing breath. Of course, you can breathe without thinking about it, but once you can intentionally sync breathing and movement, your physiology begins to shift. A study conducted by the Trinity College Institute of Neuroscience and Global Brain Health Institute shows a neurological link between respiration and focus (Melnychuk et al., 2018). The study demonstrates that people who practice intentional and consistent breathing exercises affect the level of noradrenaline in their brains. *Noradrenaline* is a natural chemical messenger that is released when we are challenged, focused, or emotionally aroused. When people experience stress, too much noradrenaline is produced, and when sluggish, too little is produced. Melnychuk and colleagues (2018) find that people who practice daily breathing exercises produce an optimum amount of noradrenaline and show greater ability to focus. The website Headspace (n.d.) offers some suggestions that include counting deep breaths, lengthening exhales, and belly breathing.

One method to help regulate noradrenaline is to use a breathing ball, which you can purchase at various retail outlets, including online. This ball promotes healthy diaphragmatic breath, allowing you to slow down your breathing by inhaling and exhaling at a healthy pace. To use the breathing ball, hold the ball with two hands in front of your lungs and inhale slowly as you hold the ball closed. As you expand the ball, expand your lungs. As you breathe out, contract the ball. Do this several times until you are more relaxed and your breathing is at a normal pace.

When tennis player Billie Jean King (2008) talks about the immense pressure she endured on the tennis court, especially when millions of people were watching her play in the Battle of the Sexes against Bobby Riggs in 1973, she explains how her breathing exercises would calm her down, relax her, and make her feel more secure. She had a breathing regimen for every serve: breathe in for four counts, and breathe out for four counts. She has continually relied on breathing exercises, whether competing in tennis or completing other tasks (King, 2008).

Movement

How and when you move requires you to purposely notice how your body responds in the moment. Mindful movement asks your body what it needs in terms of physical activity. Mindful movement encourages you to take notice and be intentional with your motion or immobility, focusing more on the surroundings and quality of movement than the quantity or challenging aspect of it (Yang & Conroy, 2018). Body movement need not be more than a short walk or a few stress-relieving yoga poses in order to achieve the benefit of reduced stress (Berbari, 2018). Harvard Health Publishing (2021), summarizing the findings of numerous studies, highly recommends yoga in particular to elevate brain function and reduce stress (more on that soon).

Sometimes we need a little reminder to move. I wear a fitness watch that tells me to move if I haven't moved in at least one hour. That *move* alert can be quite annoying, but at the same time, it does signal to me that I have been sedentary for too long. How often you move is subject to your situation, but being mindful of balancing motion with rest is essential for your body and mind.

Rest

The idea of rest here is not just about sleep (though sleep is, of course, important too). When stress builds to a point where you begin to feel overwhelmed and exerted, it's time to press the pause button. This is not the time to reflect on problems, issues, or the situation causing the stress; it is time to remove yourself completely from the cause. The best course of action to pause is to get outside and breathe the air—not to exercise but simply to *be*. In Japan, they have a name for that: *shinrin-yoku*, or forest bathing. It's not hiking, trail running, or exercising of any sort. It's actually less about being in the wilderness as it is about honoring the hybrid of nature and civilization that the Japanese have cultivated for thousands of years (Li, 2018). Instead of exercise, forest bathers might write poetry, walk slowly, and inhale the woodsy scents of the forest. It is standard preventive medicine in Japan (Li, 2018).

The hardest part might just be that you need to leave your phone and laptop behind. Find a place where you can walk slowly and aimlessly. Says Qing Li (2018), a professor of forest medicine at Nippon Medical School in Tokyo:

> The key to unlocking the power of the forest is in the five senses. Let nature enter through your ears, eyes, nose, mouth, hands and feet. Listen to the birds singing and the breeze rustling in the leaves of the trees. Look at the different greens of the trees and the sunlight filtering through the branches. Smell the fragrance of the forest and breathe in the natural aromatherapy of phytoncides. Taste the freshness of the air as you take deep breaths. Place your hands on the trunk of a tree. Dip your fingers or toes in a stream. Lie on the ground. Drink in the flavor of the forest and release your sense of joy and calm. This is your sixth sense, a state of mind. Now you have connected with nature. You have crossed the bridge to happiness.

Once you've had a chance to try out some strategies for each mindfulness technique, you can use figure 3.1 to record your favorite or most successful approaches.

Technique	Notes
Breathing	Using the breathing ball works well because it regulates my inhaling and exhaling and slows it all down.
Movement	The easiest way to get moving is to make a trip upstairs—using the stairs.
Rest	The sauna at the gym really puts my body at rest.

Figure 3.1: Mindfulness techniques organizer.

*Visit **go.SolutionTree.com/leadership** for a free reproducible version of this figure.*

 Tool: Binaural Beats

Christopher is the physical therapist I'm putting through grad school to work miracles on my neck, shoulders, and back. I endure forty-five-minute sessions of searing pain as he breaks up huge knots and scar tissue, formed from years of being what he calls a high-strung person. One day, Christopher gave me a new remedy for those ailments. He wrote three words on a sticky note while I added his college fund gratuity to my bill: *binaural beats rhythms*. He told me to look it up and start listening right away. He said I could keep coming back every two weeks for torture, or I could start teaching myself to relax, not just my tightly wound body, but the perpetual motion of my brain as well.

You can start tuning it all out by tuning in to binaural beats. *Binaural* means relating to both ears. Prussian meteorologist Heinrich Wilhelm Dove discovered binaural beats in 1839 (Inglis-Arkell, 2015). As a secondary teacher, he noticed that when he placed a tuning fork with a listening tube that ran from the fork to a subject's ear on one side and placed another tuning fork and another tube running to the other ear, the two forks didn't quite vibrate at the same frequency. The subject could hear the difference, but they would hear it as a combined sound—one slow beat, now known as a binaural beat (Inglis-Arkell, 2015).

WebMD (n.d.) writers explain that a binaural beat is essentially an illusion the brain creates when you listen to two tones with two different frequencies at the same time. The way your brain interprets the sounds can help it reach certain mental states. While there is a lack of clinical research regarding binaural beats, there is some inconclusive evidence that they can help achieve calmness and focus (WebMD, n.d.). I have listened to binaural beats using headphones at night to calm my brain and have found it a soothing way to drift off to sleep. All you need to experience binaural beats are a pair of headphones and an app.

WebMD (n.d.) cautions that while some people might find them effective, others might not. In my experience, it was worth the try. To utilize this tool, you can search any music streaming service using the binaural beats search term. There are also apps available that you can download. There are several of these to choose from, and most of them are free of charge. I'm particularly fond of the one called Binaural Beethoven—Moonlight Sonata, which I listen to for several minutes before going to sleep to help calm my brain from the day's activities. Once you've found a track or an app that you like, grab your headphones, relax, and listen. You can listen to binaural beats in your office as a brain break, at the end of the day, or anytime you feel the need to calm your brain and your body.

 Tool: Office Yoga Poses

Another tool I recommend to help you become a more stress-resistant person is yoga, which incorporates each of the mindfulness techniques—breathing, movement, and rest. The practice of yoga is ancient. It has been traced back to the dawn of civilization, with historical evidence dating it back to the Indus Valley civilization in 2700 B.C. (Basavaraddi, n.d.).

Yoga instructor and author Timothy Burgin (2022) explains that yoga can help us connect with our surroundings while accessing "inner resources to teach us about self-awareness, acceptance, compassion, patience, gratitude, forgiveness, humility, love, peace, and joy." Besides these benefits, there is also evidence that it has a measurable impact on the brain:

> With its emphasis on breathing practices and meditation—both of which help calm and center the mind—it's hardly surprising that yoga also brings mental benefits, such as reduced anxiety and depression. What may be more surprising is that it actually makes your brain work better. (Harvard Health Publishing, 2021)

Harvard Health Publishing (2021), in an article titled "Yoga for Better Mental Health," explains how yoga sharpens your brain by allowing your brain cells to make new connections. These changes that occur in brain structure result in improved cognitive functioning, including learning and memory. Yoga also strengthens the brain in areas of attention, thought, and language. According to Harvard Health Publishing (2021), studies using brain imaging technology show that people who regularly did yoga had a thicker cerebral cortex, the area of the brain responsible for processing information, and a thicker hippocampus, the area of the brain that involves learning and memory. Those two areas of the brain are the ones that typically shrink as you age, and the brains of the older yoga participants in the study showed less shrinkage than those of people who did not do any yoga.

Harvard Health Publishing (2021) also notes another plus to doing yoga is that it improves your mood. Exercise, in general, improves your mood by lowering the levels of stress hormones and increasing the levels of endorphins, the good chemicals that give you that "runner's high" by bringing more oxygenated blood to your brain. It elevates levels of gamma-aminobutyric acid, a chemical associated with better mood and decreased anxiety.

One of the best parts of yoga is that you can practice it anywhere, including in your office:

> Your yoga mat is a place to invite in stress and meet it head-on to rewire your mind on a daily basis. All the ingredients you need are there: the challenges, the resistance, the doubts, the frustrations, the fears, and the possibilities. You can either break down or break through. (Baptiste, 2002, p. 30)

Figure 3.2 shares some easy poses you can start with that just involve standing so that you can strike the pose and breathe for a few minutes at a time right in your office, without even needing a mat.

These office yoga poses are useful for a quick, calming break. For a more intensive yoga experience, there are yoga classes at just about every fitness center that offers group classes, yoga-specific centers, and health spas, and you can even find some online. All of the tools to stay calm can be used at any time during the day.

If you feel that your stress is rising, close the door. Take a few moments and reach for that breathing ball, run through these poses, throw on some headphones, or just sit and meditate. There are many calming apps to choose from if you just need a few minutes of down time. You owe it to yourself, as well as everyone else, to take the time to calm and center your brain when tensions rise. Of course, using these tools as preventive measures may help keep the tensions and stress from rising in the first place.

Standing Yoga Pose	Instructions
Warrior (Virabhadrasana II)	• Take a large step forward with your left foot, keeping it facing forward. • Bend your left knee until your thigh is parallel to the ground while keeping your right leg straight. Turn your right foot out so that it is perpendicular to your left foot. • Point your left arm forward and your right arm toward the back. Face your hips and body forward but look over your left shoulder toward your left hand. • Hold for one to five breaths and then switch legs.
Mountain (Tadasana)	• Stand with toes together and heels slightly apart. • Spread your toes and stand straight, keeping your weight even on both feet. • Reach overhead with your arms while pressing down into your feet. • Take slow, deep breaths through your nose. • Hold for three to five breaths.
Crescent Lunge (Utthita Ashwa Sanchalanasana)	• Take a large step forward with your left foot, keeping it facing forward. • Bend your left knee until your thigh is parallel to the ground. Keep your back leg straight with your heel off the ground. • Keeping your body and head facing toward your left foot, extend your arms toward the ceiling on either side of your head. • Stretch upward while pressing into the floor. • Hold for five breaths and then switch legs.
Tree (Vrksasana)	• Stand with both feet on the ground with toes together and heels slightly apart. • Lift your right foot to the inner thigh of your left leg and squeeze your foot and inner thigh together, keeping your right knee turned out. • Take as much time as you need to get your balance, then lift your hands into a prayer position either in front of your chest or over your head. • Hold for five to ten breaths and then switch sides.

Source: Adapted from Winderl, 2018.

Figure 3.2: Office yoga poses.

*Visit **go.SolutionTree.com/leadership** for a free reproducible version of this figure.*

Tip 12: Keep Your Balance

I always take trekking poles with me when going on an extended hike. They preserve my knees on the downhills and stabilize me on uneven or rocky terrain. They have truly kept me from plummeting thousands of feet off the edge of a cliff more than once. My poles provide me with the physical balance I need to stay healthy on the trails, which is essential when you are miles from civilization. What is equally important is your mental and emotional balance. This means balancing eustress and distress. Recall that *eustress* is the positive stress. It is stress that motivates us, makes us feel exhilarated at the prospect of a task that's within our capabilities, actually improving performance. Distress, on the other hand, causes anxiety and, ultimately, exertion because it's stress that comes from the prospect of a task we feel is outside of our capabilities, decreasing performance and leading to mental and physical ailments (MentalHelp.net, n.d.).

Fighting off distress is vital to a lengthy career as a principal. Keeping your balance as a principal means focusing on what keeps you healthy and happy, which is best achieved by ensuring you have a balance between professional time with personal time. The principal position does not take a vacation, so you must consciously prioritize what's important to you outside your job.

According to Gary Hopkins (2009), editor-in-chief of *Education World*, fitting in family can be a tough assignment when after-school activities and evening events keep you at school through the dinner hours and beyond: "The demands of the principal's job can't help but take a toll on marriages and families." Keeping families intact requires plenty of effort, teamwork, and a well-used calendar. Hopkins (2009) writes:

> The demands of the job—internal and external—can affect marriages, too. In the blink of an eye, the school's needs can take precedence over the immediate family's. And that can lead to Divorce Court. It happens more often than many people care to admit. In spite of the stress and the demands of the job, many families manage to hold it all together. But none of them says that happens easily. It doesn't happen without effort and planning.

So, how do you balance the demands of the job with everything else you value in life? Having a visual to help you understand your balance, or in some cases, imbalance, in life can be very beneficial. Here are tools that will give you a visual representation of your life-work balance with a fun and simple paper plate activity and a way to simplify the act of saying no.

Tool: The Full Plate Activity

As entrepreneur, coach, and author Tony Robbins (n.d.) remarks, "Too many people are caught up with making a living—and not designing their life. But to be able to design your life, you must first create your map of where you are today." Robbins's (n.d.) wheel of life is a visual tool that helps you examine the different areas of your life and assess which areas are out of balance. This tool can be helpful to identify the areas that you need to pay more attention to in order reach equanimity. Robbins (n.d.) explains, "Consider each area like a spoke of a wheel: When one of the spokes is shorter than the others, it can throw the whole thing off balance." To use this tool, you can download an app, such as the LifeWheel: Smart Goal Tracker, Balance Life: Wheel of Life, or a host of others that are free of charge.

The wheel of life activity is highly useful, and I recommend trying the full process, but here I suggest a simple variation that I first did with my school staff with the intention of illustrating this notion of balance (actually, imbalance for most). I gave them each a paper plate and some crayons and asked them to divide the plate up in segments proportional to how they usually spent their week. Try it! Choose about six to eight areas that are especially important to you, such as family, work, relationships, volunteering, hobbies, spirituality, and so on. Be sure to include time to yourself as one. In the wheel of life, each area is imagined as a spoke on the wheel, but in this activity, you portion out each area as a slice of a pie chart according to how much time you spend on it so you can see right away which parts of your life are taking up the most space.

For many of my staff who did this activity, it illustrated why they were always so exhausted. After finishing their pie charts, many staff members did not even have a sliver of color representing time solely for themselves. This visual really illustrated for many staff the imbalances in their lives. Many realized that they had to make some changes that allowed more time to rest, re-energize, and recharge their lives.

I saw one of those staff members a few years later, and she told me she still had the paper plate on her refrigerator to remind her that she needs to find some time for herself. Try this exercise on yourself and then have your staff do it as well. You will see that we are all overscheduled with things that do not include our own well-being. Look at where your plate is imbalanced and find ways to balance the demands of the job and family with time for yourself.

So, you take a look at your paper plate, and you have a whole lot going on. Taking action is the critical step here. You can continually assess your balance in life and complain about how work dominates your entire life, or you can make the changes that allow more time for yourself to do the things that recharge and re-energize your life and allow you to gear down. You are now probably saying, yes, but *how*? What gear do I shed? In some cases, you might just have to use that two-letter word.

🧭 Tool: Just Say No

In some cases, keeping your balance means saying *no*. "No, I can't fit that into my schedule today." "No, I'm not able to take on another committee obligation." *No* is a complete sentence. However, saying *no* without offering a reason is not always easy, especially if it involves your boss. Preston Ni (2012), a professor of communication studies, suggests using *I* statements when the situation is tenuous, and you really want to say *no* without actually using that two-letter word. When asked to do something you are not comfortable with or you feel exceeds your limits, Ni (2012) suggests *I* statements such as these.

- "I prefer to . . ."
- "I prefer not to . . ."
- "It doesn't work for me to . . ."
- "It's important to me that . . ."
- "Unfortunately, I'm not . . ."
- "I'm uncomfortable with . . ."
- "I made a promise to myself that . . ."

Using *I* statements, Ni (2012) explains, makes it more difficult for the other person to dispute. He adds if that person is persistent, continue to use *I* statements and stand your ground until the person ultimately realizes you are not going to relent.

As a principal, that two-letter word doesn't come naturally. We know that there is *nothing* that is not in our job description. I've been asked to be on interview committees for principal candidates, professional organization committees, and other ad hoc committees outside of my school building during the school day. If I can manage the time requirement of my involvement in external activities and they meet my criteria of high value of contribution and passion (recall the priority matrices from tip 1, page 6), I will accept; if not, I explain that the time away from my building is greater than what I feel comfortable with. You have to decide which activities you deem important and promote your professional growth and work those in.

So where do you say no? *No* can be translated to mean, *This is an area where I can delegate some work.* You might not want to start delegating more of your share of family responsibilities, so find areas of delegation at work. Use your worksheets from tip 1 (page 6) to help you decide which additional items you might want to delegate in order to keep your life more balanced and less stressful. You will see this tool again with regard to tip 15 (page 96) in this chapter.

🦉 Tip 13: Listen Up

My staff once filled out a principal survey with items that ranked the effectiveness of their principal. One of the items asked staff to rank "The principal is a good listener" from 1 to 10, 10 being an awesome listener and 1 a fairly poor listener. When I reviewed the results, the answers for that item ranged from 1 to 10, with no distinct mode. At a staff meeting, I addressed this item, asked the staff what they felt made me either a good listener or a poor listener, and what was revealed was astonishing to me. They all agreed that I listened to them, but what made me a good listener was if a suggested idea actually factored into a decision that I made. In other words, they agreed that I listened to all of the input, but the final decision, based on listening to all of the input, determined if I was deemed a good listener. That's when I started to think about what effective listening really entails and how listening and decision making are interconnected. This experience also gave rise to a mantra I have used over the years: *If I please 50 percent of the people 50 percent of the time, I'm doing a d——n good job.*

"Listen first, speak last," says Peter Drucker, the Harvard lecturer dubbed the father of modern management, quoted in Rick Bommelje's (2017) article, "Drucker's Rule." As a principal, heed that quote.

Leadership development consultants Jack Zenger and Joseph Folkman (2016) researched what great listeners actually do to be considered great listeners, and it's not always what people think. They find that most people think that not talking when others are speaking, making facial expressions and verbal sounds (like *uh huh*), and being able to repeat what others have said make a good listener. Zenger and Folkman (2016) suggest there are other more important factors in describing good listeners. In researching data from close to 3,500 managers, they grouped their results into four main findings of what distinguishes average listeners from really good listeners.

1. **Questioning:** People perceive the best listeners as those who periodically ask questions that promote discovery and insight. Instead of sitting silently and affirming what the other person is saying, asking insightful questions lets the speaker know that you have not only heard what the speaker is saying but understand it and are interested enough to want additional information. Managers consistently see good listening as a two-way dialogue rather than a one-way monologue (Zenger & Folkman, 2016).

2. **Safety:** Good listeners make the conversation a positive experience for the speaker. That means the listener is engaged and not critical of what is being said. The speaker feels supported, confident, and is in an environment that is safe enough to discuss the issue (Zenger & Folkman, 2016).

3. **Cooperation:** Managers see listening as a cooperative conversation during which feedback flows back and forth with neither party becoming defensive or offended by comments made by the other party (Zenger & Folkman, 2016). Poor listeners tend to appear competitive, listening to find errors or why the idea won't work, while good listeners may challenge the ideas or assumptions, but the speaker feels like the listener is helping the speaker come to better conclusions, rather than trying to win the argument.

4. **Feedback:** Good listeners tend to make suggestions as the other party is speaking. This surprised Zenger and Folkman (2016) because jumping in too quickly to solve the speaker's problem is a common complaint. The researchers theorize it is more about the manner in which the listener introduces suggestions. In other words, they contend that a good listener acts as someone to bounce ideas off of. You, as the listener, become someone others feel confident about bouncing ideas on, like a trampoline, rather than just telling you about them (Zenger & Folkman, 2016).

Matthew McKay, Martha Davis, and Patrick Fanning (2009) emphasize many of the same points in their advice for becoming an active listener. *Active listening* involves paraphrasing, clarifying, and giving feedback during a conversation. *Paraphrasing*, or stating what the speaker is saying in your own words, keeps you in the conversation by making sure you understand what the other person means. You should paraphrase whenever an important point or concern is raised in the conversation so that there is less chance of miscommunication or misinterpretation.

By asking *clarifying questions*, as you would during the critical friends process from tip 9 (page 52), you receive additional information and can see the larger picture. Asking clarifying questions also shows the speaker that you are interested in what they are saying. Finally, after you have paraphrased and clarified what was said, *offer feedback* in a nonjudgmental manner, sharing what you heard, felt, thought, or sensed.

Plainly the art of listening is a little more complex than might be immediately apparent, and it's also something you can develop. To guide further reflection, this tip offers a listening survey, a reflection on the four purposes of listening, a listening blocks worksheet, and a feedback tendency tracker.

Tool: Six Levels of Listening Survey

Given what we know about the effort and thought that goes into listening, consider that you can apply your listening skills in different ways depending on the situation. Zenger and Folkman (2016) agree that there are different levels of listening and that not every conversation requires the highest level of listening. To that end, they suggest six levels of listening that you can aim for.

1. **Safe environment:** You ensure that the speaker feels comfortable discussing difficult, complex, or emotional issues by providing physical and psychological safety. For physical safety, the listener can find a space that is conducive to keeping the discussion confidential. For psychological safety, the listener can set conditions for discussing more controversial topics; for example, by removing fear of retaliation and allowing for mistakes to be admitted and discussed.

2. **Focus:** During a conversation, you eliminate distractions, such as devices, and make eye contact. Zenger and Folkman (2016) point

out that besides letting the speaker know you are listening, this practice actually influences your own attitude toward the interaction, helping you be a better listener.

3. **Understanding:** You restate ideas and ask questions to ensure you understand what the speaker is saying. In doing so, you show the speaker that you are truly engaging with something this person thinks is important or has value.

4. **Nonverbal cues:** You pick up on body language, such as hand gestures and facial expressions, and even more subtle signs like perspiration and breathing rate. Zenger and Folkman (2016) advise that you "listen with your eyes as well as your ears," as they say that 80 percent of what is communicated comes from these nonverbal cues.

5. **Empathy and validation:** You show that you understand more and more of what you're hearing by identifying and acknowledging the speaker's feelings. Zenger and Folkman (2016) emphasize that at this level, the speaker should feel supported and not judged.

6. **Questions and feedback:** You ask questions that help clarify the speaker's thinking and help him, her, or them get a different perspective on the issue. While this might involve volunteering your own thoughts and ideas, Zenger and Folkman (2016) stress not to hijack the conversation. You don't want the speaker to feel you're making it about you.

These levels build on one another, so think about where you may have a weakness as a listener or where you may have been criticized in your listening skills and choose a starting point. If you're not sure how your staff members perceive your listening skills, pass out the survey in figure 3.3 and ask for feedback to help get to that starting point.

Listening Level	How Am I Doing? (Circle a number.)
1. You feel safe discussing difficult, complex, or emotional issues with me.	Never Sometimes Always 1 2 3 4 5 6 7 8 9 10
2. I don't allow our conversations to be derailed by distractions, and I make appropriate eye contact with you.	Never Sometimes Always 1 2 3 4 5 6 7 8 9 10
3. I show that I'm trying to understand what you are saying by restating your points and asking questions.	Never Sometimes Always 1 2 3 4 5 6 7 8 9 10
4. You feel that I pay attention and respond to nonverbal cues to help move the conversation along.	Never Sometimes Always 1 2 3 4 5 6 7 8 9 10
5. You feel supported and not judged during our discussions. You feel I acknowledge your feelings and truly understand what you're saying.	Never Sometimes Always 1 2 3 4 5 6 7 8 9 10
6. You are able to get clarity and even a new perspective on issues as a result of our discussion. When I bring in my own thoughts, you never feel that I'm taking over and making it about me.	Never Sometimes Always 1 2 3 4 5 6 7 8 9 10

Source: Adapted from Zenger & Folkman, 2016.

Figure 3.3: Six levels of listening survey.

Visit go.SolutionTree.com/leadership for a free reproducible version of this figure.

Tool: Four Purposes of Listening

In addition to understanding elements of effective listeners, education authors and experts Shirley M. Hord, James L. Roussin, and William A. Sommers (2010) describe four purposes of listening aligned with seven listening modes of effective listeners. These listening modes are dependent on the focus of the conversation, whether the purpose is for coaching (generative and appreciative modes); collaboration (empathic and autobiographical modes); consulting (analyzing and advising modes); or evaluation (judging). See table 3.2 for a summary.

Think about your position when listening to others, and consider your purpose for listening and responding. Think about what mode and listening filters are appropriate, as well as the factors that contribute to being a better listener. After you do your initial survey with your staff, reflect on their perceptions of you as a listener. Once you know where you need to improve your listening skills, think about at what level of listening you want to start, understand your purpose for listening in each situation, and apply some of the elements of effective listeners. Let a few months lapse, survey your staff again, and see if your listening skills are improving.

Table 3.2: Four Purposes of Listening

Purpose of Listening	Explanation
Listening as a coach	If you are listening for coaching purposes, you are listening through a generative and appreciative listening filter. As a coach, generative listening pays attention to the deeper meaning and nuances of what is being said. This allows the listener to focus on constructing meaning between you as the coach and the other party through reflection and learning. The appreciative listening filter allows us to acknowledge in others their positive qualities, and to embed positive assumptions in paraphrasing and questioning.
Listening as a collaborator	If you are in a collaborative listening mode, you are more empathic and autobiographical. As a collaborator, empathic listening acknowledges the other's self-worth through the expression of empathy and understanding. Autobiographical listening allows us to connect with the other person by finding something in common. We allow ourselves to be vulnerable and personable, which is an important step in building trust.
Listening as a consultant	Consulting requires we listen from the analyzing and advising filters. By analyzing, you are focusing on interpreting the speaker's message or situation. By advising, you are offering help in the situation that the speaker is describing, and seeking some sort of solution. The focus is on identifying the problem and offering a solution to the problem or the situation that is not working for the other party.
Listening as an evaluator	You are listening from the judging filter. You are judging the situation, problem, or idea as either good or bad. The focus of this listening mode is on making an assessment of the speaker or the speaker's situation and deciding whether it is right or wrong.

Source: Adapted from Hord et al., 2010; Roussin, 2014.

Tool: Listening Blocks Worksheet

In today's world, much of our conversation is online. We email, we text, we Zoom. Often, we use a word or two or even just an emoji to respond to others. Regardless of whether it's the old-fashioned face-to-face method of communication or the more modern phenomenon of typing (or even just speaking to a robot), good listening is critical to your leadership. Matthew McKay, Martha Davis, and Patrick Fanning (2009), authors of *Messages: The Communication Skills Book*, detail twelve blocks to listening that can derail any conversation. By understanding these blocks to listening, you can begin to have meaningful and productive conversations.

After reviewing the listening blocks in the reflection worksheet in figure 3.4 (page 88), practice listening to yourself when engaged in conversations to see if you notice yourself using one or more of these blocks and write it down. Then, you can see if there is a pattern to when and with whom you use certain listening blocks. If there is a particular listening block you tend to use more than others, concentrate on removing that block. You can even try to mentally tally how many times you are using a particular listening block in conversations with others.

In his summary of McKay and his colleagues' (2009) listening blocks, Jason Rash (2019) comments:

> Listening is a commitment and a compliment. It shows people that you care about their experiences, what has happened and what is happening to them. It also allows you to set aside your prejudice, judgments, your self-interest and your own beliefs.

I have the habit of exploiting the identifying block to listening. I know I tend to relate to what the other person is talking about or experiencing, and I tend to refer to my own experiences. I have no doubt I am guilty of engaging in some of the other eleven listening blocks as well. I'm sure when you read this list of twelve blocks, you will find an area or two in which you fall short when it comes to listening to others. McKay and his colleagues (2009) assure us that everyone uses listening blocks. The important point, they say, is becoming aware of when you are using a specific block.

Tool: Feedback Tendency Tracker

As McKay and his colleagues (2009) point out, active listening, which includes giving feedback, is essential to being a good listener and a good leader. Receiving feedback, likewise, is a critical part of being a good listener. It aligns expectations and solves problems. But unless you are open to receiving that feedback, little will improve, and this can be especially challenging when the feedback you receive doesn't feel constructive. Negative feedback especially can come from places of hurt, frustration, or even resentment, using language that feels hurtful and personal. It's your job to separate your feelings from the feedback's tone and instead focus on its motivation, the places it's truly coming from, and the reasons for that.

Hillary Clinton (2014), in her book, *Hard Choices*, describes how she dealt with receiving feedback:

> I'm often asked how I take the criticism directed my way. I have three answers: First, if you choose to be in public life, remember Eleanor Roosevelt's advice and grow skin as think as a rhinoceros. Second, learn to take criticism seriously but not personally. Your critics can actually teach you lessons your friends can't or won't. I try to sort out the motivation for criticism, whether partisan, ideological, commercial, or sexist, analyze it to see what I might learn from it, and discard the rest. Third, there is a persistent double standard applied to women [in politics]—regarding clothes, body types, and of course, hairstyles—that you can't let derail you. Smile and keep going. Granted, these words of advice result from years of trial and error and mistakes galore, but they helped me around the world as much as they did at home. (p. 699)

Douglas Stone and Sheila Heen (2014), authors of *Thanks for the Feedback*, explain that it is the receiver of the feedback who controls whether the feedback is let in or kept out. You as the receiver are in control of what you let in or don't let in, how you make sense of what you are hearing, and whether you choose to change. Many of us are resistant to receiving feedback due to how we might react when given certain information. Of course, receiving positive feedback is easy; it's the negative feedback that is much harder to swallow.

When we receive feedback, however benign it might be, it can leave us feeling frustrated, angry, threatened, and unappreciated. Stone and Heen (2014) believe that the skills needed to receive feedback well are distinct and learnable. They maintain that what makes receiving feedback so difficult is that the process strikes at the tension between two core human needs: (1) the need to learn and grow and (2) the need to be accepted just the way you are.

Block to Listening	I used this block when . . .
Comparing You try to assess who is smarter, more competent, or more emotionally healthy.	
Mind Reading You are not paying attention to what is being said. You are trying to figure out what the other person is really thinking and feeling.	
Rehearsing You don't have time to listen because your whole attention is on preparing and crafting your next comment.	
Filtering You listen to some things and not to others. You make sure you are not in any danger or trouble, and if that's the case, you let your mind wander.	
Judging You use negative labels and prejudge someone to be not as qualified as you are.	
Dreaming You are half listening. If someone says something that triggers personal association your mind begins to drift off.	
Identifying You take everything a person tells you and refer it back to your own experience.	
Advising As soon as someone begins speaking, you begin searching for advice right away.	
Sparring You are very quick to disagree. You are not listening to the whole conversation.	
Being Right You go to any length to avoid being wrong.	
Distracting You change the subject when you get bored or uncomfortable with the topic.	
Placating You want to be nice, pleasant, and supportive so people will really like you. You agree with everything.	

Source: Adapted from McKay et al., 2009.

Figure 3.4: Listening blocks worksheet.

*Visit **go.SolutionTree.com/leadership** for a free reproducible version of this figure.*

Stone and Heen (2014) identify three feedback triggers, each of which provokes a different set of reactions and responses from us. These include (1) truth triggers, (2) relationship triggers, and (3) identity triggers. *Truth triggers* are set off by the content of the feedback, *relationship triggers* are set off by the person delivering the feedback, and *identity triggers* concern the relationship with yourself, when you will struggle with your emotions of feeling overwhelmed, defensive, or off balance.

In their article "Find the Coaching in Criticism," Heen and Stone (2014) identify six steps to becoming a better receiver of feedback.

1. **Know your tendencies:** When you receive feedback, do you automatically start defending yourself, argue about the message, or strike back; do you become emotional; or are you more stoic? Once you understand and acknowledge how you operate when receiving feedback, it becomes easier to decide how to make the most of it. If you know, for instance, that you immediately become defensive, before operating like a defense attorney, step back, reflect, and decide how to proceed in a more professional manner.

2. **Disentangle the *what* from the *who*:** You have to separate the message from the messenger and then consider both. Look at the message and what you can learn from it, and then look at it from the perspective of the sender. Sometimes they are mutually exclusive, and other times they are not. Once you disentangle the message from the sender, you can have a rational conversation to help improve the situation.

3. **Sort toward coaching:** Some feedback is evaluative, and some is coaching. Most of the time, we take feedback as evaluative, jumping straight to the conclusion that we are doing something wrong. But whenever possible, sort toward coaching so as to hear the feedback as potentially valuable advice from a fresh perspective rather than as a conviction of something you've done wrong.

4. **Unpack the feedback:** Sometimes it's not immediately clear whether the feedback is valid or useful. In these cases, it's best to take the time to analyze the feedback in order to better understand it. By stepping aside from making a snap judgment regarding the feedback, you can enter into a more rich, informative discussion about your practice, and reflect on how it can improve your performance and professionalism on the job.

5. **Ask for just one thing:** When asking for feedback, it's best to be specific as to what you would like to know about your performance. So instead of saying, "I'd like some feedback on my performance," ask for specifics. When I ask for feedback from staff, I usually just ask them to write down one thing I am doing well and one thing they would like me to do differently. That encourages them to think of the things that rise to the top instead of listing a litany of things that might be much less significant. It also makes it easier to analyze the feedback and look for patterns for what you are doing well versus what you can improve upon. When my supervisor suggests next steps for improvement, I usually ask which one is the most important for me to work on right now. It's easier to concentrate on one thing at a time and experiment on that one suggestion.

6. **Engage in small experiments:** If you still have not determined exactly which bits of feedback will help you and which will not, Heen and Stone (2014) suggest conducting small experiments to find out. When someone gives you advice and you're not sure about it, test it out. If you find that it works out, it improves your performance and improves relationships.

Figure 3.5 (page 90) is a tracking tool you can use to note your tendencies when you receive feedback. This is one that you might use once in a while, and you might only notice yourself filling in certain rows. These patterns can also turn into valuable feedback.

When I receive feedback, I tend to	Yes or No	Example of a situation where I
Become defensive		Was defensive:
Argue the point		Argued the point:
Become offensive		Struck back:
Become emotional		Let my emotions get the best of me:
Become unemotional		Appeared apathetic:

Source: Adapted from Heen & Stone, 2014.

Figure 3.5: Feedback tendency tracker.

*Visit **go.SolutionTree.com/leadership** for a free reproducible version of this figure.*

Once you have accepted the feedback, if you still do not agree with some of it, you may have to find a respectful way to disagree with the origin of the feedback. Most of us would likely prefer not to have to do this, as we worry about the negative consequences that might ensue. Amy Gallo (2016), author of the article "How to Disagree With Someone More Powerful Than You," offers tips for disputing feedback with a supervisor. She says, first, be realistic about the risks of speaking up. Weigh those risks against the risk of not speaking up. Then, decide whether it is better to wait and hold off on voicing your opinion. There may be some facts that you have to find out first, and you can always get another opinion from a trusted colleague.

To experience growth as a school leader, it is just as important to receive feedback from peers and direct reports as it is to receive feedback from your boss. By openly asking for feedback, you model vulnerability and acceptance of both praise and criticism. When I received everything from 1 to 10 on that listening question in the annual principal survey, I stood up and asked the entire staff for feedback on the gamut of responses.

Kim Scott (2017), author of *Radical Candor*, offers some tips for receiving feedback from peers and your staff. Scott (2017) calls it guidance, which I consider a very nice euphemism for feedback. Scott (2017) advises the following.

- **Embrace discomfort:** Hearing honest feedback from others is difficult. They are also in a difficult position giving feedback to you, their boss. Know that going in and take what is said graciously.

- **Intend to understand, not respond:** Don't criticize the criticism. Ask for clarification if you need it, but don't debate it or become defensive. Manage your feelings so that they don't manage you.

- **Reward criticism to get more of it:** Find something in the criticism that you agree with and check to make sure you understand exactly what others mean. Let them know you will think about it and get back to them with an idea for how to improve.

- **Gauge the guidance you get:** How often are you praised, and how often are you criticized? Try to keep a running tally. Don't get headstrong if it's all praise; continue to seek out criticism so that you ultimately improve your leadership.

After receiving feedback from either your boss or a peer or staff member that you disagree with, you should first ask permission to disagree. This gives the receiver psychological safety and control. If you are granted permission, then you can confidently assume the person or group is willing to hear your perspective. Once you have that permission, you will have more credibility, says Gallo (2016), if you can connect your disagreement to a "higher purpose." In other words, if you can identify a shared goal or purpose, you are more likely to be heard. But, she says, you have to state it overtly, contextualizing your statements so that you're not seen as disagreeable but as a professional who is trying to advance a shared goal. And when you are sharing your opinion, stay calm, validate the original point (articulating the other person's or group's point of view), and lay a strong foundation for the discussion.

It's important, says Gallo (2016), to watch your language carefully and not make judgments. Avoid judgmental words and terms such as *that won't work*, *foolish idea*, or *hasty decision*. Remember, if it's your boss providing the feedback, that you are the subordinate, and that you are only offering your opinion, so stay humble, acknowledge their authority, and tell your superior, in so many words, that "this is just my opinion, but . . . and I know you will make the right call in the end."

Being able to handle negative feedback is a skill that enables you to grow in the profession and allows you to manage up more convincingly. Remember, managing in all directions is managing yourself.

This tip has given you a few tools to manage your listening efficacy. While Peter Drucker may have been quoted as saying, "Listen first, speak last" (Bommelje, 2017), when it's time to speak up, the next tip will offer several tools for managing your communication.

Tip 14: Express Yourself

You're in the produce aisle, and you overhear a conversation. You look toward the voice, and while you might not remember the name of the person talking, you say to yourself, "I recognize that voice." Angeles Arrien (1993), author of *The Four-Fold Way*, quoted in Barbara McAfee's (2011) book *Full Voice: The Art and Practice of Vocal Presence*, "discovered that voice is an essential element in indigenous societies around the world and in many of these cultures, one's voice is directly linked to the soul or spirit of a person" (p. 19). Knowing your voice and what voice to use in different situations is an essential element to managing yourself as a school leader.

Barbara McAfee (2011) describes the art and practice of vocal presence, the state where your words, facial expressions, body language, tone of voice, emotions, imagination, and spirit are completely aligned when conveying your message. In other words, ensuring that what you say and how you say it are fully aligned. McAfee (2011) explains that vocal presence does more than affect the way you speak. It also affects the way you listen. She says:

> As you become more aware of your own voice, you're able to listen more accurately for what people are saying beneath and between their words. You become a student of voices—how they sound as well as what they're saying. This kind of deep listening is a rare and precious skill, one that transforms both speaker and listener. (McAfee, 2011, p. 5)

Understanding your voice and knowing that you have different voices, choices, and tones allows you to more accurately convey your message in the manner you intend. This tip offers tools for choosing when to use your approachable voice versus your credible voice, finding the right voice at the right time, and structuring challenging communications with a trick that I call the well-dressed hamburger.

Tool: Approachable Voice Versus Credible Voice

Dynamics show your personality. Dynamics keep the flow of information more interesting and play a huge role in determining how your audience receives your information. In music, *dynamics* refers to the changes in loudness of various musical notes and phrases. Think about how important these changes are to your appreciation of a musical piece. As a drummer, I have to be conscious of when and where to pound the drums and where and when to play more subtly, as well as everything in between. Yes, it's exhilarating to be loud and rowdy on the drums, and it relieves a lot of stress, but no one wants to hear it continuously, and playing at the same volume all the time would soon become monotonous. The way you use your voice, even beyond simply its volume, can similarly affect how people receive your message.

Michael Grinder (2007), a renowned expert in nonverbal communication and author of *The Elusive Obvious: The Science of Nonverbal Communication*, explains the difference between using an approachable voice versus a credible voice. An *approachable voice* is a more friendly, lively voice used when you are gathering information or opening up a dialogue and you want people to feel comfortable speaking. When you are using your approachable voice, your nonverbal communication involves head bobbing and more spirited hand gestures. Your voice is more animated, you use more inflection, and your voice has a more rhythmic cadence. When using your approachable voice, your voice modulates and intonation regularly rises and falls (Grinder, 2007).

Your *credible voice*, on the other hand, is the voice you use when you present or send information or make a point (Grinder, 2007). When using your credible voice, your nonverbals are calmer; your head, body, face, and arms are still; your voice is flat; and you impart information using more of a soliloquy style. Your actions, voice tone, and words all communicate the same message, and nothing should distract you from the message.

Not only do you need to be mindful of what voice you are going to use to communicate, you also need to know your audience. What may be your idea of an approachable voice may not be the listener's impression of an approachable voice. As Grinder (2020) cautions, communication can become challenging when a member of one culture is speaking to members of another culture, and speakers sometimes need to adjust their communication style to their listeners. *Cross-cultural communication* "refers to the ways in which people from different cultural backgrounds adjust to improve communication with one another" (Stobierski, 2019). Marketing specialist Tim Stobierski (2019) maintains:

> In today's rapidly changing professional world, it's critical to gain an understanding of how cultural elements influence communication between individuals and groups in the workplace. Developing strong cross-cultural communication skills is the first step in creating a successful work environment that brings out the best in all of an organization's team members.

To help improve cross-cultural communication, Stobierski (2019) recommends embracing agility, being open minded, and becoming more culturally aware, all of which add up to being willing to understand and adapt to your audience.

You need to choose the voice to match the intention to bring about the result you desire. Know how to calibrate your voice and bring it to a balanced register so that people understand your intentions. When using the credible or informative voice, be aware of how long you are in that voice mode during a meeting. If you spew too much information in that information-imparting voice, you're likely to start sounding like Charlie Brown's teacher—monotonous and easy to tune out. Table 3.3 shows characteristics of both. Be mindful about which voice you're using, and be sure to choose the most appropriate one for each situation.

Table 3.3: Approachable Voice Versus Credible Voice

	Approachable Voice	**Credible Voice**
Purpose	Seeking information	Presenting information
Tone	Friendly, lively, inflective	Calm, matter of fact
Hands	Spirited, palms facing up	Less movement, palms facing down
Head	Bobs up and down	Still
Cadence	Rhythmic	Steady

Source: Adapted from Grinder, 2007.

🧭 Tool: Right Voice, Right Time Worksheet

Finding the right tone of voice is also an important aspect of knowing your voice. You want your voice to help you make the right statement and have the greatest impact, so knowing what you sound like to others is very beneficial. There are voices for large-group speaking and voices for two-way conversations. Since more intimate conversations also involve listening, refer to the tools in tip 13 (page 83) for more insight, and remember your approachable versus your credible voice. But what about when you need to communicate information to a larger group?

According to Ryan Foland (2017), who coaches leaders worldwide on public speaking, there are five of what he calls tricks that can help you use the right voice at the right time.

1. **Record yourself and review and analyze how you sound:** This is a good idea if you have to pitch an initiative or program to a large group. You can listen to how you emphasize the key ideas and words and decide whether or not you sound convincing.

2. **Listen to your voice in your head:** Read your speeches silently to yourself in a quiet room and pay attention to the rhythms of your voice in your head. When I am observing teachers, I scribe their instruction, and when I go to type it into the evaluation, I hear their voice exactly the way they expressed it in the lesson. It has the same results with reading your own script. When you read your speech, you should be able to hear your voice as you would say it out loud.

3. **Talk it out with friends:** As you are rehearsing your speech with your friend, does the friend interject and ask questions while you are speaking? If so, you can probably expect that from your audience. Ask for feedback once you have finished, go back to trick two, and rehearse it again in your head, applying the feedback.

4. **Let someone else read your script out loud:** That way, you can see what it sounds like as the audience. Listen for the speaker's tone of voice and what words and phrases they tend to emphasize.

5. **Practice in front of a group:** Tell them in advance that you are practicing and that you would like their collective feedback regarding your tone and word emphasis. You can also figure out if what you thought was humorous actually is or what you might add to give the speech greater impact.

Remember, you want to sound natural and authentic while making an impact on your audience, be it one or several hundred. This is especially important when you address community groups who may not know you, your style of speech, your humor, and so on. Be well aware of the audience, and if you have doubts about your voice, again, ask for a practice audience and explain the audience for whom you are rehearsing, listen closely to their feedback, and make necessary changes so that the message you convey is the one you intend. The worksheet in figure 3.6 (page 94) gives you a way to keep track of each trick for using the right voice at the right time. A reproducible version is available on page 104.

Using these tricks to more intentionally impart information can help meetings and other gatherings that involve a lot of information sharing go more smoothly and productively. When I overheard, "The last half of that meeting could have been sent in an email," from a teacher after a staff meeting, it made me stop and think about how much information should be imparted at any given time. I think of this often, especially when I am in a meeting listening to information that threatens sensory overload. We all have our important information to share, but once the law of diminishing returns kicks in, we've hit our saturation point. The amount of information we can absorb begins to ebb and all we start to hear is Charlie Brown's teacher droning: wah, wah, wah.

What is the optimum amount of time for a meeting? Alf Rehn (2016), Finnish professor and world-renowned leader in innovation and creativity, believes

Trick	Reflection Questions	Notes
Record yourself.	How do I sound? What should I fix?	*I'm speaking too fast. Slow it down.*
Listen to your voice in your head.	Am I using the right voice?	*Use less inflection for a credible voice.*
Talk it out with friends.	What is their feedback?	*Pause between points.*
Have someone else read the script.	How does it sound when someone else reads it? Does it convey my message?	*There are a few areas I could condense to make it less verbose.*
Practice in front of a group.	What is the group's reception?	*It's a bit long. Condense some of the ideas.*

Source: Adapted from Foland, 2017.

Figure 3.6: Right voice, right time worksheet example.

the optimal attention span for an audience is eighteen to twenty minutes. After twenty minutes, Rehn (2016) says, no matter how interested we are in the topic, our focus becomes depleted, and unless corrective action is taken, our focus will erode steadily until we are no longer listening at all. Rehn (2016) quotes author Philip Crosby, who remarks, "No one can remember more than three points." Or as McKay and colleagues (2009) indicate, make one strong point with three subpoints. The rest, they say, is wasted breath. So, focus your oral communication on a focused topic and try to stick to twenty minutes per topic.

Perfect examples of this are TED talks. TED talks are eighteen minutes, and for that span, the speaker focuses on one topic (Rehn, 2016). Depending on how long your staff meetings last, you could improve the quality by keeping segments of the meeting to between eighteen and twenty minutes. By moving to twenty-minute segments, you can make your points more succinctly and keep the attention of your audience. My staff meetings usually last about fifty minutes. That means I can schedule two twenty-minute segments or topics on the meeting agenda, which allows me to leave about ten minutes for what I call *good of the order*, a time to give staff the opportunity to ask questions or make announcements that were not on the meeting agenda.

Tool: Well-Dressed Hamburger

Attention to voice is equally important for written communication. An abrupt, terse email that says "Please see me" and one that says "Can you please come by when you have a minute?" produce very different reactions and responses. The first one can create unnecessary fear, anxiety, or stress and implies a more informational meeting, while the second one elicits more of an intrigued response such as "I wonder what she has in mind?" Always be aware that just because you intend an email to be read in a particular way does not always mean the receiver is going to interpret it in that way.

Sometimes, as I learned early in my career, you have to write more than just the point of the message. And it's not always effective to use a predictable method like the well-known feedback sandwich popularized by entrepreneur Mary Kay Ash (1984), which just alternates criticism with praise. In most of my emails, I use what I call the *hamburger approach*.

In my first year as a principal, I focused on disseminating information. People get so many emails; I figured I would just give them what they need: the meat. What I found was that though they needed the meat, they also wanted a bun, some pickles, and a little sauce. In fact, they found it rude to get just the meat. It was like taking the burger off the grill and slapping it on the plate. The bit of information, the point of the email, by itself was too dry and bland; they wanted it with the fixings: compassion, reassurance, affirmation, or acknowledgment.

When composing emails that require action, I start with the meat and make sure it's not overcooked, meaning I don't overdo the information. Then I go back and add the beginning, which you can think of as the top bun of the hamburger, with a positive introductory sentence or two. I then flourish the email with the fixings and finish the email, the bottom bun of the burger, with an additional flourish of "Thank you, I appreciate your time [your consideration, your understanding, your flexibility, and so on as necessary]." You can then add details and other comments as necessary—think condiments. Figure 3.7 helps visualize this idea.

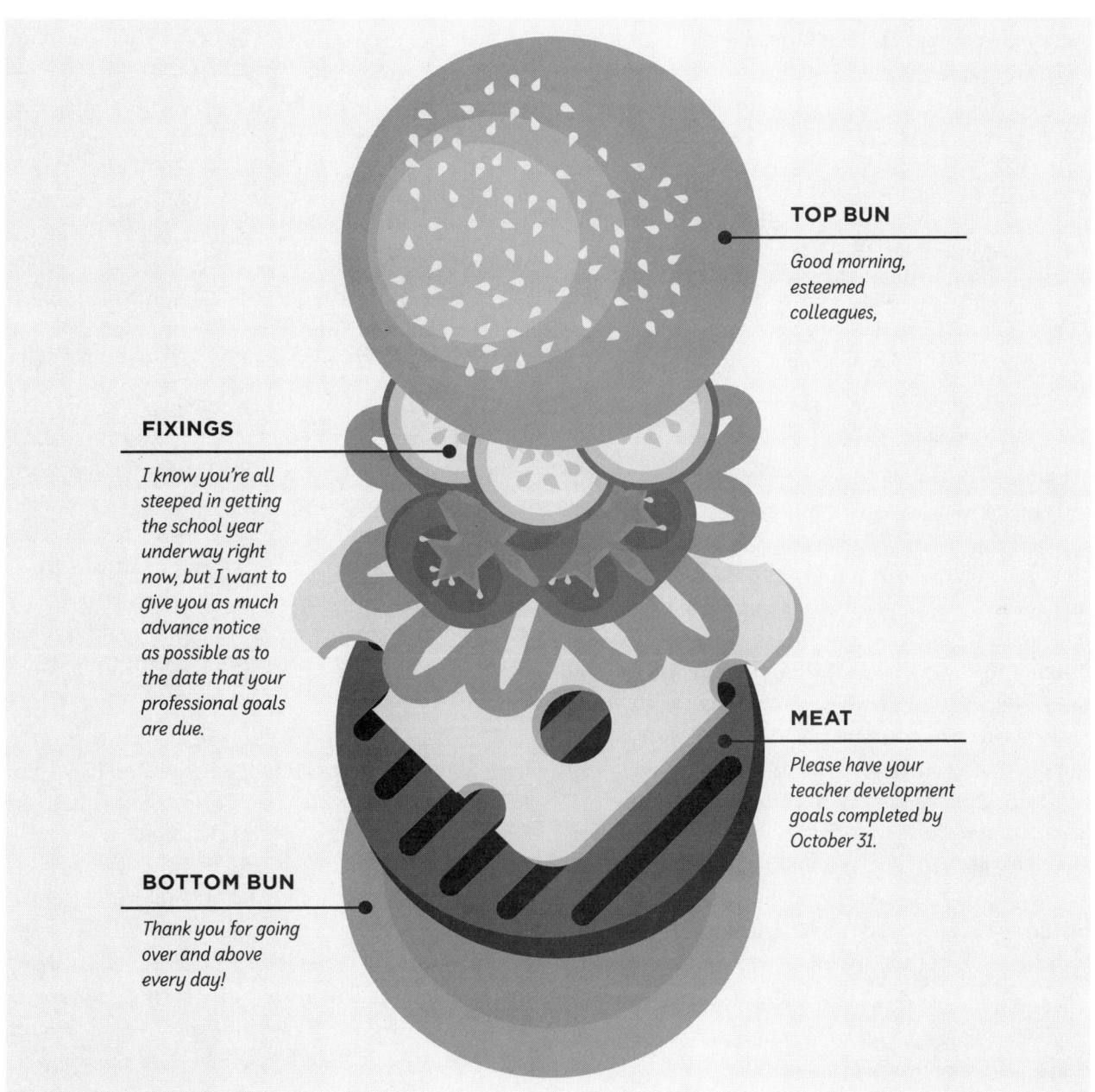

Figure 3.7: Well-dressed hamburger.

Here are some additional tips to consider when writing emails to both staff and supervisors.

- Make sure the right person or people are listed as recipients. Be sure not to use *reply all* unless everyone actually needs to see your reply.
- Check your dates and times if you are including them in the email.
- Check your spelling (especially names that may not be caught by spellcheck) and your grammar. It's a good idea to have spelling and grammar checkers turned on in your email application.
- Reread your email for tone and correct content.
- Send the email during work hours, not at midnight or four in the morning (some email programs allow you to schedule your emails for certain times of day).
- For especially important emails, have someone else read drafts and give you feedback about tone and possible interpretations.
- When in doubt, save it as a draft and revisit it at a later time.

Likewise, when you receive an email from either a staff member or a district employee, your tone and response are just as important. An email that has you reeling, and your first response is "Are you kidding me?" or "What the—?" could spell trouble if you respond too quickly. As much as you would like to respond this way, your voice in the response cannot reflect that tone. In cases where you are tempted to respond with a sarcastic tone, you need to pause before responding, sometimes for a full twenty-four hours. Depending on the content of the email, you can then decide to use the approachable voice or the credible voice in your response. You will find that things that are important to other people may be trivial in your perspective, but nevertheless they need to be respectfully heard and verified in their concerns or proposals.

Communication, whether written or oral, is a lifeline for principals. You need information, and your staff and community need information. How well you disseminate that information will define a lot of your leadership. Good communication leads to the trust and followership you desire with your community and with your superiors.

Tip 15: Stretch Your Limits (But Know Your Limitations)

My physical limitations when I'm on a mountain are pretty much defined by steepness. The steepness of Jackson Hole going down, the steepness of the Boise Mountains going up. I knew the minute I started skiing down Rendezvous Bowl at Jackson Hole that I had no business being on that part of the mountain. And when my mountain bike fell over exactly 90 degrees to the ground in the Boise Mountains, I knew that I had exceeded my limit of pedaling up a steep incline on dirt. In each of these cases, exertion outpaced exhilaration by a long shot. Both times I (over)stretched my limits, I was with my son, Aaron, who has a very different set of skiing and biking skills than I have.

On the tram ride to the peak at Jackson Hole, an announcement came on that said the area is for expert and extreme skiers only, and all other skiers should remain on the tram and take it back down. I told Aaron I was going to take the tram back down, as I did not fit the description of the skier who should exit the tram. He convinced me I had the skills to ski the bowl and to get off the tram. Against my better judgment, I got off the tram.

To make a long story short, I finally made it to the bottom of Rendezvous Bowl. Exertion had long since set in, it was dark, and the ski area had closed. As I was ready to collapse, Aaron exclaimed, "See, you skied it." To which I replied, "I think we have different definitions of 'skied it.'" He then asked me if my skis were still on, and when I admitted they were, he affirmed his position that I skied it. He felt that I had the physical ability to ski that bowl. He assured me as we started that I had the skills to get down the mountain. And while I may have had the physical ability to ski that part of the mountain, I certainly did not have the mental ability to ski the steepness of that bowl. The only things that got me down were sheer grit and a patient guide.

Knowing your emotional or mental limits may not be as clear cut as physical limitations. Overstepping your physical limits can lead to bodily injury in the form of cuts, bruises, and broken bones. As a school leader, overstepping your emotional or mental limits can lead to more of a broken psyche. How do we push ourselves *to* our limits (exhilaration) without exceeding them (exertion)? Cindra Kamphoff (2018), professor of sport psychology and author of *Beyond Grit: Ten Powerful Practices to Gain the High-Performance Edge*, says the answer is through the combination of grit and willpower (and some common sense).

I think of grit as powering through. Powering through adversity, challenges, and difficult situations. I wear a ring on my finger that says, וגם זה יעבור (V'gam zeh y'avore), which is Hebrew for *And this too shall pass* (TTSP). Sometimes you will power through a situation for a few minutes, and sometimes, as in the case of the COVID-19 pandemic, for several years. Understanding your limitations in any situation can help you power through.

Limitations can often be measured by frustration, a sense of failure, a lack of confidence, and not pushing through the ordeal. As Kamphoff (2018) puts it, "Your best self is the one at the other end of that trail of grit" (p. 14). Kamphoff (2018) defines *grit* "as having passion and perseverance toward your very long-term goals" (p. 34). I define grit by a gift I was given by a teacher during the COVID-19 pandemic. She came into my office one morning and laid a bracelet on my desk. I told her it looked like Morse code. She said, "Read the back." Sure enough, it was Morse code. Morse code for Keep F———ing Going (KFG). We had a good laugh, and I immediately put it on my wrist.

I wore the KFG bracelet right below the TTSP ring, and when I needed to power through, I said KFG and TTSP. I wore that bracelet every day until the string broke. I then carried it with me every day in my pocket. No matter what the wilderness had in store for me, I would KFG, knowing TTSP. This mindset can also help you keep your goals and focus in view and continuously stretch your limits, something the pandemic forced every principal to do. The tools in this tip, starting with directions for making your own KFG bracelet, also include a stop light grid, a grit score reflection, and a worksheet for setting boundaries.

 Tool: KFG Bracelet

You've set your goals, and you are determined to focus on achieving them. There will always be roadblocks and detours, but your grit and willpower will keep you on your journey. Sometimes you need a reminder that you have that grit and willpower to keep going. That's where the KFG bracelet (or key ring) comes in handy. Here is how you, too, can sport a KFG bracelet. You can even have a KFG bracelet party and have your colleagues join you as a team-building experience. And, of course, if the idea of KFG doesn't quite work for you, you can tailor the specific message to something that does. For example, your message could be *keep on going* (*KOG*).

At your favorite craft store, purchase a roll of elastic that can be used to string beads, a package of round beads, and a package of long beads. The elastic size needs to match the size of the beads you purchase. You can also purchase a package of key rings, some plastic lacing, and larger beads to make key rings.

Then all you have to do is string the beads in the correct order and tie the elastic or the plastic. The Morse code for this particular set of letters is in figure 3.8 (page 98).

In addition to the personal benefits you experience from having your own bracelet, doing this activity during a staff meeting is a chance for staff to relax and let off a bit of steam while doing something fun and informal with their hands. It's an opportunity to build community and remind everyone they're part of a team, working together toward the same goals. And during a rough patch, either for someone individually or collectively as a school, it is a visual reminder that, together, everyone has the collective grit to power through and carry on.

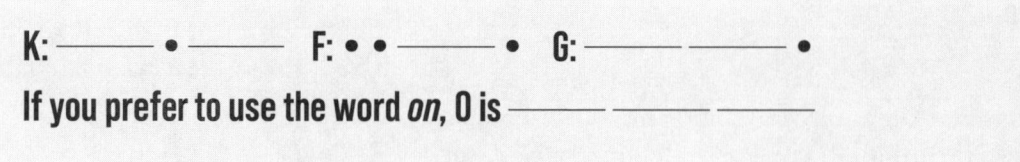

Figure 3.8: Morse code.

 Tool: Stop Light Grid

If knowing how to stretch your limits means acknowledging your limitations, it's critical to ask, "How do you know what your limits are if you don't push them? How do you test your limits safely?" It doesn't mean you walk precariously close to the edge of a cliff; it means you push yourself toward the things that you're passionate about and have the most meaning for you personally and professionally. Many times, we don't realize what we can really achieve because we believe it's beyond our reach. In her address to the Harvard graduating class of 2011, Ellen Johnson Sirleaf, former president of Liberia and winner of the Nobel Peace Prize, said, "The size of your dreams must always exceed your current capacity to achieve them. If your dreams do not scare you, they are not big enough."

Stretching your limits may be thinking well outside the box, utilizing resources and creativity that may expand your boundaries and experiences. As the Italian sculptor, architect, and poet Michelangelo is reported to have said, "The greatest danger for most of us is not that our aim is too high and we miss it, but that it is too low and we reach it" (Kamphoff, 2018, p. 62). We often let our minds and limiting beliefs get in our way. But when we dream one step more than we normally would, we grow. We are forced to push ourselves. Dreaming above your comfort zone requires you to consider all the possibilities.

Adam Thielen, wide receiver for the Minnesota Vikings, played Division II football in college and had no professional football contract coming out of school. However, being a Minnesotan, he wanted to play for the Minnesota Vikings. While the odds were against him, the Vikings signed him to their practice squad. Eventually, through perseverance and hard work, he became one of their best receivers. He credits his success to three factors: (1) focusing on taking advantage of every available opportunity, (2) keeping his mind on the opportunities he could control, and (3) being self-aware and conscious of what he does (Kamphoff, 2018). To successfully stretch your limits in the job, you have to be aware of your words and your actions and understand when and how to exert the proper force that results in the exhilaration of taking yourself to your upper limits of ability.

Many times, stretching your limits gets stifled by what Ethan Kross (2021) calls chatter. *Chatter*, he says, is your inner voice of negative thoughts and emotions that turn your capacity for introspection into a curse rather than a blessing. That is, the negative thoughts take over and drown out the positive. He explains that when your internal conversation loses perspective and gives rise to those negative emotions, "the brain regions involved in self-referential processing (thinking about ourselves) and generating emotional responses become activated" (Kross, 2021, p. 49). His solution to this problem is, rather than trying to ignore feelings, to notice them:

> In the most basic sense, introspection simply means actively paying attention to one's own thoughts and feelings. The ability to do this is what allows us to imagine, remember, reflect, and then use these reveries to problem solve, innovate and create. (Kross, 2021, p. xvii)

To perform at your optimum level, meaning stretching your limits, but not exceeding them, self-awareness is a key component of your journey. Kamphoff (2018) maintains, "The world's best understand themselves and their tendencies, and are in tune with their thoughts, emotions, and actions. They know they need to master themselves to be successful" (p. 175). An example of this is Alex Honnold, who is known for starring in the documentary *Free Solo* (Vasarhelyi & Chin, 2018) about his ascent of Yosemite National Park's El Capitan, a three-thousand-foot-high rock face, without the use of safety ropes. Why do people like Honnold seem to have no limits? He explains that he spends a tremendous amount of time thinking about the risks he takes and how to minimize them to ensure safety (Harrell, 2021). His self-awareness of what his goals entail and his exhaustive preparation helped him safely complete the climb. While Honnold has MRI evidence that his amygdala responds differently to fear stimuli than a normal amygdala, you don't need a fear-proof brain to use the same idea for more grounded pursuits. Without self-awareness, Kamphoff (2018) says, you can lose yourself by becoming overwhelmed with anxiety, doubt, and frustration. Another word for this self-awareness of one's own thinking is metacognition.

Metacognition is critical in being able to estimate the quality of decisions as well as having a reliable estimate about how well we perform in certain situations. According to Martijn Wokke (2021), a researcher in the field of metacognition, "metacognitive abilities allow adjustment of ongoing behaviour and modification of future decisions in the absence of external feedback." Wokke (2021) finds that the brain internalizes external processes to allow us to guide our behavior and decision making more effectively. "Specifically," he says, "the prefrontal cortex seems crucial when it comes to internally predicting what will happen next and in producing a sense of 'metacognitive awareness' of how our interactions with the world proceed" (Wokke, 2021).

Kamphoff (2018) compares three levels of self-awareness of how you're doing to a traffic stop light. As in an actual stop light, green means go, yellow means caution, and red means stop.

- The green light represents you when you are performing at your best. When I think of myself skiing at Jackson Hole, I'm in my green light when I am cruising down a blue (intermediate) slope with just enough challenge.
- In the yellow light, you start to lose your high-performance mentality and are in the early stages of losing your nerve, confidence, and control. I get into the yellow light when I am skiing in areas that are too icy or too steep.
- And once you hit the red light, you have completely lost your high-performance mentality and are struggling, you're tense, and you feel like you have completely lost control of the situation. That would definitely be the back bowls of Jackson Hole where I had no business being on skis.

Your goal is to live in the green light by learning more about yourself and how you typically respond to stressors. The grid in figure 3.9 (page 100) helps you develop a plan to deal with situations that tend to lead you into the yellow and red lights. A reproducible version is available on page 105. Using the stop light grid as a school leader, think of where your strengths lie, where you feel prepared and in control, and enter those into the green light. In your yellow light boxes, add the areas in which you are not as confident, make you nervous, or you feel slightly out of control. The red light boxes are reserved for the areas in which you are really struggling and you feel you have totally lost control.

Use this tool in different situations and circumstances, either personally or professionally, and over time, you'll learn how to avoid or better manage yellow and red lights. For example, by the time I realized I was in the red light at Jackson Hole, there was no way out but down. A very steep down. But I learned from that experience. In the same way, you can build the self-awareness to stretch your limits in eustress rather than overstep them and end in distress.

Inevitably, you will find yourself in that yellow or red light, and you'll need to deal with that. Kamphoff (2018) describes how a *power pause*, an intentional pause for mindful breathing, can help you move to the green light. For fifteen seconds, focus on your breathing by breathing in through your nose for six seconds, holding your breath for two seconds, and then breathing out slowly through your mouth for seven seconds. Use your breathing ball (tip 11, page 76) to do this as many times as you need to feel calm and in control. It took me a lot of power pauses to ski to the bottom of that bowl. Being self-aware of where you are will help you stay in the green light without overstepping your limits.

		I am saying to myself:	I am feeling:	I am focused on:
✕	In Your Red Light	I can't ski this terrain	Incompetent and nervous	Figuring out an easier way down—if there is one
⋯	In Your Yellow Light	This slope is icy and steep	Cautious and nervous—I'm not sure I can get down this	Slowly and cautiously making my way down
✓	In Your Green Light	My skiing skills match this terrain	Confident about skiing this terrain	Enjoying the run

Source: Adapted from Kamphoff, 2018.

Figure 3.9: Stop light grid example.

Tool: Grit Score Reflection

People with grit believe they have control over outcomes. They believe that they can move from failure to success through their own efforts (Duckworth, 2016). In her book *Grit: The Power of Passion and Perseverance*, psychologist Angela Duckworth (2016) discusses her research into the characteristics of what makes certain people successful. She argues that what is most important to success is the willingness to persevere despite difficulty and failure. Many people believe that innate talent and ability are the most important determinants of success and achievement; however, she finds that hard workers with determination can succeed in fields dominated by people with talent and genius ability. Duckworth (2016) explains that grit itself is not a fixed characteristic but one we can learn and cultivate by focusing on our own passions and cutting out distractions. Duckworth (2016) further explains, "Grit is not just about success; it is also about fulfillment. Hard work in pursuit of passion is exciting and satisfying. Determined people not only succeed but attain personal satisfaction even when they experience setbacks or failure" (p. 12). Duckworth (2016) offers several key takeaways to achieving grit:

- Talent is less important than grit for achieving success.
- The grit scale can be used to predict grit.
- To cultivate grit, it is important to identify one's passions.
- High achievers improve their skills through difficult, deliberate practice.
- Gritty people feel they have control over their fact and that hard work can change outcomes. (p. 18)

Grit comes in all sizes and shapes, depending on what you are powering through. When the COVID-19 pandemic began and schools were shuttered, our families were at home with a device most had never used for academic purposes. Tablets and laptops became lifelines for administrators, staff, students, and families. Technology definitely stretched my limits. But as it stretched my limits, it gave me new powers that I never knew were possible. It started with providing tech help for our families. Many of our families speak English as a second language, and sitting on hold with the technology department and then having them race through instructions in English didn't work well for most of them. When I found that many students could not access the lessons because of tech problems, I went to school each day and provided curbside tech assistance. No amount of grit was going to allow those families to access the technology they needed to be online without assistance, but I had the privilege and the bandwidth to take this on. It took some grit to stare down COVID-19 and take on the tech role, but I was able to solve most of the technology issues our students were having. I powered from the red light of not feeling very confident regarding my tech abilities with these devices to the green light of feeling confident enough not only to tackle technology issues but to produce Zoom presentations and create some pretty entertaining videos for morning announcements while students were learning from home.

Even in non-pandemic times, the principal position requires a certain amount of grit. Duckworth (2016) asks ten questions that can determine your level of grit. There are no right or wrong answers to these questions. If you answer the questions honestly, you will get a score that reflects how passionate and persevering you see yourself to be. Visit https://angeladuckworth.com/grit-scale to answer these questions online and see your grit score. Your grit score combines those two components of passion and perseverance. The odd-numbered questions measure your passion, while the even-numbered questions measure your perseverance, so keep track of how you answered each of the ten questions.

Figure 3.10 offers a reflection tool to help you think through your results.

At some point of course, grit runs into limitations. Sometimes it's just not a great idea to think that grit is going to get you the outcome you desire. There are instances when your self-awareness reminds you that there are limitations, and you have to heed that metacognitive advice. During that skiing ordeal in Jackson Hole, once I exited that tram, there was no other option than to get down to the bottom. I learned that even though grit got me down, skiing terrain like that is a serious limitation, and I now stick to terrain that provides exhilaration rather than exertion. I don't need to test my grit on steep, black diamond runs. So, whether you're in the wilderness of nature or the school, it's best to recognize when you face situations that may require more than grit and when you need to step back and have respect for your true limitations.

Date: 1/26/23	Your grit score: 3.9 (out of 5)
What did you notice? What could you do to improve your grit?	
For the passion questions, on only one question did I respond "mostly." On all other odd-numbered questions regarding passion, I responded either "somewhat" or "not much." On the perseverance questions, I responded "mostly" or "very much" to all five even-numbered questions. What this is telling me is that I have more perseverance than I have passion. So, I'm concluding that even if I am not terribly passionate about doing something, I will do it and finish it.	
To improve my grit score, I would have to feel more passionate about the projects and tasks that I choose.	

Figure 3.10: Grit score reflection.

*Visit **go.SolutionTree.com/leadership** for a free reproducible version of this figure.*

Tool: Setting Boundaries Worksheet

Knowing your limits means knowing your boundaries. You may know your boundaries, but unless you set them so that others know them as well, your boundaries stay invisible. Living in a high-tech world, our phones are on 24/7, but that doesn't mean you need to answer work calls 24/7. In her article "Boundaries: A Guide to Making Essential Life Decisions," Linda Esposito (2019) maintains, "Establishing boundaries is one of the best ways to preserve your emotional energy and define who and what you allow in your life. Most importantly, you internalize the message that you teach people how to treat you." You probably have your boundaries set in your head, but as a busy principal, others need to know some of your boundaries as well. The following tool gives you some parameters for setting boundaries to help you stay balanced.

Setting boundaries is all about your self-awareness, what you expect of yourself, and what you expect of others. According to Nedra Tawwab (2021), author of *Set Boundaries, Find Peace: A Guide to Reclaiming Yourself*, setting boundaries for yourself means communicating those expectations clearly. To set boundaries and be able to communicate them, you need to ask yourself a few questions.

- "Do I feel overwhelmed?"
- "Do I resent others for asking for my help?"
- "Do I avoid interacting with people who I think might ask me for something?"
- "Do I make comments about helping others and not getting help in return?"
- "Do I feel burned out?"
- "Do I have no time for myself?" (Look at your paper plate from tip 12, page 81.)

If you answered *yes* to at least a few of these questions, then according to Tawwab (2021), you need to set some boundaries. Tawwab (2021) defines *boundaries* as "expectations and needs that help you feel safe and comfortable in your relationships. Expectations in relationships help you stay mentally and emotionally well" (p. 5). In some cases, she says, knowing your limits means saying *no*.

As discussed earlier in this chapter, too many principals are working way beyond a forty-hour week. And again, if your paper plate shows you are not balanced, then setting limits and boundaries can help you maintain your mental health and your relationships. Tawwab (2021) offers several suggestions for setting boundaries at work. Begin by asking yourself these three questions.

1. "Why am I staying late?"
2. "What areas of the job are burning me out?"
3. "Can I get my work done at work?" (Set some boundaries. Go back to your priorities worksheets from tip 1, page 6, and figure out what else you can delegate.)

Figure 3.11 offers a template to work through these questions. A reproducible version is available on page 106.

Why am I staying late?

I do not give myself uninterrupted time to do work during school hours.

What areas of the job are burning me out?

Student behavior and discipline referrals

Can I get my work done at work? (Boundaries)

- **Responding to emails and phone calls:**
  - *Between 7:00 a.m. and 8:00 p.m., M–F*
  - *Between 10:00 a.m. and 10:00 p.m., weekends*
- **Responding to texts:**
  - *Between 7:00 a.m. and 10:00 p.m.*
- **Calendar:**
  - *Scheduling at least thirty minutes between meetings when possible*
- **Prioritizing and delegating tasks—delegate behavior referrals**
- **Open office hours:**
  - *7:00–7:30 a.m. and 10:30–11:00 a.m.; 3:00–4:30 p.m.*
- **Door closed hours:**
  - *12:00–12:30 p.m. and 1:30–2:30 p.m.*

Source: Adapted from Tawwab, 2021.

Figure 3.11: Setting boundaries worksheet example.

Tawwab (2021) also suggests that you be proactive and not let issues get out of control before you set boundaries. Do a check of your areas of concern (where you need to set boundaries) and influence (those boundaries you can set), and then be clear about your expectations and be consistent by respecting and modeling your own boundaries.

Summary and What's Next

Being proactive by attempting to ward off stress is crucial. However, given the nature of the job, stress will always creep its way into your pack. Some of that stress is eustress, which is good for you as it stimulates growth and creativity. But as soon as you feel that the additional weight on your shoulders is more of the distress, do your best to unpack it as soon as possible by using the tips and tools provided in this chapter. And speaking of unpacking, chapter 4, "Unpacking Your Bag," will provide you with tips and tools to assist you with reflecting and recharging as you leave the office for the day. Chapter 4, the final chapter in this guide, includes tips and tools for giving yourself a break, reflecting on your experiences, laughing about the experience, recharging for whatever lies ahead, and celebrating your accomplishments.

Right Voice, Right Time Worksheet

Trick	Reflection Questions	Notes
Record yourself.	How do I sound? What should I fix?	
Listen to your voice in your head.	Am I using the right voice?	
Talk it out with friends.	What is their feedback?	
Have someone else read the script.	How does it sound when someone else reads it? Does it convey my message?	
Practice in front of a group.	What is the group's reception?	

Source: Adapted from Foland, R. (2017, May 25). 5 ways to find the right tone when speaking. Accessed at *www.influencive.com/5-ways-find-right-tone-speaking on December 5, 2022.*

Stop Light Grid

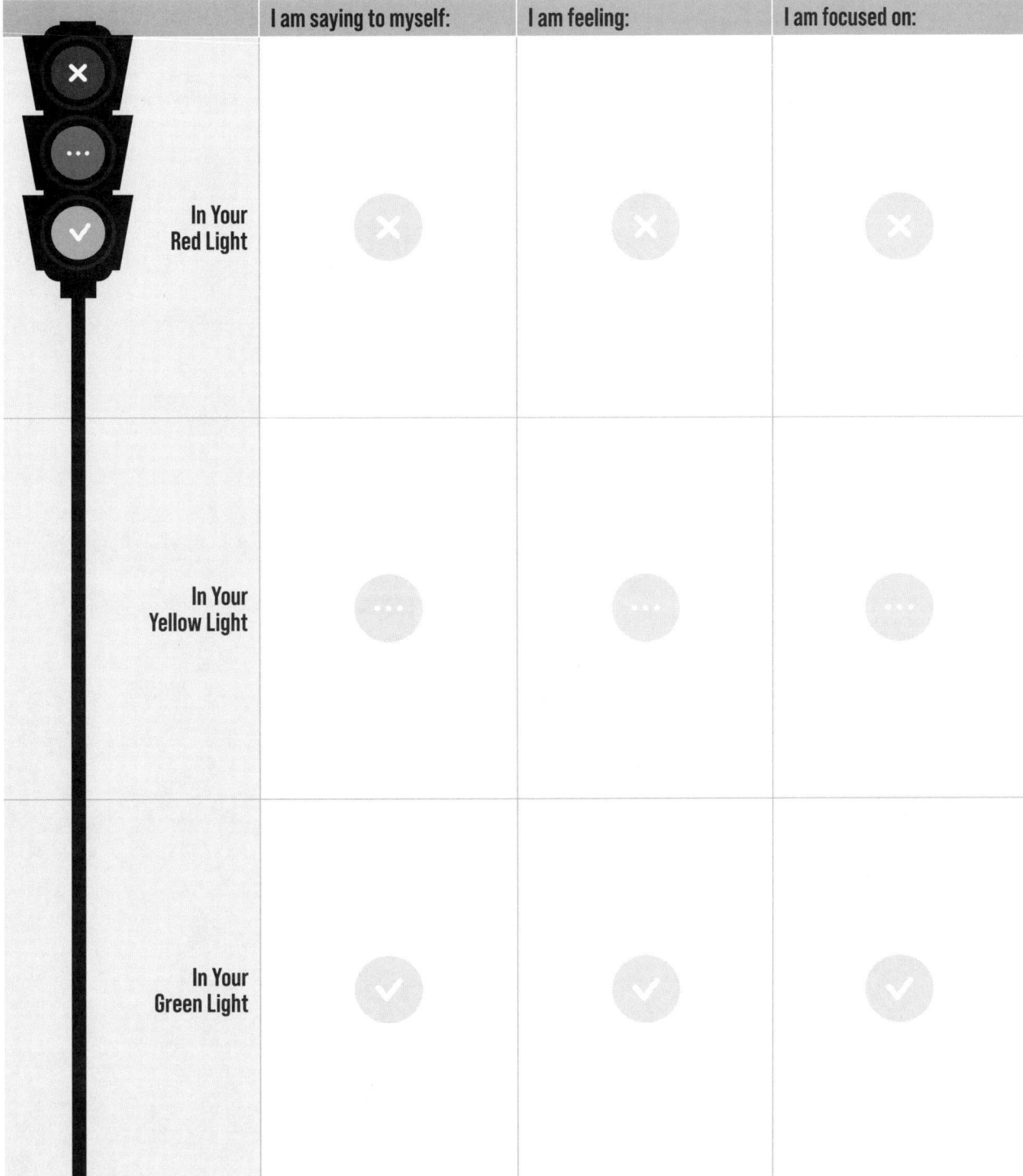

	I am saying to myself:	I am feeling:	I am focused on:
In Your Red Light			
In Your Yellow Light			
In Your Green Light			

Source: Adapted from Kamphoff, C. (2018). Beyond grit: Ten powerful practices to gain the high-performance edge. Minneapolis, MN: Wise Ink Creative.

Setting Boundaries Worksheet

Why am I staying late?

What areas of the job are burning me out?

Can I get my work done at work? (Boundaries)

Source: Adapted from Tawwab, N. (2021). Set boundaries, find peace: A guide to reclaiming yourself. New York: Penguin.

CHAPTER 4

Unpacking Your Bag

Every evening as you hoist your pack off your back for the last time that day, you feel that a huge weight has been lifted from your shoulders. You set it down and begin to unpack it. You pull out your tent, sleeping bag, stove, and your delicious freeze-dried dinner packet. Then, as you sit by the campfire sipping hot chocolate or any other beverage that comes in a pouch or a bag, you unwind and debrief the day's experience. You might be admiring the sunset while discussing both the challenging parts of the trail and the exhilaration of the day. You probably also look at the map and plan for the next day's trek or make notes in your journal.

In the office, every day is a new adventure, and it's just as important to unpack after a day on the job as it is a day on the trail. There are several ways to unpack the day: reviewing the day with key staff or your principal colleagues, writing down your thoughts and reflections in a journal, or just sitting quietly and reflecting on the day's events and preparing for the next day. Some days will require more reflection time than others. Unpacking also means unwinding and removing yourself from the hectic demands of the job. It means physically leaving the office and engaging in activities that don't have to do with work: spending time with family or friends, exercising, taking in any form of entertainment, or just relaxing. This is where you seek that elusive life-work balance, check your wheel of life or paper plate, take the pulse of your health, and do what you need to do in order to maintain your health, sanity, and relationships.

Maintaining your health, sanity, and relationships means giving yourself some grace, taking time for meaningful reflection, engaging in laughter, recharging your batteries, and celebrating, because managing yourself is the key to managing everything and everyone else and truly being an effective school leader. This chapter gives you five tips for unpacking, unwinding, and leaving the job back on the trail: give yourself some grace, reflect on it, laugh about it, recharge, and celebrate.

Tip 16: Give Yourself Some Grace

Spencer, my drum instructor, and I were working on a drum pattern simultaneously on our drum kits when I quit in exasperation after I messed it up for the third time in a row. He looked at me and said, "Give yourself some grace. It's a challenging pattern, and it's going to take a little practice." Give yourself some grace? When was the last time someone said give yourself some grace? And when was the last time you actually gave yourself some grace? Here's that permission. Give yourself some grace. Allow yourself the time to learn and improve when exploring new territory.

On one of our backpacking trips on the Superior Hiking Trail, Liz, a mutual friend, joined Jackie and me for a five-day trek. Liz did not have as much experience hiking as we did, and when we started, I paid my drum instructor's guidance forward, as I gave her one piece of advice: give yourself some grace. Rarely do any of us hike at the same pace. Some leap out in front, and others take time to literally smell the roses. On our last day, a particularly warm day with several uphill climbs, Jackie and I sat down on the trail to wait for Liz. When she arrived, all she said was, "I gave myself some grace." And my response was, "As you

so deserved." When on a learning curve, have some compassion for your limit—even if your limitation is for a moment in time. As author and poet Maya Angelou says, "It's one of the greatest gifts you can give yourself, to forgive. Forgive everybody" (as cited in Hardie Grant Books, 2019, p. 9).

Giving yourself some grace does not mean making excuses for yourself such as not meeting a deadline, not finishing a project, or being short with a colleague or staff member. It means taking a risk to learn something new, stretching your limitations, or heading into uncharted waters. Giving myself some grace meant giving myself time to learn the drum pattern, not giving excuses for why I didn't practice it and learn it.

As a principal, you will err in judgment, say something you regret, and occasionally make a poor decision. At the time, the faux pas may seem like you hit the end of the trail with nowhere to go. You immediately go to the chatter and the negative thoughts. You worry about the repercussions and your reputation. But beating yourself up is not the answer. To help you learn from mistakes and leave you in a more positive frame of mind, this tip offers tools for taking a self-compassion survey, engaging in self-compassion exercises, utilizing a growth mindset, and reframing your situation.

Tool: Self-Compassion Survey

Do you give yourself some grace? Do you notice your strengths? Do you give yourself the care you would give to others? Or, do you listen to your negative chatter and dwell on self-criticism? Kristin Neff (2011), a professor at the University of Texas at Austin and author of *Self-Compassion: Stop Beating Yourself Up and Leave Insecurity Behind*, has spent years researching self-compassion and explains how "it is a powerful way to achieve emotional well-being and contentment in our lives" (p. 11). She explains that self-compassion fosters happiness and optimism and provides a safe haven from your negative thoughts and insecurities. As Neff (2011) defines it, *self-compassion* encompasses three core components.

1. **Self-kindness:** In times of difficulty, Neff (2011) asserts that people should be gentle with themselves and avoid too much self-criticism. The reality is that things don't always go well; when you accept that and move past it, you can confront the issue with greater emotional balance.
2. **Common humanity:** Suffering and personal inadequacy are part of the shared human experience, something that everyone goes through. Neff (2011) describes how feelings of isolation can work against this natural connection and how self-compassion is about recognizing shared human experience.
3. **Mindfulness:** Neff (2011) recommends taking a balanced approach to negative emotions, neither suppressing nor exaggerating them but observing them in order to relate to others and put things in perspective.

Self-kindness means that we stop the constant self-judgment and disparaging conversations we have with ourselves. It requires that we understand our shortcomings, limitations, and failures, rather than condemning them and ourselves. It involves actively confronting ourselves and allowing ourselves to be emotionally moved by our pain. We can actually soothe ourselves as we would a friend, with warmth, gentleness, and compassion. We can actually treat ourselves as we would treat others.

Social media can definitely do a number on our self-compassion. Living in an individualistic society, we tend to judge ourselves on the accomplishments and merits of others, and when we are inundated with images of our friends, family, colleagues, celebrities, and sports legends everywhere we look, there is a temptation to say to ourselves, "I could never be that good, that smart, that beautiful." According to an article published in *Cyberpsychology, Behavior and Social Networking*, the use of social media may be associated with depressive symptoms, partly because "computer-mediated communication may lead to the altered (and often wrong) impression of the physical and personality traits of other users" (Pantic, 2014). By giving yourself compassion, you are giving yourself grace to get past expectations that not only are unrealistic but are not actually based on reality. The images we see are snapshots and moments that don't reflect the unique struggles and challenges everyone deals with in one form or another. Having self-compassion, Neff (2011) explains, allows you to break free of the chatter of negative self-talk that Kross (2021) describes and makes you more resilient.

To determine your level of self-compassion, you can visit https://self-compassion.org/self-compassion-test to take Kristin Neff's self-compassion survey. After answering a series of questions, the survey calculates your level of self-kindness, self-judgment, common humanity, isolation, mindfulness, and over-identification, and then gives you an overall self-compassion score with a rating from 1 to 5. The survey explains your scores, and Neff provides self-compassion exercises to help you improve in any of the areas the survey covers. And if you find yourself in need of other ways to improve your self-compassion, you have additional options.

Tool: Self-Compassion Exercises

While Neff's suggestions from her website are a good start toward aligning your needs with solutions, Tchiki Davis (2021), author and expert on well-being technology, also offers exercises to help you increase self-compassion.

- **Write a self-compassion letter to yourself:** Write kind things about yourself as if you were talking to a child or friend in need of kindness. We tend to treat others, especially children or friends in need, a lot more compassionately than we treat ourselves, so write to yourself as if you were talking to someone else.
- **Let go of negativity:** Stop the chatter. This goes back to what Kross (2021) advises: pay attention to your inner voice and try to manage that inner conversation to change your thoughts and your mindset. You can also reframe those negative thoughts into more positive scenarios.

- **Stand up to your inner critic:** Don't get caught up in self-criticism. Ask yourself why you listen to the negative chatter and try to reframe the negative into more positive self-talk.
- **Nix the shoulds:** From a young age, we've been told what we should and should not do, and thus we tend to continue to judge ourselves on the shoulds and should-nots. Get rid of them and stop judging yourself on what you or someone else thinks you should do.
- **Take a self-compassion break:** When you find yourself chattering, stop and turn the negative thoughts into positive ones. Find your happy place, take a walk, forest bathe, do some yoga, or just have a great big ice cream sundae—and don't feel guilty about it.
- **Forgive yourself:** Seek understanding of what happened, apologize for what happened, learn from it, and move on. Put your energy into a positive mindset so that you can KFG even when the chips are down.

It's easy to skim a list like this and quickly forget it. Be intentional about using one or more of these exercises whenever you need a dose of self-compassion. This is a good opportunity to journal.

Tool: Pathways to Enhancing Your Mindset

Neff (2011) finds that self-compassionate people are more oriented toward personal growth than those who are continually self-critical. She also finds they are more likely to achieve goals and have a more balanced life. A positive mindset that fuels personal growth is what Carol Dweck (2016), a Stanford University psychologist and author of *Mindset: The New Psychology of Success*, describes as a growth mindset.

Dweck (2016) finds that it's not just our talents or abilities that bring us success but whether we approach our goals with a fixed mindset or a growth mindset. With a *fixed mindset*, you are more about proving you are smart and talented while believing that these are innate and unchangeable qualities. Through this lens, success is about self-validation while failures are setbacks that reflect on you as a person. In contrast, a *growth mindset* is concerned with improvement, a belief you (or anyone) can continue to learn and improve.

A growth mindset encourages you to take risks, stretch your limits, and thrive on challenges. It's like climbing mountains. There are always obstacles between the base and the summit, and the challenge is to overcome the obstacles, making your way toward your goal of reaching the summit. As a principal, stuff happens, and you need to be able to deal with the obstacles and manage the stress that accompanies them. When you encounter a challenge you don't know how to handle, perhaps even something you've failed at before, you can view the situation as too stressful, inevitably leading to failure, unfixable, or too overwhelming. Alternatively, you can reframe it, seeking solutions and learning from the entire ordeal. To get started, rewind back to tip 11 (page 76). Those mindfulness techniques can calm the negative chatter and help develop that growth mindset.

If you find yourself working with a fixed mindset in certain circumstances, Dweck (2016) offers assurance that you can change your mindset. By admitting you are working with a fixed mindset in certain situations, you can start changing that mindset by thinking and reacting in new ways. While the growth mindset is a starting point for change, you need to decide for yourself where your efforts toward change would be most valuable.

Principals usually have a growth mindset. It would be difficult to succeed in the job without one. However, there are ways to enhance your mindset. Organizational change consultant Rachel Howard (2021), in her article "Cultivating a Growth Mindset," offers pathways into believing that you can enhance the potential of your abilities. Figure 4.1 is a tool to come up with your own map to follow each pathway.

Pathway	Map to Get There
Seek out learning opportunities.	*Coach, critical friends group, professional organizations*
Add the word *yet*.	*I don't know the answer to that versus I don't know the answer to that yet. Do some research and find answers.*
Push out of your comfort zone and challenge yourself.	*Stretch your limits.*
Set goals.	*Challenge yourself, but keep them SMART.*
Find purpose.	*Look to your beliefs and values.*
Be resilient.	*KFG*
Take feedback as a gift.	*Be open to critical information about yourself.*
Transform your thinking.	*Replace judgment with compassion.*
Be realistic.	*All of this takes time.*

Source: Adapted from Howard, 2021.

Figure 4.1: Pathways to enhancing your mindset.

Visit **go.SolutionTree.com/leadership** *for a free reproducible version of this figure.*

Principals with growth mindsets focus on improving their performance rather than protecting themselves from failure. Failure doesn't always mean you've failed; it means you have to try something else. Goals, purpose, grit, and resilience yield performance. Serena Williams, one of the greatest tennis players of all time, explained in an interview with journalist Gayle King what she learned from losing:

> I would not take any of them [the losses] away, because every time I lose, it takes a really long time for me to lose again because I learn so much from it. . . . If you lose or if something happens—not just in sports—in business or in school—learn from it. Don't live in the past, live in the present, and don't make the same mistakes in the future. (Williams & King, 2017)

There are numerous surveys and inventories you can take to assess your level of mindset by searching the internet for growth versus fixed mindset questionnaires. Here are some websites with inventories with which you can assess your mindset.

1. **https://bit.ly/3I7OkHD:** This is a fifteen-question mindset quiz.
2. **https://blog.mindsetworks.com/what-s-my-mindset:** This one has eight questions and little more variability possible in the answers.
3. **https://bit.ly/3JQUrBJ:** This assessment has twenty questions as well as an inventory to determine which mindset you exhibit.

After analyzing your results, you can take a look at the pathways tool to help you work on enhancing your mindset.

Tool: Cognitive Reframing Worksheet

As you reflect on your day, you may find yourself thinking about a situation that you wish you had handled differently. You start to ruminate on what you felt you did wrong, and all of a sudden, your emotions take over, and it becomes difficult to see the big picture. Cognitive reframing involves looking at the broader picture and transforming it from a negative interpretation of what has happened to a more positive interpretation. Cognitively reframing a situation can also help you give yourself some grace.

Cognitively reframing any situation involves looking at it from a different angle, one that creates less stress and anxiety and provides you with more control over the situation. In many instances, you cannot control the circumstances, but you can control how you respond to them. The way you frame the situation "can turn a stressful event into either highly traumatic or a challenge to bravely overcome" (Scott, 2020a).

Positively reframing a situation can involve recognizing what can be learned from a challenging situation. First, weigh the evidence you have pertaining to a particular situation. Look at the assumptions you are making about how you are viewing the situation and how you feel others are viewing it. Are your assumptions valid? Remind yourself that thoughts aren't necessarily facts, and the best way to interpret a situation is to get a different perspective.

According to Lee Bolman and Terrence Deal (1997), the essence of reframing is looking at the same situation from multiple vantage points. The ability to reframe an experience enriches and broadens a principal's repertoire. In fact, "it is a powerful antidote to self-entrapment" (Bolman & Deal, 1997, p. 6). Expanded options help principals generate more creative ideas and solutions to the broad range of issues we face every day. Different frames yield different ways to respond to situations—by rescripting or generating new scenarios. If you need a better view, head to the balcony and look at it from a different vantage point.

By reframing a situation, we alter our perception of the stressor, and as a result, relieve ourselves of significant amounts of stress that keep us from handling the situation with a clear thought process. Psychologist and author Elizabeth Scott (2020a) offers four reframing techniques that you can use to help you reframe challenging situations.

1. **Learn about thinking patterns:** What are some of the negative thinking patterns that greatly increase your stress levels? Take a look at your cognitive distortions—the tendencies and patterns of your mind's thoughts and beliefs—for unproductive reactions. Then, when you know what to look out for when you begin thinking in this direction, you can begin to change the way you experience stressors in your life.

2. **Notice your thoughts:** Become aware of when you find yourself slipping into negative and stress-inducing patterns of thinking. As you become observant of them, it's easier to notice and change your thoughts rather than get caught up in them.

3. **Challenge your thoughts:** Examine the truth and accuracy of the thoughts. Instead of seeing the thought or situation in a negative light, see if you can reframe it in such a way that it still fits your situation but appears in a more positive light or at least one with potential for a positive outcome.

4. **Replace your thoughts with more positive thoughts:** When you're in a stressful situation or see something negative, try to change your self-talk to use fewer strong or negative emotions. Try to view the potentially stressful situation as a challenge versus a threat, and see if you can keep your stressors in a more positive, optimistic frame.

You still need to keep the situation real and acknowledge the severity, but reframing can have a big, positive impact on your stress and the way you view your daily situations.

Personal coach and author Blaž Kos (n.d.) explains that when you are sizing up a situation, you go to your default frames, or *schemata*, those mental structures that provide a framework for representing some aspect of the world. These default frames help you organize information in a manageable way. Kos (n.d.)

offers three goals you want to achieve by cognitively reframing a situation.

1. **Describe your situation as accurately as possible:** Erase the negative thoughts and make sure you see reality as accurately as possible. You need to view the negative aspects, but don't skew them as larger than they actually are. Your reality, says Kos (n.d.), is "anchored in your core beliefs, values, past life experiences, expectations and many other factors."

2. **Illuminate personal power:** Don't portray yourself as less powerful than you actually are. Put the situation into a circles of concern and influence model (Covey, 1989; see tip 3, page 17) to get a more accurate picture of what you can control. You may see that you have more ability to deal with the situation than you originally thought.

3. **Brainstorm alternative views:** Find better alternative views of the situation at hand. You want to seek what Kos (n.d.) calls a *redemptive narrative* or frame that tells the story of where tough events bring something good (at least with time).

The next step is to neutralize the negative thoughts by asking yourself the right questions. These, says Kos (n.d.), are called *optimal thinking questions*, which will help you reframe the situation in a positive light. Ask yourself what went right with the situation, what is the best way to act in this type of situation, and how you can turn the disaster into a win or at least a lesson learned.

Kamphoff (2018) explains that "reframing helps us stay stoked and excited despite hardships, no matter how awful things might feel in the moment" (p. 157). Use the cognitive reframing worksheet in figure 4.2 to view a stressful situation in a more optimistic and positive light. A reproducible version is available on page 129. One note of caution, though. When reframing, be honest about and acknowledge any mistakes you made, add them to the pocket where you keep your lessons learned, and KFG.

Event or situation:			
I did not get the mentorship position I wanted.			
What happened? (My original interpretation)	**What were my thoughts and assumptions?**	**What was my schema?**	**What was my reaction?**
I applied to be a mentor for new principals and did not get the position.	*My assumption was that I was well qualified to be a mentor and I thought I was a good candidate for the position.*	*My belief is that new principals need support in order to succeed in the position, and I felt a strong purpose to pay my experiences forward.*	*I was annoyed and perplexed as to why I was not chosen as a mentor.*
Reframing scenario	**Evidence: What are the facts?**	**What can I control?**	**What went right?**
There are other avenues to mentoring new principals.	*There were more applicants than there were mentor positions and others were chosen.*	*I can still mentor new principals in a different manner.*	*I would not be adding additional responsibilities and hours to the job. I would now be mentoring new principals in the form of a book.*
Lesson learned			
There are always opportunities if you seek them out. If something doesn't work out, try a different avenue.			

Source: Adapted from Bolman & Deal, 1997; Kamphoff, 2018; Kos, n.d.; York-Barr, Sommers, Ghere, & Montie, 2006.

Figure 4.2: Cognitive reframing worksheet example.

Tip 17: Reflect on It

Reflection is a critical aspect of a principal's job. The sheer number of decisions and actions in a day, coupled with the tremendous amount of communication that flows in every direction, requires principals to unwind at the end of the day and reflect. The practice of reflection allows us to think about our practice and consider ways to improve our practice in the future. It should become standard practice as an organizer for your thoughts and learning. Reflection is not just talking or thinking about our work; it includes action steps for continuous improvement. There are many different models for reflective practice, and all of them include action steps you can take to further improve your practice.

Reflective practice requires you to pause, either intentionally or because of a crisis or dilemma. Pausing gives you the opportunity to consider options for action. This break in the action gives you the time to write down the thoughts you want to reflect on. You can start by asking yourself some questions: What happened? What did I learn? What went well? What didn't go as well as I had planned? What made the situation difficult? What resources do I have to help me? What do I want to improve on for the future?

Jennifer York-Barr and her colleagues (2006), authors of *Reflective Practice to Improve Schools*, offer a profile of a reflective leader:

- Stays focused on education's central purpose: Students' learning and development
- Is committed to continuous improvement of practice
- Assumes responsibility for his or her own learning—now and lifelong
- Demonstrates awareness of self, others, and the surrounding context
- Develops the thinking skills for effective inquiry
- Takes action that aligns with new understandings
- Holds great leadership capacity within a school community
- Seeks to understand different types of knowledge, internally and externally generated (p. 16)

Reflection is a process, explain York-Barr and her colleagues (2006), that includes both experience and uncertainty. It involves identifying questions and key elements of a situation that have emerged and having a dialogue with yourself and with others, which will help provide insight about the perspectives of others, your values and beliefs, and the greater context. Women's leadership thought leader Susan Madsen (2020) considers critical reflection the key to effective leadership development.

The reflection process is a synthesis of many of the practices already discussed in this book. The reflection process sends you back to your purpose and values and to your why of a decision. Like with your critical friends from tip 9 (page 52), as you reflect with others, you need to listen without judgment or blame. Ask questions, trying to shift your questions from how to the what and why. As you reflect, you are also reframing the situation. By reframing the situation, you acknowledge that your current view or practice may be inaccurate or incomplete; you might need to think about the situation differently from another perspective. Methods of reflecting include the tools of journal writing, the ladder of inference process, and the decide, enact, analyze, reflect model.

 Tool: Journal Writing

One of the best ways to document your reflection processes is to keep a journal. Keeping a journal helps to organize your thoughts and reflections and allows you to refer back to them along your journey: "Journaling is a relatively safe means by which you can think through uncomfortable, complex, and challenging issues you need to sort out before discussing them with others" (York-Barr et al., 2006, p. 49). Journaling can actually act as a stress-management tool. Scientific evidence shows that "writing removes mental blocks and allows you to use all of your brainpower to better understand yourself, others, and the world around you" (Dibdin, 2022).

I purposely journal when the activity of the day has wound down, either by the creek at the campground after a day's trek or in my office at school, once the literal or figurative pack has been lifted off my shoulders. Journaling allows you to put your thoughts down in any random manner without regard to spelling, grammar, or syntax. York-Barr and her colleagues (2006) explain that "journaling makes invisible thoughts visible. It provides a means of describing practice and of identifying and clarifying beliefs, perspectives, challenges, and hopes for practice" (p. 87). Journaling offers a private place for honest reflection of your daily encounters.

As a principal, I have kept a journal throughout my entire career. It contains thoughts, messages, ideas, poetry, and things I've heard, things I've seen, and things I've felt. I also use a journal to clear my head by purging the tempest of chatter that can rule my few hours of sleep. Journaling is something you can do quickly, even in the middle of the night. Having a journal allows you to go back at any time to any entry and reflect on your observations, emotions, and situations. In fact, this book is a compilation of those stories, situations, ideas, poems, speeches, data, statistics, models, strategies, and activities I have been writing about for over twenty years. I keep a separate journal of my backpacking adventures, which someday may become another book.

Journaling is an important part of professional growth as a school leader. Remember the importance of self-awareness and metacognition from tip 15 (page 96)? Journaling helps you work explicitly in that space and make connections between theory and practice (York-Barr et al., 2006). Journaling can also be used "to gain insight about how organic impulse and idea generations are evoked within ourselves" (York-Barr et al., 2006, p. 94). When you reflect on what you have written, you can begin to look at situations using multiple lenses, and should a similar situation arise in the future, you may have strategies and models that have been proven successful.

Besides the benefits of self-awareness and professional growth, there is quite a bit of research and science behind the impact journaling has on your mental and physical health. On the physical side, journaling improves your brain function and your immune system. A study conducted at Michigan State University (Schroder, Moran, & Moser, 2017) finds that "expressive writing can clear your mind's worries and free up resources in your brain that could be put to use on other tasks" (Intelligent Change, n.d.). It can help calm your brain in the state of worrying.

When you're worried about one thing, it is difficult to concentrate on other tasks and responsibilities because your cognitive efforts are being exhausted on that worry, making it more difficult to be present in the moment (Intelligent Change, n.d.). According to Siri Carpenter (2001) of the American Psychological Association, journaling can also help decrease the emotional impact of negative events, which have a greater cognitive impact than positive events.

A second health benefit of journaling is how it impacts your immune system. James Pennebaker, a social psychologist whose career focused on expressive writing, finds that it can strengthen your immune system (Pennebaker, Kiecolt-Glaser, & Glaser, 1988). He believes that journaling can be used as a stress-relieving tool by reducing the number of sensors on your immune system cells. He finds that journaling could lower your chances of getting ill and improve your recovery from surgery and wounds (Baikie & Wilhelm, 2018; Intelligent Change, n.d.).

Along with the physical benefits of journaling are the mental health benefits. We know that mental health affects physical health, and by confronting our struggles, situations, and events, writing down our thoughts and feelings helps reduce stress (Baikie & Wilhelm, 2018). Journaling on a daily basis can help us overcome negative emotional responses (Baikie & Wilhelm, 2018), as we are better equipped to reflect on our situations from multiple perspectives, enabling us to find alternative solutions. A journal is also a place to write about your accomplishments, celebrations, good news, and situations and problems you solved effectively. And of course, it can be anything you feel like putting down on paper.

The one thing you do not want your journal writing to become is a chore—another thing you have to do in your busy day. Journal writing should feel cathartic, so write first when you need to and second when you can relax and have the time to reflect. In other words, when you find yourself in a predicament or precarious situation, or you hear something or see something you want to remember, jot it down immediately. Take a minute to write it down, even if it's a few choice words on a sticky note. You can always rewrite those notes in your journal at a later time. When you have time to truly relax and reflect, find a quiet, comfortable place to purge the negative chatter that occupies your mind, and then add all the positive talk as well. Always try to find something to celebrate at the end of each day.

Along with feeling cathartic, journal writing should also help you organize and prepare yourself for meetings. The writings in your journal should serve as fodder for your critical friends process or coaching discussions (tip 9, page 52). Having your thoughts on paper keeps you from coming up with just any old topic so that your time with your critical friends and coach is meaningful and productive.

Here are a few tips to start.

- Have a notebook or journal dedicated solely to journaling.
- Keep a pen or pencil attached to it.
- Date the entries.
- Keep your journal handy, and when possible, take it with you to work (or keep a sticky note pad in your pocket).
- Write quickly when you need to put down a few words; then find an uninterrupted time that allows you to relax and find your inner voice for more thoughtful entries.
- Reflect on patterns and trends.
- Balance negative entries with positive entries.
- Have a separate journal or pad of paper at home, especially by your bed for those middle-of-the-night worries or great ideas.
- Either rewrite or paste your scraps of notes into your journal as soon as possible.
- Review your entries at a later date and look at them through a different lens.

Free writing is always a perfectly acceptable manner of capturing your thoughts and reflections, but the next two tools offer more structure for reflection and subsequent action steps.

Tool: Ladder of Inference Process

The ladder of inference is a model of the steps you can use to make sense of a situation in order to act. It's a model for metacognition that helps us to think about our thinking and to coordinate our thinking with others.

Chris Argyris (1986), behavior theorist and professor emeritus at Harvard University, developed the ladder of inference model that describes your thinking process to get from problem to actionable solutions. Using the ladder of inference allows you to become more aware of your own thinking and reasoning, the basis of reflection. It also makes your reasoning more visible to others when it is shared. The model was included in *The Fifth Discipline Fieldbook* (Senge, Kleiner, Roberts, Ross, & Smith, 1994) and became a popular and enduring method of engaging in action research (McArthur, 2014).

You begin at the bottom rung with observable data and experiences that relate to your problem. This is what you see as if you were recording it. This is where you start your written reflection. You record people's words, tone of voice, nonverbal communication, statistical data, and any actions that were observed. You then move up the ladder to where you select data that you decide to use. Be careful not to ignore certain data that might be uncomfortable to attend to. You then add your own meanings to those data by paraphrasing the data and interpreting the meaning of people's actions. Here again, you are deciding what data to use and interpreting what you see and believe. The next rung up the ladder is naming what is happening by characterizing what is happening and making assumptions based on the meanings you added. Here you put a name to the problem. The next step involves explaining and evaluating what is happening and why it is happening, and finally, you take action based on your conclusions of what happened and why it happened.

The ladder is a reflexive loop that illustrates your assumptions, values, and beliefs. It shows how your interpretations influence your decisions. This helps you reflect on how you see things and how they align with your own assumptions, values, and beliefs. Once you understand how you interpret a situation, you can look into how others perceive the situation as you make decisions and transparently show others how you perceived the situation and arrived at a particular decision. While this is a valuable tool to use to reflect on your practice, it's always important to look at situations and interpretations from as many different perspectives as possible when deciding action steps.

Figure 4.3 reverses the ladder, allowing you to work through it as a step-by-step process; a reproducible version is available on page 130.

Data observed:
A high number of office referrals

Selected data:
The number of office referrals for the past month

What the data mean:
There are issues with classroom management

The problem:
We do not have schoolwide systems for classroom management in place

Why the problem exists:
We are not all on the same page with behavior expectations and strategies

Action steps:
Create a schoolwide system of steps for student behavior expectations and strategies and build schoolwide commitment to adhere to the system

Source: Adapted from Argyris, 1986; Senge et al., 1994.
Figure 4.3: Ladder of inference process example.

 Tool: Decide, Enact, Analyze, Reflect Model

Another action model for reflecting is one that I created, based on the well-known and often-used plan, do, study, act (PDSA) model, which originated in the work of Walter Shewhart and was refined by W. Edwards Deming in the 1980s (Taylor et al., 2014). The PDSA cycle of evaluating an outcome has been used extensively in education settings, especially to assess whether an initiative or program is showing continuous improvement in academic achievement. The PDSA model recognizes *act* as the final step in the process, in which you act on the changes that need to be made in the initiative or program that was introduced. I, however, believe that *reflection* is a more relevant process on which to conclude whether or not your implementation was successful. I have reworked the PDSA method to exemplify a more reflective model. I call this model decide, enact, analyze, reflect (DEAR).

In the DEAR model, the first step is to decide—to make a decision, possibly using one of the decision tools in tip 3 (page 17). The second step is to enact the decision by implementing the plan, initiative, or program. Throughout this implementation stage, you will collect both quantitative and qualitative data. In step 3, you will compile the data into spreadsheets, charts, or graphs so that you can analyze the results of the program implementation. The final step is to reflect on what areas of the program were successful and what areas of the program could be improved. This process lends itself perfectly to conducting action research in an education setting. You can work your way through the DEAR model using the template in figure 4.4 (page 118).

Decide	Continue the prekindergarten program with outside funding.
Enact	Implement one half-day session.
Analyze	Look at enrollment, budget, classroom observations, and parent and community surveys.
Reflect	The program successes included maximizing enrollment and staying within the budget. Classroom observations indicated appropriate curriculum and schedule, and parent and community surveys illustrated the demand and satisfaction with the program. The one area for improvement was to look for ways to avoid attrition due to students leaving the school after preK.

Figure 4.4: Decide, enact, analyze, reflect.

Visit **go.SolutionTree.com/leadership** *for a free reproducible version of this figure.*

Tip 18: Laugh About It

I once hightailed it through forest, brush, and streams, making as much noise as possible due to seeing a couple of bears behind us on the trail. When we finally figured it was safe to stop and catch our breath, my companion, Jackie, commented on how she'd never seen me move so fast with thirty pounds on my back. We were both stressed (scared!), but at that point, we just broke into a roaring laughter, immediately relieving us of the stress of that sighting. That short burst of laughter allowed our cortisol levels to retreat, and thus, we were back to our normal pace and feeling the weight of our heavy loads.

This same mechanism applies to office stresses. Feeling stressed out? Laugh! Your workplace needs laughter. *Harvard Business Review* writer Alison Beard (2014) explains:

> According to research from institutions as serious as Wharton, MIT, and London Business School, every chuckle or guffaw brings with it a host of business benefits. Laughter relieves stress and boredom, boosts engagement and well-being, and spurs not only creativity and collaboration but also analytic precision and productivity.

"Laughter is a social phenomenon," says neuroscientist Sophie Scott, as quoted by journalist Daryl Austin (2023). Scott, who has studied laughter for over two decades, finds in a cowritten study (Warren et al., 2006) on laughter that "the brain responds to the sound of laughter by preparing one's facial muscles to join in, laying the foundation for laughs to spread from person to person" (Austin, 2023). You know how when someone yawns, you start to yawn? It's the same phenomenon scientists find with laughing (Austin, 2023). Researchers also find that laughter can strengthen relationship connections because "people naturally want to be around those who make them feel good the way laughing does" (Austin, 2023).

Mayo Clinic (2021) has also proven that laughter is a great source of stress relief. Data show it can contribute to a lot of welcomed and surprising effects, such as stimulating your heart, lungs, and brain; helping circulation; aiding muscle relaxation; improving your immune system; and relieving pain (Mayo Clinic, 2021). There is evidence that laughter works similarly to an antidepressant by helping control serotonin in the brain (Gibson, 2020). Even a stressful event can elicit some laughter, though usually after the fact.

Laughter can be a healthy coping mechanism. It's what Jackie and I used on the trail to manage our bear-induced stress. When researching people's laughter, psychologists found that the more laughter they experienced, the lower they reported their stress levels (Gibson, 2020). Further, a growing number of therapists recommend laughter to help clients build trust and improve work environments (Gibson, 2020). Erin Lynn Raab (2020) writes that laughter contributes to growing more resilient. *Resilience*, Raab (2020) says, "is the psychological strength that allows some people to adapt, thrive, and/or return to their baseline faster after adverse experiences happen." As a principal, you will inevitably deal with change, setbacks, tragedy, and grief in one way or another. Raab (2020) says that you can grow more resilient with positive emotions.

Look for places in your school where you can laugh for even a minute. On the hundredth day of school, I knew I could find a good laugh by visiting the kindergarten rooms. The teachers digitally enhanced photos of themselves and their students to make them look like they were one hundred years old. They were hysterical. Walking by those classrooms could immediately lighten my mood. The bulletin boards in my office are always filled with fun photos of smiling faces of students and staff I've taken throughout the years, not with work documents or information. There are several ways you can indulge yourself in a nice helping of laughter. Here are two tools you can use to help induce more laughter in your daily routine: laughter yoga and humorous media.

 Tool: Laughter Yoga

Laughter yoga is no joke. Laughter yoga is both a preventive and therapeutic program, incorporating aerobic exercise and a cardio workout. It works by releasing endorphins, which are natural painkillers, and can help those who suffer from migraines or any other type of pain (Laughter Yoga International, n.d.). It also unwinds the negative effects of stress and strengthens your immune system. It increases oxygen to the brain and body, gives you an energy boost, and makes you feel healthy. It's not yoga in the sense that you are contorting your body into different positions; it combines laughter exercises with yoga breathing techniques (Laughter Yoga International, n.d.). Studies in stressful work environments find that laughter therapy such as laughter yoga lessened pro-stress factors and elevated mood-elevating anti-stress factors, which reduces anxiety and depression (Akimbekov & Razzaque, 2021).

Laughter yoga started in Mumbai in 1995 when physician Madan Kataria (2018) had the idea that his patients and friends would be happier if they laughed more often. He started the first laughter club in a park with a few participants but found that after a few sessions, the jokes became stale. He then decided to find a way to keep the laughter rolling by creating simple exercises to get people laughing without any jokes. Kataria (2018) wrote an entire book on the subject, called *Laughter Yoga: Daily Laughter Practices for Health and Happiness*. He realized one day that the yoga breathing exercise of exhaling while saying "ho ho" and "ha ha" could simulate laughter. Even fake laughter has benefits (Scott, n.d.), but Kataria (2018) finds that simulated laughter, especially in a group setting, can become real and contagious. Rather than a spontaneous response to a funny joke, Kataria (2018) turns laughter into a "complete delivery system that allowed laughter to be prescribed as part of a daily routine in order to realize all the health benefits it has to offer" (p. xv).

One of the reasons Kataria (2018) pursued this form of laughter was because he found that while children can laugh up to four hundred times in a day, adults laugh fewer than twenty times in the same span (Scott, n.d.). Children, he says, laugh more than adults because they do not place conditions on laughter. They laugh just because they want to. Adults look for reasons to laugh and rely on their level of happiness, satisfaction, sense of humor, and reason.

Kataria (2018) maintains that by laughing for at least ten minutes per day, you will enjoy health benefits that include increased oxygen levels in the blood, relaxed muscles, better blood circulation, and the release of certain hormones, including endorphins and serotonin. So, what is the link between yoga and laughter? As discussed in tip 11 (page 76), yoga has its origins in ancient Indian philosophy; the word is Sanskrit for *union* (Basavaraddi, n.d.; Burgin, 2022): "It means getting ahold of our lives, integrating all aspects, and harmonizing our bodies with our minds, spirits, and society" (Kataria, 2018, p. 19).

To practice laughter yoga, you have to have a willingness to laugh and a positive mindset to get over any awkwardness, which Kataria (2018) says can be a hang-up to many people because it's not genuine laughter. To try it out, use the following steps.

1. **Chant:** Warm up by chanting "ho, ho" and "ha, ha" while standing. As you say "ho, ho," push your hands forward away from your chest, and as you say "ha, ha," put your hands toward the ground, with your palms facing the ground.

2. **Breathe:** Straighten your arms out in front of you with your palms facing up. Inhale through your nose and bring your arms, using a fist, close to your chest. Hold your breath for three to four seconds, then exhale in laughter. Repeat this three times.

It may sound like a very weird and unusual way to improve your mental and physical health, but when other things are not working, and you're desperate to change the work environment, it might be worth a try. Presently, there are thousands of laughter social clubs around the world (Laughter Yoga International, n.d.). Besides the social clubs, laughter yoga is practiced in schools, colleges, senior centers, corporations, factories, police stations, and prisons (One Billion Rising, 2015).

There is a questionnaire in Kataria's (2018) book that reveals your laughter quotient after you have answered twenty questions. When I took this quiz, I scored 58 out of 100, and according to Kataria (2018), if you score between 40 and 59, you laugh very little and need to be happier. I'm going to have to work on that.

 Tool: Humorous Media

Need to relax? Watch a funny sitcom or other humorous television program, search for an entertaining video or podcast, read the comics section of your local newspaper, find or reread a funny book, or arrange a night out at a comedy club. I am a self-professed sitcom junkie. We already know that laughter provides stress relief, and while you may not want to schedule anything else in your day, you can just turn on the TV or any other device. There are now countless channels, streaming services, apps, and other options for finding just about anything you want to watch.

Nothing screams stress like a pandemic. Masks, positive virus tests, quarantines, staff shortages, substitute shortages, bus driver shortages, schedule changes, digital learning, Zoom drops, another "You're on mute." For the three years, starting in 2020 at the beginning of the COVID-19 pandemic, I'd come home, fill a glass with wine, and watch a rerun of some sitcom. Nothing satisfies my media entertainment needs like a good thirty minutes of comedy. Well-written, hilarious lines, even ones I've seen or heard many times, allow me to laugh out loud all by myself on the couch. This is my ultimate therapy at the end of the school day, and I soon realized it was a lot healthier to spend a good thirty minutes laughing rather than drinking that glass of wine.

At the time, I didn't really know why I found solace in the sitcom reruns, but researchers have found "measurable restorative effect from a familiar fictional world" (Jayne Derrick, as quoted by Scott, 2020b). Derrick, one of the researchers who analyzed the relationship between television habits and task completion, found that if study participants had to do energy-consuming tasks (a principal's job description), they were more likely to seek out a rerun of their favorite television show, rewatch a familiar movie, or reread a favorite book (Scott, 2020b). They reported that doing so restored their energy levels and allowed them to do more afterward. Derrick notes in her analysis that it was reruns, not just any television viewing, that tended to make the difference. The reason for this, she explains, is that "there is something about the 'social surrogacy' of watching favorite characters, and there is a relaxing element to already knowing what will happen" (as cited in Scott, 2020b).

Janet M. Gibson (2020) explains, "Laughter, like humor, typically sparks from recognizing the incongruities or absurdities of a situation." This could explain why we laugh at the absurdities of sitcoms. I continue to laugh at the lines even when I've heard them several times over. So, if you feel that you should be doing something more constructive with your very limited free time besides engaging in something "frivolous," here is permission to unhook yourself from the workload you brought home and give yourself a reprieve to do nothing but immerse in something fun and light-hearted for thirty minutes.

Tip 19: Recharge

Mountain air is thin, especially if you're somewhere like the Andes, up at over fifteen thousand feet. At this altitude, you need to give your body, lungs, and mind a rest at regular intervals. It's definitely easier to say, "I need a break," on the trail than it is in the office, but the principal position is a 24/7 position, a position that doesn't take a vacation. And while the position doesn't take a vacation, the principal needs to take a vacation from the position. You don't need to climb mountains or move mountains on vacation; you simply need to separate yourself from the daily grind of the job and do something you enjoy.

When I say take a vacation, I don't mean work twenty grueling weeks and then go away for two weeks. Honor Jones (2018) suggests in *The New York Times* that traditional vacations are a good thing, but only allowing them to serve as a release valve normalizes letting the pressure mount for the rest of the year. Jones (2018) asks, "What if I'd taken all the money and enthusiasm I'd put into the past 10 years of vacations and devoted it, instead, to making my own life, the real one, a little bit better?" You need both a physical and a psychological break. Taking a psychological break means stepping away from work, not just physically but mentally. It means disconnecting from technology, taking in some fresh air, and enjoying the effects of nature, all of which give us the time to breathe, clear our heads, and release the stress of the job.

Recharging is not the same as resting; it's taking a break from your normal routine and doing something you enjoy so that you are ready to resume working. Rest is about *not* doing; the focus is on repose. Both are important, but the distinction can sometimes get lost. Sometimes the doing means letting go and making space for fulfillment. This tip offers tools for finding your happy place, unplugging and disconnecting, and creating a nature log.

Tool: Your Happy Place

Your work is relentless. On top of your work hours, you are fitting in family, friends, hobbies, sports, and more. Where do you go when you need to disconnect from everything and feel peace? Though it will differ by individual, we all need a happy or safe place to retreat to in order to improve our mood and lift our spirits. According to the Australian Medical Association (2022):

> A benefit of having a happy place is that it provides us with an escape and the opportunity to ground ourselves. This helps us to put things in perspective and diverts our mind away from negative or stressful thoughts. It also increases our feelings of gratitude and decreases anxiety and panic.

Happy places can be physical or imaginary. If I just need a few minutes, I'll throw on some headphones and listen to some of my favorite tunes. Memories are also an important way to access an imaginary happy place. They empower you to visit a virtual or imaginary happy place, something you can do by looking at photos or visualizing it in your mind for a few moments. When you think about happy memories that you want to relive, seek to laugh a little—don't forget the benefits of laughter discussed in tip 18 (page 118). That way, you're engaging two of the tools to help reduce stress.

There are also physical places to go when you need a break. Use your vacation time! Take advantage of the non–student contact days and try to escape for some much-needed rest and relaxation or some exhilarating adventure. When I need to be physically away from work, I try to line up a trip to a happy place. Even if the trips are local excursions, I look forward to being in a different milieu. But, again, don't let a traditional vacation become your *only* time away. Outside of school, I still find daily solace in nature, running, music, and watching sitcoms.

If I need a quiet place during the school day, I'll sit outside in the courtyard (during the three or so months a year without snow in Minnesota), or if I need to uplift my mood, I'll head to a prekindergarten classroom. Watching four-year-olds learning and playing, I can't help but smile.

Nancy Mramor (n.d.), a psychologist who leads workshops on achieving happiness, offers these five tips to finding your happy place.

1. Remember places with sounds that you liked, such as birdsong, ocean waves, or a particular type or piece of music.

2. Think of places that were enjoyable visually, like a spot where you witnessed a sunset, a place with beautiful trees, seascapes, or places with wonderful artwork or architecture.

3. Select a place that has the elements to contribute to *your* happiness. Depending on your needs, this might be a busy spot with

lots of people, laughter, and bustle, or it might be a calm environment of peace and stillness.

4. Think of a time when you were deeply content, and remember where you were. This might be a favorite restaurant, a house where you spend time with family, or any other place that has special meaning.

5. Be open minded and willing to look for new or different places that provide that happiness and serenity.

The Australian Medical Association (2022) also advises that when you are seeking your happy place, make sure it is safe and secure, a place where people don't judge, where you are comfortable in your own skin, and where you can truly enjoy every moment of the break. When you think about your happy place, keep it a place free from others who are complaining about work, your coworkers, or other topics of conversation that might elevate stress rather than relieve it. We all need this escape. Keep it solitary and peaceful—if only for brief moments at a time.

Tool: Unplug and Disconnect Tracker

We all know the principal job can be 24/7, but that's if you allow it to be a 24/7 job. Technology just reinforces that 24/7 mentality, because people expect that you will answer 24/7. And if you allow it to be a 24/7 job, you are not allowing your body to take a break from the stress. It's really hard to completely detach yourself from technology, but by doing so, you can help keep your stress under control. When you allow yourself to be available to your work 24/7, you expose yourself to all the stressors associated with the job all the time. By turning off the phone and shutting down the computer, you give your body a break from that constant source of stress. It's really hard to enjoy a romantic dinner or any nonwork event when your phone is constantly dinging, ringing, and pinging.

A 2022 phone usage statistic shows that the average American touches his, her, or their phone 2,617 times a day (Flynn, 2022). For those who are awake sixteen hours a day, that means they touch their phone every twenty-two seconds. Another 2022 usage statistic shows that average Americans spend five hours and twenty-four minutes a day using their phones (Flynn, 2022). With these kinds of statistics, we are really overconnected. Being overconnected can lead to being depressed and burned out. It can also lead to insomnia by interrupting sleep cycles and inactivity due to sedentary screen time (Gomes, 2018). The benefits to unplugging from your devices include reduced stress, anxiety, and feelings of loneliness, and more free time for your hobbies, spending time with family, or volunteering (Gomes, 2018).

A research study published in the *Journal of Occupational Health Psychology* (Park, Fritz, & Jex, 2011) finds:

> Unplugging after work can make a big difference in your quality of life, health, and happiness. Researchers found that when people "unplugged" from work-related tasks, such as checking their work email after hours, they reported feeling fresher and better recharged when beginning work the following day. (Higgins & Thorpe, 2020)

Unplugging also allows time to reflect on appreciation and gratitude, or engage in other activities such as playing games (the kind that come in a box) or reading books (the ones with actual pages). It also gives you the opportunity for face-to-face conversations and to go out and connect with nature.

You might have to start off with small amounts of unplugged time to make it manageable, because at first, being unplugged might feel stressful. You can even put your phone on airplane mode for a little while to ensure that you are not available for a bit of time and then work up to more manageable amounts of time. To get into the routine of unplugging, schedule a time to be technology-free. Be up front with your staff and your boss. Explain to them that you are not answering the phone or emails during the dinner hour, or at certain hours during the evening and weekend when you are enjoying family time, participating in an activity, watching a show, reading a good book, or just giving yourself a break. Review the tools in tip 15 (page 96) for setting boundaries. If you haven't set boundaries for answering emails, texts, and phone calls, go back to that tool and set those boundaries.

I always say one of the best things about backpacking is that I'm off the grid—sometimes for several weeks at a time. At first, it was hard to disconnect, even for a short time. Once I did it, I found it liberating to be free of the constant barrage of emails, texts, and phone calls. Start small and work your way up, but at some point every day, unplug, disconnect, and give yourself the break you need from work and the screen. If you do not have dedicated unplugged time in your setting boundaries worksheet from tip 15 (page 96), you can use figure 4.5 to monitor just how much time you are allowing yourself from the tether of your devices, particularly your phone and your laptop. Monitor the time only until it becomes a habit to disconnect for a certain amount of time each day, even if it's for a very short time.

Device	Date	Time Unplugged
Phone	1/14/23	9:00 a.m.–12:30 p.m.
Laptop	1/14/23–1/24/23	10 days

Figure 4.5: Unplug and disconnect tracker.

Visit **go.SolutionTree.com/leadership** *for a free reproducible version of this figure.*

 **Tool: Nature Log**

Given the importance of disconnecting, you may be able to open up some time for something better. While you're disconnected, get some fresh air. A principal's schedule is usually quite full and demanding of your time, but finding just ten minutes a day to take a walk and get some fresh air will refresh and recharge your body and your brain.

Let's start with the brain. Oxygen is vital for maintaining healthy brain function and growth, as 20 percent of the oxygen you breathe in is used by your brain to function (Starling, n.d.). Your brain is extremely sensitive to oxygen levels, so taking a walk outside, breathing in fresh air, improves brain function and the efficiency of every cell in your body, your thinking, your focus, and your ability to concentrate (Ross, 2020; Starling, n.d.).

David Strayer, cognitive scientist at the University of Utah, who has studied cognitive attentiveness and interaction with nature, finds that higher-order cognitive skills improve with prolonged exposure to the outdoors (Damiano, 2020). He explains that "being in nature activates the default mode network in the brain, which is normally engaged when we daydream or spend time in introspection," while the use of technology has been shown to disrupt that default mode, emphasizing the importance of being outdoors in natural environments (Damiano, 2020). While Strayer talks about prolonged exposure to the outdoors improving cognition, Florence Williams (2017), author of *The Nature Fix*, believes that even small amounts of exposure to the living world can improve our creativity and enhance our mood. "Short exposures to nature," she says, "can make us less aggressive, more creative, more civic-minded, and healthier overall" (Williams, 2017, p. 236).

As for the rest of your body, when you are outside walking, you increase your diaphragmatic breathing, meaning you breathe more deeply, drawing more air deep into the bottom of your lungs. This deep breathing brings more oxygen into your cells and helps the lungs expel more airborne toxins from your body. Time you spend outside also carries with it a lower risk of airborne illnesses because viral particles have a reduced chance of survival in fresh air (Wang et al., n.d.). Also, the amount of serotonin your brain releases is affected by the amount of oxygen you have in your blood (Starling, n.d.). Serotonin is responsible for your sense of happiness and well-being, so the more fresh air you have, the more relaxed and refreshed you will feel.

The physical benefits are good, but the mental benefits are arguably even better. Richard Louv (2011), author of *The Nature Principle*, holds "that a reconnection to the natural world is fundamental to human health, well-being, spirit, and survival" (p. 3). While the nature principle is primarily a statement of philosophy, Louv (2011) purports that it is supported by a growing body of theoretical, anecdotal, and empirical research that backs the restorative power of nature and its impact on our senses, intelligence, and physical, mental, and spiritual health.

In his book *Last Child in the Woods*, Louv (2005) introduces what he terms the nature-deficit disorder. While not a medical diagnosis, he uses this term to describe a growing gap in children: "Nature-deficit disorder describes the human costs of alienation from nature; among them: diminished use of the senses, attention difficulties, and higher rates of physical and emotional illnesses" (Louv, 2005, p. 36). Since he first introduced the nature-deficit disorder as it pertained to children, he has heard from many adults about their own sense of loss with nature (Louv, 2005). The good news is that it's easy to do something about it.

"Cool things happen when you're exposed to nature for two hours a week," says Brent Bauer (as quoted by Barker, 2019) of the Mayo Clinic in Rochester, Minnesota. Doctors write prescriptions for all kinds of ailments, but those usually involve ingesting or injecting medication. Patients usually follow through with written prescriptions but do not do as well with just oral suggestions, such as spending some time outside. Now, Bauer recommends doctors hand out prescriptions for time outdoors amid legitimate science that points to nature's health benefits (Barker, 2019). A formal mechanism, such as a written prescription, makes it easier for patients to follow through and sends the message that being outdoors is a legitimate form of therapy.

Bauer founded Mayo Clinic's complementary and integrative medicine program in the early 2000s grounded in the theory of *biophilia*—that humans have an innate need to be connected with nature (Barker, 2019). He has seen a "scientification" of our need for nature, something he notes has been studied and measured. While Bauer will admit a walk in the park is not going to cure hypertension, it can be used in conjunction with other therapies, including medication, if necessary (Barker, 2019).

Another study conducted by researchers from the University of Michigan aims to determine the association between nature and stress hormone levels (Hunter, Gillespie, & Chen, 2019). The researchers had asked a group of adults to take what they termed "nature pills"; the dose of which called for them to spend some time sitting or walking in nature. They were required to spend a minimum of ten minutes in nature at least three times a week for a period of eight weeks. The participants could choose the time of day, duration, and place of their nature experience, defined as anything outside and which made them feel connected to nature. After analyzing the results, the researchers found that having a twenty-minute nature experience reduced cortisol levels, and those who spent thirty minutes outside had the greatest decrease of cortisol levels (Hunter et al., 2019; Parker, 2019). To help keep track of your own time spent recharging in nature, you could use figure 4.6.

Place	Date	Time
Walked around the block	5/5/22	20 minutes
Hiked in state park	5/7/22	2 hours
Sat and read in my garden	5/8/22	1 hour
Ate lunch in the courtyard	5/9/22	15 minutes

Figure 4.6: Nature log.

Visit **go.SolutionTree.com/leadership** *for a free reproducible version of this figure.*

Even ten minutes connected to nature can do a body good, and if you can manage thirty, all the better. Like the research says, "Managing stress is a core component of being a successful leader, and spending time in nature can reduce stress while also improving cognitive performance" (Damiano, 2020). Taking a hike doesn't mean you need to lace up hiking boots and put thirty pounds on your back for a week. You can take urban hikes around the corner, through parks, along designated trails, or anywhere you feel describes nature. It can be walking through your own backyard among the trees, the grass, the sand, the flowers, and the bugs. Use the nature log to account for your time away from your desk. The idea is not so much where; it's *that* you take the time to relax, refresh, and recharge, and if those words have not been in your job description, add these: "Take a hike!"

Tip 20: Celebrate!

As immunologist Anthony Fauci was retiring from his leadership position at the U.S. National Institutes of Health (NIH), he was asked in an interview if he was discouraged that HIV/AIDS and COVID-19 were still with us after he spent fifty-four years at the NIH developing tests and drugs to fight the viruses (Healy, 2022). He reframes the question, explaining that he was responsible for the science, "and the science has been an overwhelming success story when it comes to therapy and prevention. So am I discouraged? No, I think it's cause for celebration!" (as cited in Healy, 2022, p. A8).

There is evidence that the most successful celebrations require a social gathering with food and drink that intentionally marks a positive life event (Brick, Wight, Bettman, Chartrand, & Fitzsimons, 2022). Those who participate in celebrations with these ingredients receive a reinforced sense of social support and the belief that their social network will be there for them (Brick et al., 2022). While you might not be able to throw a catered party every time there is something to celebrate, this might be helpful to remember the next time you're making decisions about which elements of a party are most important.

Richard DuFour, Rebecca DuFour, Robert Eaker, Thomas W. Many, and Mike Mattos (2016), authors of the seminal professional learning community guidebook *Learning by Doing*, explain how celebrations are a particularly powerful tool for communicating what you deem valuable and for building community. Celebrations allow you and your staff and colleagues to express appreciation and admiration for something valued. They also provide an opportunity to tell a story, and good stories are remembered and recalled. According to DuFour and his colleagues (2016), "Good stories appeal to both the head and the heart and are more compelling and convincing than data alone. . . . Good stories personify purpose and priorities" (p. 224). Stories put a human touch on the data or goal.

When your school culture embraces the power of celebration, everyone benefits, from students to school leaders. DuFour and his colleagues (2016) offer four suggestions for incorporating celebrations into the school culture.

1. **Explicitly state why you're celebrating:** Remind everyone involved how important celebration is to reinforce the school's mission and goals and keep improving.

2. **Make sure everyone can be involved:** Everyone should have the opportunity to recognize colleagues. If you as the principal are the only one who initiates celebration, the rest of the staff is less likely to respond.

3. **Clearly link recognition with the behavior or commitment you are reinforcing:** Think about what you want to encourage by recognizing a particular person or behavior.

4. **Create opportunities for many winners:** Give everyone a chance for recognition. Making celebration exclusive can be distracting and divisive. Recognition should be meaningful but attainable.

This tip offers I honor cards, a questionnaire for gathering information about celebrations in your school, and an accomplishments checklist to help you remember to celebrate yourself.

Tool: I Honor Cards

One of my favorite celebrations at school is our Honor Ceremony at the end of every school year. The very last thing we do as an entire staff is honor each other. On our last day together, I print out hundreds of what I call *I honor* cards that I distribute to staff at our final gathering together. I had experienced a similar celebration years before at a retreat, and the memory of the jubilance of the participants gave me the idea of a formal ceremony for my staff. Everyone has the opportunity to write honor cards to coworkers expressing gratitude for their work and honoring them for specific accomplishments or help. So many times we're not aware of how acknowledging even the smallest favors can have such an overwhelming effect on our psyche. Inevitably, every year I have to make a mad dash to the copier during the ceremony to print additional copies. You can use the simple card template in figure 4.7. The reproducible version on page 131 is set up to print eight at a time; just make sure you make plenty of copies! As Oprah Winfrey has said, "The more you praise and celebrate your life, the more there is in life to celebrate" (as quoted by Smith, 2016, p. 1).

I honor

Figure 4.7: I honor cards.

You certainly don't have to wait until the end of the year to do these honors. Recognizing staff one way or another, whether it is weekly, monthly, or even better, whenever, keeps the working environment positive and upbeat.

 **Tool: Celebrations Questionnaire**

When you celebrate, endorphins are released inside your body, and you feel a sense of euphoria (Carmody, 2015). If you fail to recognize your accomplishments, you are training your brain to believe that what you are doing is inconsequential. Celebrating with colleagues brings you closer and strengthens your networks. And when you recognize the success of others around you, they are bound to build upon the success and be motivated to continue on the path to even greater success (Carmody, 2015).

There are many options for celebrations at work with both students and staff. We continually recognize students and staff for individual and schoolwide accomplishments. As a leader, it's essential to foster a culture of celebration. Encourage teachers to celebrate their students, and celebrate with your staff. Even if coming up with ideas and organizing is not your forte, you can delegate that part to others. What's important is that you support celebrations throughout the school.

As a staff at school, we always celebrate the end of the week with breakfast treats. On Friday mornings, we can always count on some delicious goodies to signal the end of another week. We celebrate the end of the year with the Honor Ceremony as well as a softball game against a colleague's school. While we always manage to lose that game (and lose big), I harness that "winner" strength of mine, and we *all* celebrate together at the local watering hole. After all, we all won. We made it through another year together. When you take the time to celebrate even the smallest of wins, the world seems a lot brighter.

Could you celebrate more often in your school? The best way to find out is to talk to your staff. Here are some questions you can ask (DuFour et al., 2016).

- What gets publicly celebrated in our school?
- Who gets publicly celebrated in our school?
- Do our public celebrations reinforce our purpose and priorities?
- Have we created opportunities for lots of people in our organization to be recognized and celebrated?

- What celebrations are the most meaningful?
- What areas of celebrations could we improve upon?

These questions can be a handout or survey you give to your staff to help assess how celebrations are perceived in your school culture and find opportunities for improvement. A reproducible version is available on page 132.

Tool: Accomplishments Checklist

When you have accomplished a goal that you set for yourself, regardless of how large or small the goal, it is reason to celebrate. Your celebration doesn't have to be an extravagant gala; it can be as small as acknowledging to yourself that you accomplished that goal, you finished that task, you've realized your dream, you crossed the finish line, victory. Some accomplishments do warrant a larger celebration. The celebration is up to you. Informed by a list provided by eWomenNetwork (n.d.), an organization for women entrepreneurs, here are five reasons to celebrate.

1. **Your mindset:** When you celebrate something, dopamine is released into your brain and endorphins are released into your body (Carmody, 2015). This feels so great, and you want more. That is why celebrating small goals and achievements is important. That steady stream of dopamine helps feed into a positive mindset and motivates you to move on to other goals. Conversely, if you don't take the time to celebrate, you are robbing yourself of the sensation that accompanies success.

2. **Your confidence:** When you acknowledge what you have accomplished, you are more likely to continue to do what you are good at. Recognizing your strengths means you can better use them. Success breeds success, and the more you acknowledge success, the more likely you are to succeed both individually and as a member of a team.

3. **Your gratitude:** Take the time to acknowledge those who helped you achieve the goal and accomplish the tasks. It shows others how much you appreciate their time and effort. It also strengthens your network, and when people feel appreciated and acknowledged for their hard work, they will be more likely to contribute to enhancing the culture of the workplace.

4. **Your motivation:** Celebrating increases your motivation to set additional goals and move on to others that are somewhere on your action priority matrix. It proves you can attain your goals and motivates you to try to achieve goals that may seem like more of a stretch.

5. **Your inspiration:** When you share your celebrations with others, it inspires them to work toward their own goals. They see how the celebration positively affects your mindset, and they want that dopamine as well. Encourage others to celebrate and tell them that you want to be part of their celebrations.

Sometimes it's easier to see what others have accomplished when they are posted on social media, plastered on the front page of the sports section, or emblazoned on pages of entertainment media. Your accomplishments don't need to be widely publicized; they just need to be acknowledged.

Think about all that you have accomplished over a period of time and use the checklist (figure 4.8, page 128) to record small wins, ambitious goals, and the dates you accomplish them. When you enter the date, that's effectively checking them off your list. You can use more than one copy to keep track of various professional and personal goals. The following example shows how small wins enabled me to finish the manuscript for this book and ultimately receive a contract to publish it, which were two of my ambitious professional goals. Your small wins do not need to be directly related to your ambitious goals, but small wins usually contribute in some way to managing yourself, a prerequisite for ultimately attaining your more ambitious goals.

Date	Small Wins	Date	Ambitious Goals
July 2019	Conceptual framework	October 2021	Finished manuscript
December 2019	Outline and format	July 2022	Received book contract
March 2020	Introduction		
December 2021	Manuscript edited		
May 2022	Manuscript submitted to publisher		

Figure 4.8: Accomplishments checklist.

Visit **go.SolutionTree.com/leadership** *for a free reproducible version of this figure.*

Keep the professional checklist handy so that when you are meeting with your supervisor, rewriting your résumé, or interviewing for another position, you have a written record with which to articulate your accomplishments. Keep your personal checklist handy as well so that you are motivated to continue working toward your personal goals.

Summary and What's Next

Now that you have unpacked your bag, you have nearly reached the end of the book, and you have twenty tips and dozens of tools at your disposal. When you reflect on where you are on your journey toward more effective school leadership right now, you can pick and choose which tips and tools to load back into your bag. You may not need a few of them at any given time, and you may desperately need one or two, to which you'll want to have easy access. When you repack, store what you don't immediately need at the bottom of the pack and what you do need near the top and in those outer pockets. Your bag will be repacked differently at different times as you continually navigate the trail on your journey through each school day. Always carry what you need for survival, but make sure you pack a few items of "luxury" that you'll enjoy along the way.

Cognitive Reframing Worksheet

Event or situation:

What happened? (My original interpretation)	What were my thoughts and assumptions?	What was my schema?	What was my reaction?

Reframing scenario	Evidence: What are the facts?	What can I control?	What went right?

Lesson learned

Source: Adapted from Bolman, L., & Deal, T. (1997). Reframing organizations: Artistry, choice, and leadership (2nd ed.). San Francisco: Jossey-Bass; Kamphoff, C. (2018). Beyond grit: Ten powerful practices to gain the high-performance edge. Minneapolis, MN: Wise Ink Creative; Kos, B. (n.d.). Cognitive reframing—It's not about what happens to you, but how you frame it. Accessed at www.blazkos.com/cognitive-reframing/ on December 19, 2022; York-Barr, J., Sommers, W. A., Ghere, G. S., & Montie, J. (2006). Reflective practice to improve schools: An action guide for educators (2nd ed.). Thousand Oaks, CA: Corwin Press.

The Principal's Backpack © 2024 Solution Tree Press • SolutionTree.com
Visit **go.SolutionTree.com/leadership** to download this free reproducible.

Ladder of Inference Process

- **Data observed:**

- **Selected data:**

- **What the data mean:**

- **The problem:**

- **Why the problem exists:**

- **Action steps:**

Source: Adapted from Argyris, C. (1986). Skilled incompetence. Accessed at https://hbr.org/1986/09/skilled-incompetence on December 22, 2022; Senge, P. M., Kleiner, A., Roberts, C., Ross, R. B., & Smith, B. J. (1994). The fifth discipline fieldbook. New York: Currency.

I Honor Cards

I honor		I honor

I honor		I honor

I honor		I honor

I honor		I honor

The Principal's Backpack © 2024 Solution Tree Press • SolutionTree.com
Visit **go.SolutionTree.com/leadership** to download this free reproducible.

Celebrations Questionnaire

What gets publicly celebrated in our school?

Who gets publicly celebrated in our school?

Do our public celebrations reinforce our purpose and priorities?

Have we created opportunities for lots of people in our organization to be recognized and celebrated?

What celebrations are most meaningful?

What areas of celebrations could we improve upon?

Source: Adapted from DuFour, R., DuFour, R., Eaker, R., Many, T. W., & Mattos, M. (2016). Learning by doing: A handbook for Professional Learning Communities at Work® *(3rd ed.). Bloomington, IN: Solution Tree Press.*

Conclusion

As I mentioned in the introduction, as a principal, you never know what you are going to encounter in the wilderness on any given day. Unfortunately, these days, the news reports are filled with accounts of terrifying events at schools. While the events we encounter in our own wilderness are hopefully more about success stories than tragedy, there will certainly be challenges along your journey. This book would not have been written had I never tripped on the trail, dangled off a ledge, or been eaten alive by poison ivy. There were definitely some challenging times during my years as a principal when I coped with stress in an unhealthy manner. Realizing that I had to manage myself in a better way so that I could more effectively manage everything else, I researched and ultimately began using many of the self-management tips and tools described in this book. I also had a strong collegial network, including a coach, a super ally, and a critical friends group, that provided the support so I could successfully navigate the trail. As I sought and used tools for improving my self-management, I continually built up resilience and strengthened my leadership skills so that I was not only able to survive on my journey but also able to thrive.

The American Psychological Association (n.d.b) defines *resilience* as being able to adapt to difficult or challenging experiences, and be mentally, emotionally, and behaviorally flexible in order to adjust to external and internal demands. This is the definition of a principal's job. We meet challenges head on, we adapt, and we're flexible in order to meet demands. Challenges come in all sizes and shapes. These tips and tools are designed not just to take you through a rough patch or two; they are designed to help you stay clear of them as well, so use them before things get overchallenging.

As I finish writing this book, I'm in the seventh stage of Erik Erikson's (1950) eight stages of psychosocial growth, and in what Sara Lawrence-Lightfoot (2009) calls the *third chapter*. Erikson's (1950) penultimate stage, generativity versus stagnation, is described as the time in one's life to nurture and guide the next generation through teaching, writing, and service (McLeod, 2018; Sutton, 2020). Lawrence-Lightfoot's (2009) book *The Third Chapter* describes a time in people's lives when "they can look backward into the future; they can look back and journey home" (p. 66). Both stages describe a time in people's lives when they can look backward and forward at the same time. They look back on their experiences and lessons learned and look forward for ways of giving back.

As I thought about how I wanted to move into the third chapter of my life, I knew I wanted to pay my experiences forward. I had over two decades' worth of experience penciled in journals that I thought might be valuable in some way. In a discussion with my coach about my transition to life after a principal and my desire to somehow give back to the future generation of school leaders, we discussed the possibility of morphing those journal entries into a book. I then set a goal to publish a "thrival" book that helps guide school leaders as they navigate the wilderness of school leadership—in other words, a guide for not just surviving as a school leader but thriving.

There are a lot of tools embedded in the tips in this book. Not all tools will relate to your needs at any given time. You may find that some tools resonate with you now, while others may not be needed until sometime in the future. And some may never resonate with you.

To kick-start your exploration of self-management, I've included a list of tasks involving some of the strategies, inventories, and surveys from this book. Try them, practice using them, and make the ones that work best for you part of your self-management regimen. It would certainly be difficult to try all of them at once, so I encourage you to try whichever ones you feel you need to start with first. If there are other tools you feel you would like to start with, make your own list.

- Look at your calendar one month out and determine which projects, tasks, and assignments are due. Use the priority score worksheet from tip 1 (page 6) to determine your quick wins, major projects, fill-ins, and thankless tasks.

- Set a SMART goal for yourself (see tip 2, page 13). Look at your priorities and choose one goal that is specific, measurable, achievable, results oriented, and time bound.

- Think of a recent concern you or your staff have been wrestling with. Use the concern and influence organizer from tip 3 (page 17) to determine which areas of concern can be moved to the circle of influence and by what methods.

- Take Brené Brown's (2018) values assessment and fill out the values organizer from tip 4 (pag 23). This is one of the more difficult tasks, as it makes you really delve into your values and choose which are truly the ones that define you.

- Create an emergency procedures one-pager for yourself and your school (tip 6, page 40). There may be a district template that you can use, but make it relevant to your building and your student and staff population.

- Purchase a copy of the *StrengthsFinder* book (Rath, 2007), do the inventory, and use the strengths assessments organizer from tip 8 (page 48). Once you have discovered your strengths, read about how these strengths work to your benefit, and understand how they actually can work against you.

- Join a critical friends group (tip 9, page 52). Be the one who invites the principals to join you, teach them the process, and make it a scheduled meeting at least once per month so that you build trust with one another.

- Discover your balance in life by examining the different areas of your life through the paper plate activity from tip 12 (page 81). Pay attention to where you are out of balance and how you might change certain things in order to reach equanimity.

- Record yourself giving a speech—either to a live audience or in private—as part of using the right voice, right time worksheet from tip 14 (page 91). Listen to the tone of your voice, your inflection, and your vocabulary, and ensure that you are conveying the message you wish to convey.

- Write an email to your boss regarding a situation that has you stirred up or stressed out, using the well-dressed hamburger method from tip 14 (page 91) to include appropriate amounts of detail. Let the email sit, and then edit it so that the email you send has the information you want to convey, but sans the emotions.

- Take a recent stressful situation you encountered and use the cognitive reframing worksheet from tip 16 (page 108) to notice your patterns and thoughts. Challenge those thoughts and replace them with more positive ones.

- Journal, using the tools in tip 17 (page 114). Write down your thoughts, your questions, your trials and tribulations. What lessons you've learned and what you would like to learn more about. You can type these, but writing is cathartic, and having a special notebook with those thoughts is very meaningful.
- And finally, take a hike! Get outdoors and use the nature log from tip 19 (page 120), even if it means taking a walk around the block. Nature does wonders for the psyche, and if nothing else, relieves the stress of the job.

Try them out by yourself, with colleagues, or with staff. As you navigate your journey, continue to ask yourself, "Where do I want to go? What do I need to pack? Do I have the tools I need?" Hopefully your journey as principal will be as exhilarating and rewarding as it has been for me.

Stay strong, stay calm, and trek on!

References and Resources

Achuthappa, K. (2015, January 12). *Communicate better with the left-hand column technique.* Accessed at www.psd.gov.sg/challenge/ideas/work-better/communicate-better-with-the-left-hand-column-technique on January 20, 2023.

Ackerman, C. E. (2017, June 23). *Big Five personality traits: The OCEAN model explained.* Accessed at https://positivepsychology.com/big-five-personality-theory on January 17, 2023.

Adams, M. (2009). *Change your questions, change your life: 10 powerful tools for life and work.* San Francisco: Berrett-Koehler.

Advanced Neurotherapy. (2020, June 19). *4 reasons why walking outside benefits the brain.* Accessed at www.advancedneurotherapy.com/blog/2015/09/10/walking-outside-brain on December 22, 2022.

Akimbekov, N. S., & Razzaque, M. S. (2021). Laughter therapy: A humor-induced hormonal intervention to reduce stress and anxiety. *Current Research in Physiology, 2021*(4), 135–138. https://doi.org/10.1016/j.crphys.2021.04.002

American Institute of Stress. (n.d.). *What is stress?* Accessed at www.stress.org/daily-life on January 3, 2023.

American Psychological Association. (n.d.a). *Personality.* Accessed at www.apa.org/topics/personality on January 11, 2023.

American Psychological Association. (n.d.b). *Resilience.* Accessed at www.apa.org/topics/resilience on January 9, 2023.

American Psychological Association. (2018, November 1). *Stress effects on the body.* Accessed at www.apa.org/topics/stress/body on January 19, 2023.

Anderson, M. (n.d.). *Mind styles—Anthony Gregorc.* Accessed at https://facultyweb.cortland.edu/andersmd/learning/Gregorc.htm on November 11, 2022.

Appleby, J. (1998). *Becoming critical friends: Reflections of an NSRF coach.* Providence, RI: Annenberg Institute for School Reform at Brown University.

Argyris, C. (1986). *Skilled incompetence.* Accessed at https://hbr.org/1986/09/skilled-incompetence on December 22, 2022.

Arneson, S. (2014). *What your boss really wants from you: 15 insights to improve your relationship.* San Francisco: Berrett-Koehler.

Arrien, A. (1993). *The four-fold way: Walking the paths of the warrior, teacher, healer, and visionary.* New York: HarperCollins.

Ash, M. K. (1984). *Mary Kay on people management.* New York: Warner Books.

Atkins, S., & Murphy, K. (1994). Reflective practice. *Nursing Standard, 9*(45), 31–37.

Austin, D. (2023, January 15). *Laughter really is contagious—and that's good.* Accessed at www.washingtonpost.com/wellness/2023/01/15/laughing-is-contagious/ on June 23, 2023.

Australian Medical Association. (2022, June 8). *The importance of finding your happy place.* Accessed at https://amavic.com.au/news---resources/stethoscope/the-importance-of-finding-your-happy-place on January 29, 2023.

Baikie, K. A., & Wilhelm, K. (2018). *Emotional and physical health benefits of expressive writing.* Accessed at www.cambridge.org/core/journals/advances-in-psychiatric-treatment/article/emotional-and-physical-health-benefits-of-expressive-writing/ED2976A61F5DE56B46F07A1CE9EA9F9F on March 17, 2023.

Baptiste, B. (2002). *Journey into power: How to sculpt your ideal body, free your true self, and transform your life with yoga.* New York: Simon & Schuster.

Barker, S. (2019, September 2). *"Go for a walk and call me in the morning": How prescriptions for outdoors time are taking root.* Accessed at www.startribune.com/go-for-a-walk-and-call-me-in-the-morning-how-prescriptions-for-outdoors-time-are-taking-root/558703192 on January 6, 2023.

Basavaraddi, I. V. (n.d.). *Yoga: Its origin, history and development.* Accessed at https://yoga.ayush.gov.in/Yoga-History on February 1, 2023.

Beard, A. (2014). *Leading with humor.* Accessed at https://hbr.org/2014/05/leading-with-humor on January 18, 2023.

Berbari, G. (2018, July 2). *The easiest workout to try for less stress and more happiness, according to science.* Accessed at www.elitedaily.com/p/what-is-mindful-movement-science-says-this-type-of-workout-is-easy-way-to-release-stress-9648181 on January 3, 2023.

Birt, J. (2022, June 23). *What are 4 working styles? (And how to learn yours).* Accessed at www.indeed.com/career-advice/career-development/working-styles on October 19, 2022.

Bolman, L., & Deal, T. (1997). *Reframing organizations: Artistry, choice, and leadership* (2nd ed.). San Francisco: Jossey-Bass.

Bommelje, R. (2016, December 29). *12 blocks to listening.* Accessed at www.listeningpays.com/12-blocks-listening on December 2, 2022.

Bommelje, R. (2017, February 27). *Drucker's rule.* Accessed at www.listeningpays.com/druckers-rule/ on June 29, 2023.

Borges, P. (2019, July 21). *Angeles Arrien – Connecting to the wilderness within* [Video file]. Accessed at www.youtube.com /watch?v=a9IpsK11z_s&ab_channel=PhilBorges on November 14, 2022.

Bradberry, T. (2014, February 6). *How successful people stay calm.* Accessed at www.forbes.com/sites/travisbradberry/2014/02/06/how-successful-people-stay-calm on November 30, 2022.

Brick, D. J., Wight, K. G., Bettman, J. R., Chartrand, T. L., & Fitzsimons, G. J. (2022). Celebrate good times: How celebrations increase perceived social support. *Journal of Public Policy and Marketing, 42*(2). https://doi.org/10.1177/07439156221145696

Brook, J., & Brewerton, P. (2016). *Optimize your strengths: Use your leadership strengths to get the best out of you and your team.* Chichester, United Kingdom: Wiley.

Brooke, C. (2016, September 6). *How to build psychological safety on your team.* Accessed at www.business2community.com/human-resources/build-psychological-safety-team-01648729 on November 25, 2022.

Brown, B. (2018). *Dare to lead: Brave work. Tough conversations. Whole hearts.* New York: Random House.

Brunnermeier, M. K, Papakonstantinou, F., & Parker, J. A. (2008, August). *An economic model of the planning fallacy* (NBER working paper no. 14228). Accessed at www.nber.org/system/files/working_papers/w14228/w14228.pdf on November 8, 2022.

Buckingham, M., & Clifton, D. O. (2001). *Now, discover your strengths.* New York: Free Press.

Burgin, T. (2022, July 18). *What is yoga?* Accessed at www.yogabasics.com/learn/yoga-101-an-introduction/what-is-yoga/ on February 8, 2023.

BWell Health Promotion. (n.d.). *What are the effects of caffeine?* Accessed at www.brown.edu/campus-life/health/services/promotion/content/what-are-effects-caffeine on March 15, 2023.

Cabral, C. (2021, January 7). *The grit test: Your score and what it means.* Accessed at www.shortform.com/blog/grit-test on January 26, 2023.

Carmody, B. (2015, August 12). *3 reasons celebrating your many accomplishments is critical to your success.* Accessed at www.inc.com/bill-carmody/3-reasons-celebrating-your-many-accomplishments-is-critical-to-your-success.html on January 6, 2023.

Carpenter, S. (2001). *A new reason for keeping a diary: Research offers intriguing evidence on why expressive writing boosts health.* Accessed at www.apa.org/monitor/sep01/keepdiary on February 25, 2023.

Celestine, N. (2019, June 7). *9 strengths finding tests and assessments you can do today.* Accessed at https://positivepsychology.com/strength-finding-tests on November 22, 2022.

Centers for Medicare and Medicaid Services. (n.d.). *Guidance for performing root cause analysis (RCA) with performance improvement projects (PIPs).* Accessed at www.cms.gov/medicare/provider-enrollment-and-certification/qapi/downloads/guidanceforrca.pdf on October 31, 2022.

Chamorro-Premuzic, T. (2017). *Could your personality derail your career?* Accessed at https://hbr.org/2017/09/could-your-personality-derail-your-career on January 24, 2023.

Cherry, K. (2022a). *Understanding the optimism bias.* Accessed at www.verywellmind.com/what-is-the-optimism-bias-2795031 on November 2, 2022.

Cherry, K. (2022b). *What are heuristics? These mental shortcuts can help people make decisions more efficiently.* Accessed at www.verywellmind.com/what-is-a-heuristic-2795235 on November 2, 2022.

Cherry, K. (2022c). *What are the big 5 personality traits? Openness, conscientiousness, extraversion, agreeableness, and neuroticism.* Accessed at www.verywellmind.com/the-big-five-personality-dimensions-2795422 on November 11, 2022.

Cherry, K. (2022d). *What leads to bad decision-making.* Accessed at www.verywellmind.com/why-you-make-bad-decisions-2795489 on November 2, 2022.

Chukwuemeka, E. S. (2022, April 9). *Differences between a law and a policy.* Accessed at https://bscholarly.com/differences-between-a-law-and-a-policy on January 25, 2023.

Clinton, H. R. (2014). *Hard choices.* New York: Simon & Schuster.

Conzemius, A., & O'Neill, J. (2014). *The handbook for SMART school teams: Revitalizing best practices for collaboration* (2nd ed.). Bloomington, IN: Solution Tree Press.

Costa, A. L., & Kallick, B. (1993, October 1). *Through the lens of a critical friend*. Accessed at www.ascd.org/el/articles/through-the-lens-of-a-critical-friend on November 25, 2022.

Covey, S. R. (1989). *The 7 habits of highly effective people: Powerful lessons in personal change*. New York: Simon & Schuster.

Covey, S. R. [@StephenRCovey]. (2021, April 6). *"The key is not to prioritize what's on your schedule, but to schedule your priorities."—Stephen R. Covey #Schedule #Priorities* [Image attached] [Tweet]. Accessed at https://twitter.com/stephenrcovey/status/1379396050507735044?lang=en on October 19, 2022.

Creatively Communicate. (2021, September 3). *Approachable vs. credible voice* [Video file]. Accessed at www.youtube.com/watch?v=4CUOhoAD_Gc on December 5, 2022.

Creighton, S. (2022, October 10). *Kaoru Ishikawa: The man who invented the fishbone diagram*. Accessed at https://blog.lifeqisystem.com/kaoru-ishikawa on January 10, 2023.

Cross, R., & Thomas, R. J. (2011). *Managing yourself: A smarter way to network*. Accessed at https://hbr.org/2011/07/managing-yourself-a-smarter-way-to-network on November 24, 2022.

Crowley, K., & Elster, K. (2010). *Working for you isn't working for me: How to get ahead when your boss holds you back*. New York: Penguin.

Cuevas, J. (2015, November). Is learning styles–based instruction effective? A comprehensive analysis of recent research on learning styles. *Theory and Research in Education, 13*(3), 308–333.

Curley, B. (2019, August 10). *Why short-term stress and anxiety can actually be good for you*. Accessed at www.healthline.com/health-news/why-stress-and-anxiety-arent-always-bad-for-you on January 6, 2023.

Cutright, A. (n.d.). *Importance of joining a professional organization*. Accessed at https://abrid.alabama.gov/about-interior-design/importance-of-joining-a-professional-organization on November 22, 2022.

Damiano, M. (2020, June 4). *The profound effects of nature on our brain health*. Accessed at www.aboutmybrain.com/blog/the-profound-effects-of-nature-on-our-brain-health on January 6, 2023.

Davis, T. (2021, January 13). *6 science-based self-compassion exercises*. Accessed at www.psychologytoday.com/us/blog/click-here-happiness/202101/6-science-based-self-compassion-exercises on December 21, 2022.

DePaul, K. (2022, January 4). *This is why you keep missing deadlines*. Accessed at https://hbr.org/2022/01/this-is-why-you-keep-missing-deadlines on November 8, 2022.

Dibdin, E. (2022, March 31). *The mental health benefits of journaling*. Accessed at https://psychcentral.com/lib/the-health-benefits-of-journaling on December 22, 2022.

Doran, G. T. (1981, November). There's a S.M.A.R.T. way to write management's goals and objectives. *Management Review, 70*(11), 35–36.

Drexel University Counseling Center. (n.d.). *Bull's eye values exercise*. Accessed at https://drexel.edu/~/media/files/studentlife/counseling/bulls%20eye%20values%20exercise.ashx?la=en on March 31, 2023.

Driver, M. (2011). *Coaching positively: Lessons for coaches from positive psychology*. New York: Open University Press.

Drucker, P. (2008). *Managing oneself*. Boston: Harvard Business Press.

Duckworth, A. (2016). *Grit: The power of passion and perseverance*. New York: Simon & Schuster.

DuFour, R., DuFour, R., Eaker, R., Many, T. W., & Mattos, M. (2016). *Learning by doing: A handbook for Professional Learning Communities at Work* (3rd ed.). Bloomington, IN: Solution Tree Press.

Duhigg, C. (2016, February 25). *What Google learned from its quest to build the perfect team*. Accessed at https://centre.upeace.org/wp-content/uploads/2020/09/7.1-what-google-learnt.pdf on January 25, 2023.

Dweck, C. (2016). *Mindset: The new psychology of success* (Updated ed.). New York: Ballantine Books.

Eastridge, S. (2017, January 10). *Signs and symptoms of burnout: Learning about how the work we do affects us*. Accessed at https://slideplayer.com/slide/13250647 on November 20, 2022.

Edmondson, A. C. (2004). Psychological safety, trust, and learning in organizations: A group-level lens. In R. M. Kramer & K. S. Cook (Eds.), *Trust and distrust in organizations: Dilemmas and approaches* (pp. 239–272). New York: Russell Sage Foundation.

Edmondson, A. C., & Lei, Z. (2014). *Psychological safety: The history, renaissance, and future of an interpersonal construct*. Accessed at www.researchgate.net/publication/275070993_Psychological_Safety_The_History_Renaissance_and_Future_of_an_Interpersonal_Construct/link/55b7f06f08ae092e96587280/download on November 21, 2022.

Eisenhower. (n.d.). *Introducing the Eisenhower matrix*. Accessed at www.eisenhower.me/eisenhower-matrix on April 4, 2023.

Erikson, E. H. (1950). *Childhood and society*. New York: Norton.

Esposito, L. (2019, June 4). *Boundaries: A guide to making essential life decisions: Learning when to say yes and when to say no to others and yourself*. Accessed at www.psychologytoday.com/us/blog/anxiety-zen/201906/boundaries-guide-making-essential-life-decisions on December 6, 2022.

eWomenNetwork. (n.d.). *5 reasons why you should celebrate your accomplishments.* Accessed at www.ewomennetwork.com/blog/ewomennetwork-1/post/5-reasons-why-you-should-celebrate-your-accomplishments-263#blog_content on January 6, 2023.

Fischetti, J., & Imig, S. (2015, December 9). *Why is being a school principal one of the most dangerous jobs in the country?* Accessed at http://theconversation.com/why-is-being-a-school-principal-one-of-the-most-dangerous-jobs-in-the-country-52004 on January 3, 2023.

Florentine, S. (2016, January 20). *6 tips to improve your self-promotion skills.* Accessed at www.cio.com/article/3024416/6-tips-to-improve-your-self-promotion-skills.html on December 7, 2022.

Flynn, J. (2022, October 20). *20 vital smartphone usage statistics [2022]: Facts, data, and trends on mobile use in the U.S.* Accessed at www.zippia.com/advice/smartphone-usage-statistics on January 5, 2023.

Foland, R. (2017, May 25). *5 ways to find the right tone when speaking.* Accessed at www.influencive.com/5-ways-find-right-tone-speaking on December 5, 2022.

Frankel, D. (Director). (2006). *The devil wears Prada* [Film]. Fox 2000 Pictures; Wendy Finerman Productions; Dune Entertainment.

Gabarro, J. J., & Kotter, J. P. (1993). Managing your boss. *Harvard Business Review, 71*(3), 150–157.

Gaines, J. (2020, November 17). *The philosophy of ikigai: 3 examples about finding purpose.* Accessed at https://positivepsychology.com/ikigai on September 21, 2022.

Gallo, A. (2016, March 17). *How to disagree with someone more powerful than you.* Accessed at https://hbr.org/2016/03/how-to-disagree-with-someone-more-powerful-than-you on January 23, 2023.

Gibson, J. M. (2020, November 26). *Things are dark right now, but a little laughter is genuinely good for your well-being.* Accessed at www.fastcompany.com/90579863/things-are-dark-right-now-but-a-little-laughter-is-genuinely-good-for-your-well-being on December 21, 2022.

Goldberg, L. R. (1990). An alternative "description of personality": The Big-Five factor structure. *Journal of Personality and Social Psychology, 59*(6), 1216–1229.

Gomes, M. (2018, April 25). *Five reasons to take a break from screens.* Accessed at https://greatergood.berkeley.edu/article/item/five_reasons_to_take_a_break_from_screens on January 6, 2023.

Gordon, A. M. (2020, February 12). *In defense of the Myers-Briggs: A comprehensive counter to anti-MBTI hype.* Accessed at www.psychologytoday.com/us/blog/my-brothers-keeper/202002/in-defense-the-myers-briggs on January 11, 2023.

Gregorc, A. F. (1982). *An adult's guide to style.* Columbia, CT: Gregorc Associates.

Gregorc, A. F. (2020, February 4). *On the power of style information.* Accessed at www.anthonyfgregorc.com/post/10-ways-to-start-loving-yourself-the-way-you-deserve-to-be-loved on January 10, 2023.

Grinder, M. (2007). *The elusive obvious: The science of nonverbal communication.* Battle Ground, WA: Michael Grinder & Associates.

Grinder, M. (2020). *Cross-cultural communication: Getting the elephant out—Credibility and approachability.* Accessed at https://michaelgrinder.com/getting-the-elephant-out on March 10, 2023.

Haavik, E. (2019, April 18). *St. Paul police: 2nd-grader brought loaded gun to school.* Accessed at www.kare11.com/article/news/local/st-paul-police-2nd-grader-brought-loaded-gun-to-school/89-39eebae4-4b09-4ea8-a88c-9d7066624f77 on January 25, 2023.

Hardie Grant Books. (2019). *Pocket Maya Angelou wisdom: Inspirational quotes and wise words from a legendary icon.* New York: Author.

Harrell, E. (2021). *Life's work: An interview with Alex Honnold.* Accessed at https://hbr.org/2021/05/lifes-work-an-interview-with-alex-honnold on March 17, 2023.

Harris, R. (2009). *Your values.* Accessed at https://img1.wsimg.com/blobby/go/15bc8817-f2c2-4fe5-9665-4e247f46a902/downloads/ACT%20Bullseye.pdf?ver=1618327659995 on April 3, 2023.

Harvard Health Publishing. (2021, June 12). *Yoga for better mental health.* Accessed at www.health.harvard.edu/staying-healthy/yoga-for-better-mental-health on December 1, 2022.

Harvard University Stress & Development Lab. (n.d.). *Positive reframing and examining the evidence.* Accessed at https://sdlab.fas.harvard.edu/cognitive-reappraisal/positive-reframing-and-examining-evidence on January 23, 2023.

Hatfield, R. (n.d.). *Critical friends: A process built on reflection.* Accessed at www.dr-hatfield.com/educ216/CriticalFriends.pdf on November 25, 2022.

Hayes, S. (n.d.). *How to find your life purpose.* Accessed at https://stevenchayes.com/how-to-find-your-life-purpose on November 17, 2022.

Headspace. (n.d.). *Breathing exercises to reduce stress.* Accessed at www.headspace.com/meditation/breathing-exercises on January 3, 2023.

Healy, M. (2022, December 25). Fauci still celebrating science. *Minneapolis Star Tribune,* p. A8.

Heen, S., & Stone, D. (2014). *Find the coaching in criticism.* Accessed at https://hbr.org/2014/01/find-the-coaching-in-criticism on January 23, 2023.

Herrmann, N. (1996). *The whole brain business book.* New York: McGraw-Hill.

Higgins, M., & Thorpe, J. R. (2020, July 31). *Experts explain why unplugging from tech really is that good for you*. Accessed at www.bustle.com/wellness/188786-5-scientifically-proven-benefits-to-unplugging-from-technology on January 6, 2023.

Hogan, R., & Hogan, J. (2001). Assessing leadership: A view from the dark side. *International Journal of Selection and Assessment, 9*(1–2), 40–51.

Holt, L. (Anchor). (2023, January 9). NBC nightly news (Season 2023, Episode 9) [TV series episode]. In M. Rafferty (Executive Producer), *NBC nightly news with Lester Holt*. NBC News Productions.

Hopkins, G. (2009, December 1). *Marriage, family, and the principalship: Making it all work—Part 1*. Accessed at www.educationworld.com/a_admin/admin/admin478_a.shtml on January 3, 2023.

Hord, S. M., Roussin, J. L., & Sommers, W. A. (2010). *Guiding professional learning communities: Inspiration, challenge, surprise, and meaning*. Thousand Oaks, CA: Corwin Press.

Houston, E. (2019, April 9). *What is goal setting and how to do it well*. Accessed at https://positivepsychology.com/goal-setting on November 8, 2022.

Howard, R. (2021). *Cultivating a growth mindset*. Accessed at www.leadingagile.com/2021/06/how-to-cultivate-a-growth-mindset on December 19, 2022.

Hunter, M. R., Gillespie, B. W., & Chen, S. Y.-P. (2019). *Urban nature experiences reduce stress in the context of daily life based on salivary biomarkers*. Accessed at www.frontiersin.org/articles/10.3389/fpsyg.2019.00722/full on January 6, 2023.

Ian. (2022, October 28). *10 founders who went from failure to successful companies*. Accessed at https://press.farm/startups-fail-founders-bounced-back-and-build-successful-company on December 19, 2022.

Indeed. (n.d.). *How to celebrate success in the workplace*. Accessed at www.indeed.com/hire/c/info/celebrating-success on December 23, 2022.

India.co.in. (n.d.). *History of yoga*. Accessed at www.india.co.in/info/health/yoga/history-of-yoga on February 7, 2023.

Inglis-Arkell, E. (2015, November 16). *How a scientist's least important discovery became his most famous*. Accessed at https://gizmodo.com/how-a-scientists-least-important-discovery-became-his-m-1742623371 on January 19, 2023.

Intelligent Change. (n.d.). *Benefits of journaling: The science and philosophy behind keeping a diary*. Accessed at www.intelligentchange.com/blogs/read/benefits-of-journaling on February 24, 2023.

International Sports Sciences Association. (2021, July 1). *Top habits of stress-resilient people (that you'll want too)*. Accessed at www.issaonline.com/blog/post/top-habits-of-stress-resilient-people-that-youll-want-too on March 7, 2023.

Ishikawa, K. (1968). *Guide to quality control*. Tokyo: Union of Japanese Scientists and Engineers.

Johnson, W. (2014, December 15). *Managing up without sucking up*. Accessed at https://hbr.org/2014/12/managing-up-without-sucking-up on November 25, 2022.

Jones, H. (2018, July 21). *The trouble with vacations*. Accessed at www.nytimes.com/2018/07/21/opinion/sunday/trouble-vacations.html on January 5, 2023.

Kabat-Zinn, J. (1990). *Full catastrophe living: Using the wisdom of your body and mind to face stress, pain, and illness*. New York: Random House.

Kamphoff, C. (2018). *Beyond grit: Ten powerful practices to gain the high-performance edge*. Minneapolis, MN: Wise Ink Creative.

Kataria, M. (2018). *Laughter yoga: Daily laughter practices for health and happiness*. Gurugram, India: Ebury Press.

Keirsey, D. (1998). *Please understand me II: Temperament, character, intelligence*. Del Mar, CA: Prometheus Nemesis.

Kelly, K. R., & Jugovic, H. (2001). Concurrent validity of the online version of the Keirsey Temperament Sorter II. *Journal of Career Assessment, 9*(1), 49–59.

Kemp, N. (Host). (2020, January 19). Rock star neuroscientist, Ken Mogi's 5 pillars of ikigai [Audio podcast episode]. In *The ikigai podcast*. Accessed at https://ikigaitribe.com/podcasts/podcast06 on November 16, 2022.

King, B. J. (2008). *Pressure is a privilege: Lessons I've learned from life and the Battle of the Sexes*. New York: LifeTime.

Kos, B. (n.d.). *Cognitive reframing—It's not about what happens to you, but how you frame it*. Accessed at www.blazkos.com/cognitive-reframing/ on December 19, 2022.

Kross, E. (2021). *Chatter: The voice in our head, why it matters, and how to harness it*. New York: Crown.

Laughter Yoga International. (n.d.). *What is laughter yoga and how can it help you?* Accessed at https://laughteryoga.org/about-laughter-yoga on December 21, 2022.

Lawrence-Lightfoot, S. (2009). *The third chapter: Passion, risk, and adventure in the 25 years after 50*. New York: Farrar, Straus & Giroux.

Levitt, S. (2015, July 21). *5 tips to find your own happy place*. Accessed at www.livehappy.com/self/5-tips-to-find-your-own-happy-place on December 18, 2022.

Li, Q. (2018, May 1). *'Forest bathing' is great for your health. Here's how to do it*. Accessed at https://time.com/5259602/japanese-forest-bathing on January 26, 2023.

Lima, A. C. E. S., & de Castro, L. N. (2019). *TECLA: A temperament and psychological type prediction framework from Twitter data*. Accessed at www.ncbi.nlm.nih.gov/pmc/articles/PMC6413941/ on January 17, 2023.

Lindberg, S. (2019, January 3). *Eustress: The good stress*. Accessed at www.healthline.com/health/eustress on November 29, 2022.

Lindsey, R. B., Nuri-Robins, K., Terrell, R. D., & Lindsey, D. B. (2019). *Cultural proficiency: A manual for school leaders* (4th ed.). Thousand Oaks, CA: Corwin Press.

Litsa, T. (2018, April 2). *How to explore your real potential by testing your limits.* Accessed at https://medium.com/swlh/how-to-explore-your-real-potential-by-testing-your-limits-ce56af6bfcf9 on December 6, 2022.

Locke, E. A., & Latham, G. P. (2019). The development of goal setting theory: A half century retrospective. *Motivation Science, 5*(2), 93–105.

Loevinger, N. J. (n.d.). *If not now, when? Rashi understands Moses' final words to the people as an expression of Hillel's philosophy of self-examination.* Accessed at www.myjewishlearning.com/article/if-not-now-when on December 21, 2022.

Louv, R. (2005). *Last child in the woods: Saving our children from nature-deficit disorder.* Chapel Hill, NC: Algonquin.

Louv, R. (2011). *The nature principle: Reconnecting with life in a virtual age.* Chapel Hill, NC: Algonquin.

Lundgren, T., Luoma, J. B., Dahl, J., Strosahl, K., & Melin, L. (2012). *The bull's-eye values survey: A psychometric evaluation.* Accessed at www.researchgate.net/publication/232239325_The_Bull's-Eye_Values_Survey_A_Psychometric_Evaluation on September 21, 2022.

Mackay, H. (2005). *Swim with the sharks without being eaten alive: Outsell, outmanage, outmotivate, and outnegotiate your competition.* New York: HarperCollins.

Mackay, H. (2022, October 23). *Harvey Mackay: Hold yourself accountable by publicly announcing your goals.* Accessed at www.startribune.com/harvey-mackay-hold-yourself-accountable-by-publicly-announcing-your-goals/600218342/ on January 10, 2023.

MacMillan, A. (2022, August 25). *Good stress: What are the benefits?* Accessed at www.health.com/condition/stress/5-weird-ways-stress-can-actually-be-good-for-you on November 29, 2022.

Madsen, S. (2020, May 26). *The key to leadership development is critical reflection.* Accessed at www.forbes.com/sites/forbescoachescouncil/2020/05/26/the-key-to-leadership-development-is-critical-reflection/?sh=d38c4f73d7db on March 3, 2023.

Marewski, J. N., & Gigerenzer, G. (2012). Heuristic decision making in medicine. *Dialogues in Clinical Neuroscience, 14*(1), 77–89.

Matthews, G. (2020, February). *Goals research summary.* Accessed at www.dominican.edu/sites/default/files/2020-02/gailmatthews-harvard-goals-researchsummary.pdf on November 4, 2022.

Mawri, S. (2022, August 23). *Beware high levels of cortisol, the stress hormone.* Accessed at www.premierhealth.com/your-health/articles/women-wisdom-wellness-/beware-high-levels-of-cortisol-the-stress-hormone on March 10, 2023.

Mayo Clinic. (2021, July 29). *Stress relief from laughter? It's no joke.* Accessed at www.mayoclinic.org/healthy-lifestyle/stress-management/in-depth/stress-relief/art-20044456 on January 5, 2023.

McAfee, B. (2011). *Full voice: The art and practice of vocal presence.* San Francisco: Berrett-Koehler.

McArthur, P. W. (2014). Ladder of inference. In D. Coghlan & M. Brydon-Miller (Eds.), *The SAGE encyclopedia of action research* (pp. 486–488). Thousand Oaks, CA: SAGE.

McKay, M., Davis, M., & Fanning, P. (2009). *Messages: The communication skills book* (3rd ed.). Oakland, CA: New Harbinger.

McLeod, S. (2018). *Erik Erikson's stages of psychosocial development.* Accessed at www.simplypsychology.org/Erik-Erikson.html on December 30, 2022.

Meier, J. (n.d.). *Strengths and weaknesses vs. personality profiles.* Accessed at https://sourcesofinsight.com/strengths-and-weaknesses-vs-personality-profiles on January 29, 2023.

Melnychuk, M. C., Dockree, P. M., O'Connell, R. G., Murphy, P. R., Balsters, J. H., & Robertson, I. H. (2018). Coupling of respiration and attention via the locus coeruleus: Effects of meditation and pranayama. *Psychophysiology, 55*(9), e13091.

MentalHelp.net. (n.d.). *Types of stressors (eustress vs. distress).* Accessed at www.mentalhelp.net/stress/types-of-stressors-eustress-vs-distress on January 3, 2023.

Miglianico, M., Dubreuil, P., Miquelon, P., Bakker, A. B., & Martin-Krumm, C. (2020). Strength use in the workplace: A literature review. *Journal of Happiness Studies, 21*(2), 737–764.

Mind Tools. (n.d.a). *Successful delegation: Using the power of other people's help.* Accessed at www.mindtools.com/pages/article/newLDR_98.htm on October 27, 2022.

Mind Tools. (n.d.b). *The action priority matrix: Making the most of your opportunities.* Accessed at www.mindtools.com/pages/article/newHTE_95.htm on October 3, 2022.

Mind Tools. (n.d.c). *The wheel of life.* Accessed at www.mindtools.com/ak6jd6w/the-wheel-of-life on January 3, 2023.

Mindful Staff. (2022, August 31). *The science of mindfulness: The ultimate guide to the research on the effects of mindfulness and meditation for our health, psyche, and overall quality of life.* Accessed at www.mindful.org/the-science-of-mindfulness on March 6, 2023.

MindManager. (n.d.). *Guide to mental mapping.* Accessed at www.mindmanager.com/en/features/mental-map on September 30, 2022.

Mogi, K. (2018). *Awakening your ikigai: How the Japanese wake up to joy and purpose every day.* New York: The Experiment.

Moss, T. (2020). *Angels and tahina: 18 lessons from hiking the Israel Trail.* Jerusalem, Israel: Goat Path.

MoveMindfullyConnect. (2021, January 6). *Kathy welcome* [Video file]. Accessed at www.youtube.com/watch?v=f69TkhABγEE on January 3, 2023.

Mramor, N. (n.d.). *Five ways to find your happy place.* Accessed at https://drnancyonline.com/five-ways-to-find-your-happy-place on January 5, 2023.

Myers & Briggs Foundation. (n.d.). *MBTI basics.* Accessed at www.myersbriggs.org/my-mbti-personality-type/mbti-basics/home.htm on January 11, 2023.

Nardi, D. (2011). *Neuroscience of personality: Brain savvy insights for all types of people.* Los Angeles: Radiance House.

National Heart, Lung, and Blood Institute. (2022, March 24). *What are sleep deprivation and deficiency?* Accessed at www.nhlbi.nih.gov/health/sleep-deprivation on March 15, 2023.

Neff, K. (2011). *Self-compassion: Stop beating yourself up and leave insecurity behind.* New York: HarperCollins.

Ni, P. (2012, February 25). *Seven ways to say "no" and keep good relations: Keep your boundaries without feeling guilty.* Accessed at www.psychologytoday.com/us/blog/communication-success/201202/seven-ways-say-no-and-keep-good-relations?collection=88636 on December 6, 2022.

Nittle, N. (2022, February 4). *Principals are expected to be the "rock" of schools, but they're stressed out.* Accessed at https://19thnews.org/2022/02/school-principals-women-covid-job-stress on November 29, 2022.

Noor, M. M., & Shafee, A. (2021). The role of critical friends in action research: A framework for design and implementation. *Practitioner Research, 3,* 1–33.

Ondreicsik, A. (2020, February 19). *Use a fishbone diagram template online: Free guide.* Accessed at https://conceptboard.com/blog/fishbone-diagram-template-example on October 31, 2022.

One Billion Rising. (2015). *1 Billion Rising events.* Accessed at www.onebillionrising.org/events/v-day-dance-empowering-laughter-yoga-at-media-borough-hall-mediapa-philadelphia-area on February 8, 2023.

Pantic, I. (2014). *Online social networking and mental health.* Accessed at www.ncbi.nlm.nih.gov/pmc/articles/PMC4183915 on January 28, 2023.

Park, Y., Fritz, C., & Jex, S. M. (2011). Relationships between work-home segmentation and psychological detachment from work: The role of communication technology use at home. *Journal of Occupational Health Psychology, 16*(4), 457–467.

Parker, N. (2019, April 21). *Feeling stressed out? Get some help from Mother Nature.* Accessed at www.startribune.com/feeling-stressed-out-get-some-help-from-mother-nature/508772712 on January 6, 2023.

Pekel, K., Kemper, S., Parr, A., Evenson, A., & Zhao, Y. (2022). *Report of findings from the first Biennial Minnesota Principals Survey 2022.* Accessed at https://drive.google.com/file/d/1xg3u7iwwgoymtN26Ty6Nyw0T1W8fdFcY/view on February 3, 2023.

Pennebaker, J. W., Kiecolt-Glaser, J. K., & Glaser, R. (1988). Disclosure of traumas and immune function: Health implications for psychotherapy. *Journal of Consulting and Clinical Psychology, 56*(2), 239–245.

Pennsylvania Adult Education Resources. (2017, December 13). *Overview of critical friends model.* Accessed at www.paadultedresources.org/wp-content/uploads/2016/10/Overview-of-Critical-Friends-Model-12-13-17.pdf on November 25, 2022.

Perlmutter, D. D. (2007, January 5). *Managing up.* Accessed at www.chronicle.com/article/managing-up on November 28, 2022.

Perrine, J. (2019, May 7). *The benefits of understanding personality types in the workplace.* Accessed at www.allthingsadmin.com/benefits-understanding-personality-types-workplace on January 11, 2023.

Raab, E. L. (2020, April 20). *Laughter really is great medicine: We grow more resilient through positive emotion.* Accessed at https://erinraab.medium.com/laughter-really-is-great-medicine-we-grow-more-resilient-through-positive-emotion-ff4d1fda9f93 on December 20, 2022.

Rampton, J. (2017, November 6). *Stepping away from technology is possible. Research says it's needed to recharge your motivation.* Accessed at www.inc.com/john-rampton/stepping-away-from-technology-is-possible-research-says-its-needed-to-recharge-your-motivation.html on December 22, 2022.

Rash, J. (2019, November 28). *12 listening blocks that are ruining your conversations.* Accessed at https://jasonrash.medium.com/12-listening-blocks-that-are-ruining-your-convers-36316d236028 on January 3, 2023.

Rath, T. (2007). *Strengthsfinder 2.0.* New York: Gallup Press.

Ravishankar, R., & Alpaio, K. (2022, August 30). *5 ways to set more achievable goals.* Accessed at https://hbr.org/2022/08/5-ways-to-set-more-achievable-goals on October 21, 2022.

Rehn, A. (2016, April 11). *The 20-minute rule for great public speaking—On attention spans and keeping focus.* Accessed at https://medium.com/the-art-of-keynoting/the-20-minute-rule-for-great-public-speaking-on-attention-spans-and-keeping-focus-7370cf06b636 on December 5, 2022.

Reio, T. G., & Wiswell, A. K. (2006, June). An examination of the factor structure and construct validity of the Gregorc Style Delineator. *Educational and Psychological Measurement, 66*(3), 489–501.

Riley, P. (2015). *The Australian principal occupational health, safety and wellbeing survey.* Accessed at www.principalhealth.org/reports/2015_Final_Report.pdf on January 3, 2023.

Riley, P. (2018). *The Australian principal occupational health, safety and wellbeing survey: 2017 data.* Accessed at www.principalhealth.org/reports/2017_Report_AU_FINAL.pdf on January 3, 2023.

Robbins, M., & Ross, C. (2020). Keirsey Temperament Sorter. In V. Zeigler-Hill & T. K. Shackelford (Eds.), *Encyclopedia of personality and individual differences* (pp. 2518–2521). Cham, Switzerland: Springer Nature.

Robbins, T. (n.d.). *Wheel of life: Close the gaps from where you are to where you want to be.* Accessed at https://core.tonyrobbins.com/wheel-of-life-4 on January 3, 2023.

Roberts, L. M., Spreitzer, G., Dutton, J. E., Quinn, R. E., Heaphy, E. D., & Barker, B. (2005, January). *How to play to your strengths.* Accessed at https://hbr.org/2005/01/how-to-play-to-your-strengths on November 25, 2022.

Robinson, N. (2018, February 20). *School principals at higher risk of burnout, depression due to workplace stress, survey finds.* Accessed at www.abc.net.au/news/2018-02-21/principals-overwhelmed-by-workplace-stress-acu-survey-finds/9468078 on January 3, 2023.

Ross, J. (2020, June 19). *4 reasons why walking outside benefits the brain.* Accessed at www.advancedneurotherapy.com/blog/2015/09/10/walking-outside-brain on January 6, 2023.

Ross, R., & Roberts, C. (1994). Balancing inquiry and advocacy. In P. M. Senge, A. Kleiner, C. Roberts, R. B. Ross, & B. J. Smith, *The fifth discipline fieldbook* (pp. 253–259). New York: Currency.

Rousmaniere, D. (2015, January 23). *What everyone should know about managing up.* Accessed at https://hbr.org/2015/01/what-everyone-should-know-about-managing-up on November 25, 2022.

Roussin, J. (2013). *Questions to prepare for being coached* [Coaching session handout]. Stillwater, MN: Generative Consulting.

Roussin, J. (2014). *Seven listening modes* [Coaching session handout]. Stillwater, MN: Generative Consulting.

Russo, M., Morandin, G., & Bergami, M. (2021, September 2). *What you need to build a good relationship with your new boss.* Accessed at https://hbr.org/2021/09/what-you-need-to-build-a-good-relationship-with-your-new-boss on March 7, 2023.

Schlitz, M. (2014, May 15). *A tribute to Angeles Arrien.* Accessed at https://marilynschlitz.com/a-tribute-to-angeles-arrien on November 14, 2022.

School Superintendents Association. (n.d.). *School safety and crisis planning.* Accessed at http://aasacentral.org/school-safety on November 21, 2022.

Schroder, H. S., Moran, T. P., & Moser, J. S. (2017). The effect of expressive writing on the error-related negativity among individuals with chronic worry. *Psychophysiology, 55*, e12990.

Scott, E. (n.d.). *The stress management and health benefits of laughter.* Accessed at www.silverinnings.com/old_docs/Health%20n%20Fitness/Alternate%20Therapies/The%20Stress%20Management%20and%20Health%20Benefits%20of%20Laughter.pdf on February 8, 2023.

Scott, E. (2020a, September 28). *How to reframe situations so they create less stress.* Accessed at www.verywellmind.com/cognitive-reframing-for-stress-management-3144872? on December 12, 2022.

Scott, E. (2020b, November 24). *Why watching TV reruns can help ease stress.* Accessed at www.verywellmind.com/the-surprising-benefits-of-re-runs-3144586 on January 5, 2023.

Scott, K. (2017). *Radical candor: Be a kick-ass boss without losing your humanity.* New York: St. Martin's Press.

Senge, P. M. (2006). *The fifth discipline: The art and practice of the learning organization* (Rev. ed.). New York: Currency.

Senge, P. M., Kleiner, A., Roberts, C., Ross, R. B., & Smith, B. J. (1994). *The fifth discipline fieldbook.* New York: Currency.

Sinek, S. (2009). *Start with why: How great leaders inspire everyone to take action.* New York: Penguin.

Sirleaf, E. J. (2011, May 26). *Harvard commencement remarks (as prepared for delivery).* Accessed at https://news.harvard.edu/gazette/story/2011/05/text-of-ellen-johnson-sirleafs-speech/ on January 4, 2023.

Smith, A. (2016). *The best quotes from Oprah Winfrey.* CreateSpace Independent Publishing Platform.

Smith, J. (2022). *Why has nobody told me this before?* New York: HarperCollins.

Sostrin, J. (2017, October 10). *To be a great leader, you have to learn how to delegate well.* Accessed at https://hbr.org/2017/10/to-be-a-great-leader-you-have-to-learn-how-to-delegate-well on October 19, 2022.

Starling, K. (n.d.). *The health benefits of fresh air.* Accessed at https://physiofalmouthplus.co.uk/health-benefits-fresh-air on January 6, 2023.

Steiner, E. D., Doan, S., Woo, A., Gittens, A. D., Lawrence, R. A., Berdie, L., et al. (2022). *Restoring teacher and principal well-being is an essential step for rebuilding schools: Findings from the State of the American Teacher and State of the American Principal surveys.* Accessed at www.rand.org/pubs/research_reports/RRA1108-4.html on December 6, 2022.

Stobierski, T. (2019, November 12). *How to improve cross-cultural communication in the workplace.* Accessed at www.northeastern.edu/graduate/blog/cross-cultural-communication on March 11, 2023.

Stone, D., & Heen, S. (2014). *Thanks for the feedback: The science and art of receiving feedback well.* New York: Penguin.

Su, A. J. (2017, January 24). *How to prioritize your work when your manager doesn't.* Accessed at https://hbr.org/2017/01/how-to-prioritize-your-work-when-your-manager-doesnt on October 3, 2022.

Sutton, J. (2020, August 5). *Erik Erikson's stages of psychosocial development explained.* Accessed at https://positivepsychology.com/erikson-stages on December 30, 2022.

Systems Thinker. (n.d.). *The ladder of inference.* Accessed at https://thesystemsthinker.com/the-ladder-of-inference/ on December 22, 2022.

Tate, C. (2015a, January 26). *Assessment: What's your personal productivity style?* Accessed at https://hbr.org./2015/01/assessment-whats-your-personal-productivity-style on January 10, 2023.

Tate, C. (2015b). *Work simply: Embracing the power of your personal productivity style.* New York: Penguin.

Tawwab, N. (2021). *Set boundaries, find peace: A guide to reclaiming yourself.* New York: Penguin.

Taylor, M. J., McNicholas, C., Nicolay, C., Darzi, A., Bell, D., & Reed, J. E. (2014). *Systemic review of the application of the plan-do-study-act method to improve quality in healthcare.* Accessed at www.ncbi.nlm.nih.gov/pmc/articles/PMC3963536 on March 17, 2023.

Therapist Aid. (2021). *My strengths and qualities.* Accessed at www.therapistaid.com/therapy-worksheet/my-strengths-and-qualities on November 22, 2022.

Todoist. (n.d.). *The Eisenhower matrix: Avoid the "urgency trap" with Dwight D. Eisenhower's famous prioritization framework.* Accessed at https://todoist.com/productivity-methods/eisenhower-matrix on April 4, 2023.

Vagianos, A. (2015, June 2). *Ruth Bader Ginsburg tells young women: "Fight for the things you care about."* Accessed at www.radcliffe.harvard.edu/news-and-ideas/ruth-bader-ginsburg-tells-young-women-fight-for-the-things-you-care-about on January 10, 2023.

van Dernoot Lipsky, L. (2009). *Trauma stewardship: An everyday guide to caring for self while caring for others.* San Francisco: Berrett-Koehler.

Vasarhelyi, E. C., & Chin, J. (Directors). (2018). *Free solo* [Film]. National Geographic Documentary Films; Parkes+MacDonald Image Nation; Little Monster Films; Itinerant Media.

Vinall, M. (2021, September 1). *How sleep can affect your hormone levels, plus 12 ways to sleep deep.* Accessed at www.healthline.com/health/sleep/how-sleep-can-affect-your-hormone-levels on March 15, 2023.

Wang, C. C., Prather, K. A., Sznitman, J., Jimenez, J., Lakdawala, S., Tufekci, Z., & Marr, L. C. (2021, August 27). *Airborne transmission of respiratory viruses.* Accessed at www.science.org/doi/10.1126/science.abd9149 on March 3, 2023.

Warren, J. E., Sauter, D. A., Eisner, F., Wiland, J., Dresner, M. A., Wise, R. J. S., et al. (2006). Positive emotions preferentially engage an auditory–motor "mirror" system. *The Journal of Neuroscience, 26*(50), 13067–13075.

WebMD. (n.d.). *What are binaural beats?* Accessed at www.webmd.com/balance/what-are-binaural-beats on November 29, 2021.

Will, M. (2022, June 15). *Stress, burnout, depression: Teachers and principals are not doing well, new data confirm.* Accessed at www.edweek.org/teaching-learning/stress-burnout-depression-teachers-and-principals-are-not-doing-well-new-data-confirm/2022/06 on November 25, 2022.

Wille, S. (2004). *Colorful leadership: Harnessing the power of human ingenuity.* Accessed at https://colorfulleadership.info/papers/concrete.htm on January 23, 2023.

Williams, F. (2017). *The nature fix: Why nature makes us happier, healthier, and more creative.* New York: Norton.

Williams, S., & King, G. (2017). *On tennis, love and motherhood* [Video file]. Accessed at www.ted.com/talks/serena_williams_and_gayle_king_on_tennis_love_and_motherhood on January 5, 2023.

Wilson, V. (n.d.). *What is cultural identity and why is it important?* Accessed at www.exceptionalfutures.com/cultural-identity on November 14, 2022.

Winderl, A. (2018, August 28). *12 must-know yoga poses for beginners.* Accessed at www.self.com/gallery/must-know-yoga-poses-for-beginners on February 2, 2023.

Wokke, M. (2021, July 30). *Exploring metacognition in decision-making.* Accessed at https://cordis.europa.eu/article/id/430481-exploring-metacognition-in-decision-making on March 12, 2023.

Wokke, M., Achoui, D., & Cleeremans, A. (2020). *Action information contributes to metacognitive decision-making.* Accessed at www.nature.com/articles/s41598-020-60382-y on March 12, 2023.

Woo, A., & Steiner, E. D. (2022). *The well-being of secondary school principals one year into the COVID-19 pandemic.* Accessed at www.rand.org/pubs/research_reports/RRA827-6.html on January 3, 2023.

Yang, C.-H., & Conroy, D. E. (2018). Momentary negative affect is lower during mindful movement than while sitting: An experience sampling study. *Psychology of Sport and Exercise, 37,* 109–116.

Yasar, K. (2022, June). *SMART (SMART goals).* Accessed at www.techtarget.com/whatis/definition/SMART-SMART-goals on November 6, 2022.

York-Barr, J., Sommers, W. A., Ghere, G. S., & Montie, J. (2006). *Reflective practice to improve schools: An action guide for educators* (2nd ed.). Thousand Oaks, CA: Corwin Press.

Zeeman, A. (2019, June 8). *Atkins and Murphy model of reflection.* Accessed at www.toolshero.com/personal-development/atkins-murphy-model-of-reflection on December 22, 2022.

Zenger, J., & Folkman, J. (2016, July 14). *What great listeners actually do.* Accessed at https://hbr.org/2016/07/what-great-listeners-actually-do on January 3, 2023.

Index

A

abstract-random thinking styles, 10, 11. *See also* thinking and productivity styles reflection
abstract-sequential thinking styles, 11. *See also* thinking and productivity styles reflection
accomplishment mindset and narrative, 61. *See also* mindsets
accomplishments checklist, 127–128
active listening, 84. *See also* listening
advocacy, 63
agreeableness, 29. *See also* Big Five/five-factor model of personality
American Institute of Stress, 74
American Psychological Association (APA), 28
Angelou, M., 108
approachable voice versus credible voice, 91–92. *See also* expressing yourself; voice
arrangers, 12. *See also* whole-brain model
Arrien, A., 26–27, 91
artisans, 29. *See also* Keirsey Temperament Sorter
Austin, D., 118
Australian Medical Association, 121
automatic thinking, 23. *See also* decision making; heuristics

B

balance/keeping your balance
    about, 81–82
    full plate activity, 82
    just say no, 83
    self-management and, 134
    unpacking your bag and, 108

Bauer, B., 124
Beard, A., 118
beliefs, 23
belonging, 25. *See also* values
Big Five/five-factor model of personality, 28–29, 31. *See also* personalities
binaural beats, 79–80
biophilia, 124
boundaries
    reproducibles for, 106
    setting boundaries worksheet, 101–103
"Boundaries: A Guide to Making Essential Life Decisions" (Esposito), 101
breathing
    mindfulness techniques, 77–78, 79
    in nature, 123
    power pause, 99
    stress and, 76
Brown, B., 25
Buckingham, M., 49
bullying, 43

C

caffeine, 77
calm. *See* staying calm
celebrations
    about, 125
    accomplishments checklist, 127–128
    celebrations questionnaire, 126–127, 132
    I honor cards, 126, 131
Celestine, N., 49
chatter, 98

circles of concern and influence, 19–21
clarifying questions, 84. *See also* questions/questioning
Clifton, D., 49
Clinton, H., 87
coaches
    coaching referral and contact log, 54
    feedback and, 89
    four purposes of listening and, 86
    hiring a coach, 53–54
    questions to prepare for being coached, 54
    reproducibles for, 71
cognitive reframing
    cognitive reframing worksheet, 112–113, 129
    self-management and, 134
common humanity, 109
communication. *See also* expressing yourself; voice
    cross-cultural communication, 92
    principal-supervisor relationships and, 59
    well-dressed hamburger and, 94–96
concern and influence organizers
    decision making and, 19–21
    reproducibles for, 36
    self-management and, 134
concrete-random thinking styles, 10–11. *See also* thinking and productivity styles reflection
concrete-sequential thinking styles, 10, 11. *See also* thinking and productivity styles reflection
connections, seven critical kinds of, 52–53
conscientiousness, 29. *See also* Big Five/five-factor model of personality
contributions chart, 60–62
cortisol, 75, 118
Costa, A., 55
Covey, S., 6, 20
COVID-19, 2, 74, 97, 100, 120
credible voice, approachable voice versus, 91–92. *See also* expressing yourself; voice
crises
    one-pager emergency procedures and, 40–42
    role-playing scenarios and, 42
critical friends
    critical friends process worksheet, 55–57, 72
    self-management and, 134
Crosby, P., 94
cross-cultural communication, 92. *See also* communication

D

deadlines
    planning fallacies and, 16
    priorities and, 6

decide, enact, analyze, reflect (DEAR) model, 117–118
decision fatigue, 23. *See also* heuristics
decision making
    about, 17
    concern and influence organizers and, 19–21
    fishbone diagram and, 21–22
    heuristics and, 22–23
    starting with the why process and, 19
    two-tine litmus test and, 18–19
default frames, 112
delegation, 9. *See also* sharing the load spreadsheet
detail-oriented productivity style, 12. *See also* productivity styles
distress, 74, 81
Drucker, P., 83, 91
Duckworth, A., 100
DuFour, R., 125

E

Eisenhower matrix, 7. *See also* priorities
emergency procedures one-pager
    reproducibles for, 65
    safety and, 40–42
    self-management and, 134
emotional well-being, 2
empathy, 50, 85
Esposito, L., 101
eustress, 74, 81
expressing yourself
    about, 91
    approachable voice versus credible voice, 91–92
    right voice, right time worksheet, 93–94, 104
    well-dressed hamburger, 94–96
extraversion, 29. *See also* Big Five/five-factor model of personality

F

Fauci, A., 125
feedback
    becoming a better receiver of, 89, 90
    feedback cycle and critical friends groups, 56
    feedback sandwich, 94
    feedback tendency trackers, 87, 89–91
    listening and, 84, 85
    SMART goals and, 14
    strengths and talents and, 48
fill-ins, 7. *See also* priorities
fishbone diagram, 21–22. *See also* decision making
five-factor model of personality. *See* Big Five/five-factor model of personality
fixed mindset, 110–111. *See also* mindsets

Flynn, N., 26–27
Folkman, J., 85
forest bathing, 78
forgiveness, 110
four archetypes reflection, 26–27
four Ds process worksheet, 62–64
full plate activity, 82

G

Gabarro, J., 59
generativity versus stagnation, 133
Genovese, M., 74
Gibson, J., 120
giving yourself some grace. *See* grace for oneself
goals. *See also* SMART goals
    about, 13
    growth mindset and, 111
    Ikigai and, 24
    my boss under a microscope organizers and, 58–59
    progress reports and, 16–17
    purpose and, 23
    strengths and, 49
    why of goal process, 15–16, 34
Golden Circle, 19
grace for oneself
    about, 108
    cognitive reframing worksheet and, 112–113
    pathways to enhancing your mindset and, 110–111
    self-compassion exercises and, 109–110
    self-compassion survey and, 108–109
Gregorc, A., 11
grit
    grit score reflection, 100–101
    growth mindset and, 111
    limitations and, 97
growth
    feedback tendency trackers and, 87
    strengths and talents and, 49
    values and, 25
growth mindset, 110–111. *See also* mindsets
guardians, 29. *See also* Keirsey Temperament Sorter

H

happy place, your, 121–122
Hard Choices (Clinton), 87
healers, 26, 27. *See also* four archetypes reflection
heuristics, 22–23. *See also* decision making
High 5 strengths test, 49, 51. *See also* strengths and talents
Hopkins, G., 82
humanity, common, 109

I

I honor cards
    celebrations and, 126
    reproducibles for, 131
I statements, 83
idealists, 29. *See also* Keirsey Temperament Sorter
idea-oriented productivity style, 12. *See also* productivity styles
identity triggers, 89
Ikigai, 23–24
impact
    delegation and, 9
    priority score worksheet and, 7, 8
inclusion, 25, 44. *See also* values
influence. *See* circles of concern and influence; concern and influence organizers
inquiry, 63
introduction
    about self-management, 1
    about this book, 2–3
    preparing for the journey, 1–2

J

Jones, H., 121
Journal of Occupational Health Psychology, 122
journal writing
    reflection and, 114–116
    self-management and, 135

K

Kallick, B., 55
Kamphoff, C,, 97, 98, 113
Kataria, M., 119
Keirsey Temperament Sorter, 29–31
KFG bracelet, 97–98, 110
King, B., 2
Kos, B., 113
Kotter, J., 59
Kross, E., 98
Krueger, J., 45

L

ladder of inference process
    reflection and, 116–117
    reproducibles for, 130
laughter
    about, 118–119
    humorous media, 120
    laughter yoga, 119–120
Lawrence-Lightfoot, S., 133

laws and policies
    about, 45
    law and policy reference guide, 46–47, 66–68
    web resources for, 45
leadership, profile of a reflective leader, 114
Li, Q., 78
limitations
    about, 96–97
    grit score reflection and, 100–101
    KFG bracelet and, 97–98
    setting boundaries worksheet and, 101–103
    stop light grid and, 98–100
listening
    about, 83–84
    feedback tendency trackers, 87, 89–91
    four purposes of listening, 86
    listening blocks worksheet, 86–87, 88
    six levels of listening survey, 84–85
logical productivity style, 12. *See also* productivity styles
Louv, R., 124

M

Mackay, H., 13, 17
major projects, 6. *See also* priorities
managing up, 58, 61
mapping your route
    about, 5–6
    decision making, 17–23
    getting organized/priorities, 6–13
    knowing your purpose, 23–27
    psyching yourself up/personalities, 28–32
    reproducibles for, 33–38
    setting goals, 13–17
    summary and what's next, 32
McAfee, B., 91
meditation, 76
mental health and preparing for the journey, 2
metacognition, 99, 115, 116
Michelangelo, 98
Michigan State University, 115
mindfulness
    self-compassion and, 109
    stress and, 76
mindfulness techniques organizers
    about, 77
    breathing, 77–78
    example for, 79
    movement, 78
    rest, 78

mindsets
    accomplishment mindset and narrative, 61
    accomplishments checklists and, 127
    pathways to enhancing your mindset, 110–111
Mindful Staff, 77
Mogi, K., 24
Moss, T., 9
multitasking, 23. *See also* heuristics
my boss under a microscope organizers, 58–60, 61
Myers-Briggs Type Indicator, 28, 31. *See also* personalities

N

nature
    forest bathing, 78
    self-management and, 135
nature logs, recharging with, 123–125
nature-deficit disorder, 124
navigating the trail
    about, 73–75
    expressing yourself, 91–96
    keeping your balance, 81–83
    listening, 83–91
    reproducibles for, 104–106
    staying calm, 76–81
    stretching your limits/knowing your limitations, 96–103
    summary and what's next, 103
networks
    about, 52–53
    critical friends process worksheet, 55–57, 72
    hiring a coach, 53–54
    professional organizations, 57–58
    super allies, 55
neuroticism, 29. *See also* Big Five/five-factor model of personality
neurotrophins, 74
noradrenaline, 77

O

one-pager, emergency procedures. *See* emergency procedures one-pager
openness, 29. *See also* Big Five/five-factor model of personality
optimal thinking questions, 113. *See also* questions/questioning
optimism bias, 22–23. *See also* heuristics

P

packing your bag
    about, 39–40

creating a network, 52–58
discovering your strengths, 48–52
knowing the laws, 45–47
reproducibles for, 65–72
safety first, 40–44
studying your boss/supervisors, 58–64
summary and what's next, 64
paraphrasing, 84
passion
delegation and, 9
priority score worksheet and, 7, 8
pathways to enhancing your mindset, 110–111. *See also* grace for oneself; mindsets
Perlmutter, D., 62
personalities. *See also* thinking and productivity styles reflection
about, 28
big picture (staff chart), 31–32
personality and temperament self-reflection chart, 28–31
strengths and talents and, 48
upsides and downsides to personality traits, 30
physical safety, 40. *See also* safety
physical well-being, 2
plan, do, study, act (PDSA) model, 117
planners, 12. *See also* whole-brain model
planning fallacies, 16–17
power pause, 99
principal-supervisor relationships. *See also* my boss under a microscope organizers; relationships
Four Ds process and, 63
questions for understanding your boss, 59–60
priorities
about, 6
priority score worksheet, 6–9
self-management and, 134
sharing the load spreadsheet, 9–10
thinking and productivity styles reflection, 10–13
this book and, 3
prioritizers, 12. *See also* whole-brain model
productivity styles, 10–13
professional development, 53–54
professional organizations, 57–58
progress reports
goals and, 16–17
reproducibles for, 35
psychological breaks, 121
psychological safety. *See also* safety
physical safety and, 40
promoting, 44
psychological safety assessment, 43–44
studying your boss/supervisors and, 62, 63
purpose
four archetypes reflection and, 26–27
growth mindset and, 111
Ikigai and, 23–24
knowing your purpose, 23
values organizers and, 24–25

Q

questions/questioning
celebrations questionnaire, 126–127, 132
clarifying questions, 84
listening and, 84, 85
optimal thinking questions, 113
questions for understanding your boss, 59–60
questions to prepare for being coached, 54, 71
quick wins, 6, 7. *See also* priorities

R

Raab, E., 118
Rash, J., 87
Rath, T., 49
rationals, 29. *See also* Keirsey Temperament Sorter
recharging
about, 120–121
nature logs and, 123–125
unplugging and disconnecting trackers and, 122–123
your happy place and, 121–122
redemptive narrative, 113
reflection
about, 114
decide, enact, analyze, reflect (DEAR) model and, 117–118
four archetypes reflection, 26–27
grit score reflection, 100–101
journal writing and, 114–116
ladder of inference process and, 116–117
personality and temperament self-reflection chart, 28–31
strengths self-evaluation and, 48
thinking and productivity styles reflection, 10–13
this book and, 3
unplugging and disconnecting from technology and, 122
relationships. *See also* my boss under a microscope organizers; networks
connections, seven critical kinds of, 52–53
critical friends, 55–57, 72, 134
four Ds process and, 63
questions for understanding your boss, 59–60
super allies, 2, 55

relationship triggers, 89
reproducibles for
    big picture (staff chart), 38
    celebrations questionnaire, 132
    cognitive reframing worksheet, 129
    concern and influence organizer, 36
    critical friends process worksheet, 72
    emergency procedures one-pager, 65
    I honor cards, 131
    ladder of inference process, 130
    law and policy reference guide, 66–68
    progress reports, 35
    questions to prepare for being coached, 71
    right voice, right time worksheet, 104
    setting boundaries worksheet, 106
    SMART goal template, 33
    stop light grid, 105
    strengths assessment organizer, 70
    strengths self-evaluation, 69
    values organizer, 37
    why of my goal process, 34
resilience, 111, 118, 133
respect, 25. *See also* values
rest
    mindfulness and, 78, 79
    versus recharging, 121
right voice, right time worksheet. *See also* expressing yourself; voice
    about, 93–94
    reproducibles for, 104
    self-management and, 134
Robbins, T., 82
Roberts, C., 63
Robinson, N., 74
role-playing scenarios, 42
root-cause analysis, 21
Ross, R., 63
Rousmaniere, D., 58

S

safety
    about, 40
    emergency procedures one-pager, 40–42
    listening and, 84
    psychological safety assessment, 43–44
    role-playing scenarios and, 42
    U.S. Homeland Security website and, 43
schemata, 112
Scott, S., 118
self-awareness
    journal writing and, 115
    stop light grid and, 98–99
self-compassion
    self-compassion exercises, 109–110
    self-compassion survey, 108–109
self-kindness, 109
self-management
    about, 1
    steps for, 134–135
self-promotion skills, 61
sharing the load spreadsheet, 9–10
shinrin-yoku, 78
Sinek, S., 19
Sirleaf, E., 98
situational awareness, 3
sleep
    versus recharging, 121
    stress and, 77
SMART goals. *See also* goals
    about, 13–15
    reproducibles for, 33
    self-management and, 134
Sostrin, J., 9
staff
    big picture (staff chart), 31–32, 38
    sharing the load spreadsheet, 9–10
staying calm
    about, 76–77
    binaural beats and, 79–80
    mindfulness techniques organizers and, 77–79
    office yoga poses and, 80–81
Stobierski, T., 92
stop light grid
    limitations and, 98–100
    reproducibles for, 105
Strayer, D., 123
strengths and talents. *See also* personalities; thinking and productivity styles reflection
    about, 48
    contributions chart and, 60
    self-management and, 134
    strengths assessments organizers, 49, 51–52, 70
    strengths self-evaluation, 48, 69
    thirty-four talents, 50
strengths wheel, 51
StrengthsFinder test, 49
stress
    about, 74–75
    cognitive reframing and, 112–113
    laughter and, 118

staying calm and, 76
stress types and what they can lead to, 75
super allies, 2, 55. *See also* networks
supervisors
    contributions chart, 60–62
    four Ds process worksheet, 62–64
    my boss under a microscope organizers, 58–60, 61
    questions for understanding your boss, 59–60
supportive productivity style, 12. *See also* productivity styles

T

talents
    about, 49
    strengths and, 48
    thirty-four talents, 50
Tate, C., 12
Tawwab, N., 102
teachers, 26, 27. *See also* four archetypes reflection
TED talks, 94
thankless tasks, 7. *See also* priorities
thinking and productivity styles reflection. *See also* personalities; strengths and talents
    productivity styles/style assessments, 12
    thinking styles/style assessments, 10–11
    whole-brain model and, 11–12
Third Chapter, The (Lawrence-Lightfoot), 133
thought patterns and cognitive reframing, 112
trust, 55
truth triggers, 89
two-tine litmus test, 18–19. *See also* decision making

U

unpacking your bag
    about, 107–108
    celebrating, 125–128
    giving yourself some grace, 108–113
    laughing about it, 118–120
    recharging, 120–125
    reflecting on it, 114–118
    reproducibles for, 129–132
    summary and what's next, 128
unplugging and disconnecting trackers, 122–123. *See also* recharging
U.S. Homeland Security website, 43

V

values
    purpose and, 23
    self-management and values assessments, 134
    values organizers, 24–25, 37
van Dernoot Lipsky, L., 77
visionaries, 26, 27. *See also* four archetypes reflection
visualizers, 12. *See also* whole-brain model
voice
    approachable voice versus credible voice, 91–92
    right voice, right time worksheet, 93–94, 104, 134

W

warriors, 26, 27. *See also* four archetypes reflection
well-being, 2, 25. *See also* values
well-dressed hamburger
    expressing yourself, 94–96
    self-management and, 134
"What Everyone Should Know About Managing Up" (Rousmaniere), 58
wheel of life activity, 82, 108
"When All Else Fails, Dance!" (Flynn), 26–27
whole-brain model, 11–12
why, the
    starting with the why process and decision making, 19
    two-tine litmus test and, 19
    why of goal process, 15–16
    why of goal process template, 34
Williams, F., 123
Williams, S., 111
Winfrey, O., 125
Wokke, M., 99

Y

yoga
    laughter yoga, 119–120
    movement and, 78
    office yoga poses, 80–81
York-Barr, J., 115
your happy place, 121–122

Z

Zenger, J., 85

The Deliberate and Courageous Principal
Rhonda J. Roos
Fully step into your power as a school principal. By diving deep into five essential leadership *actions* and five essential leadership *skills*, you will learn how to grow in your role and accomplish incredible outcomes for your students and staff.
BKG013

Women Who Lead
Edited by Janel Keating and Jasmine K. Kullar
Yvette Jackson, Carmen Jiménez, Joellen Killion, Janel Keating, Julie A. Schmidt, Suzette Lovely, Heather Friziellie, Jessica Kanold-McIntyre, Jasmine K. Kullar, Tina H. Boogren, Bob Sonju, and Jason A. Andrews
Women Who Lead offers insight and strategies on effective women in educational leadership practices and how to nurture your professional growth in this male-dominated field.
BKF991

Benches in the Bathroom
Evisha Ford
Educational leadership can help ensure teachers are at their best by taking steps to create and maintain a safe, comfortable culture for all staff. A leader who's committed to establishing and maintaining an environment that prioritizes wellness and teacher stress management will find answers in this book.
BKG094

All Other Duties as Assigned
Ryan Donlan
Delve into the extensive scope of responsibilities inherent to being an assistant principal. Grow in your instructional leadership, fortify your adaptive communication skills, and gain strategies to achieve success and happiness.
BKG026

Lead From the Start
Tommy Reddicks and Tina Merriweather Seymour
Whether you are a brand-new principal or an experienced leader in a new job, *Lead From the Start* will help you succeed in your role. Use this resource to overcome the biggest leadership challenges principals face, and gain firsthand knowledge from educators like you to form best management practices at your school.
BKF924

Solution Tree | Press
a division of Solution Tree

Visit SolutionTree.com or call 800.733.6786 to order.

Global PD teams
Collaborative Learning for School Improvement

Quality team learning **from authors you trust**

Global PD Teams is the first-ever **online professional development resource designed to support your entire faculty on your learning journey.** This convenient tool offers daily access to videos, mini-courses, eBooks, articles, and more packed with insights and research-backed strategies you can use immediately.

GET STARTED
SolutionTree.com/**GlobalPDTeams**
800.733.6786